Ronald R. Wlodyga

The Foolishness of God

Is wiser than men (I Cor. 1:25

Volume 1

Copyright Statement

Any articles may be reproduced in whole, but not the book in its entirety under the following provisions: proper credit of book title and author must be given at the end of each article. There can be no charge of articles to the recipient. It is my desire to encourage, and inspire the Christian into further study with the fundamental belief of giving freely.

ISBN 978-0-9996000-2-3

Acknowledgements

Since my conversion in 1969 I have read thousands of Christian articles, books and booklets as well as hearing countless valuable sermons relating to God's plan and Christian living.

If I have done anything for the service of my Creator toward helping mankind, it is in accumulating this knowledge and presenting it to you in a way that will be easy to read and understand.

I would like to think of myself as a "help" to those that are laboring for Jesus Christ in preparing His Church to be without spot or wrinkle (1 Cor. 12:28).

A Minister's burden is heavy, and like Aaron and Hur that lifted up the arms of Moses to fulfill God's commission (Ex. 17:12), it is my hope that I have helped to make God's Ministers' burden a little lighter through this work.

In reality, there have been dozens of men who penned this book, yet all with God's Holy Spirit guiding their pen. God Himself is the Pen that deserves credit for this book——may we glorify Him!

First of all, let me state emphatically in this book that although God's plan for mankind has been a never ending Bible study for me personally, I fully realize this is not the average Christian's "cup of tea".

Secondly, let me say that it is not my intention to change the minds of any other theological belief system in this book, for I know as do other adherents of different persuasions that only Almighty God can do that!

I am merely stating my opinions as to the conclusions that I have come to on the issues after reading countless books and articles on the subject matter along with reading several translations of the Bible over the past 40 years.

The conclusions that I have come to do not necessarily mean that I am right or wrong, only that they are my current beliefs. I also realize that beliefs are subject to change based upon new evidence or revelation.

Furthermore, I believe as other writers have stated more eloquently than I, that as Christians we should be concentrating on the things that unite us rather than the things we have differences of opinion.

As one man put it so succinctly, in essentials we have unity, in nonessentials we have liberty, in all things we have charity.

Although there are many different viewpoints regarding the interpretation of the end times (eschatology) as we shall see, it would be an inaccurate impression of what unites these same Christians, namely the belief in grace through the precious blood of our Savior, His imminent return and a kingdom that will last forever after a judgment has taken place.

Vol. 1

TABLE OF CONTENTS

Page

Chapter One
In the Beginning

1. The "Word " is also God 1
2. Christ the Creator of the Universe 2
3. Was the Holy Spirit present at Creation? 4
4. The perfect creation of Elohim 5
5. Is God a Family? 6
6. The Spirit in Man 7
7. Heirs of God 8
8. Predestination of the "Elect" 9
9. Does God know everything 11
10. Creation of Angels 15
11. Lucifer rebels against God 18
12. Lucifer becomes Satan the Devil 20
13. Earth in Chaotic Confusion 21

Chapter Two
Satan becomes God

1. Christ Qualifies to be Ruler 25
2. Pagans knew of Promise of Eternal Life 29
3. Nimrod becomes Priest of Serpent-Sun-worshippers 29
4. Nimrod and Semiramis become Gods 30
5. Idolatry spreads Everwhere 39

Chapter Three
God's Plan of Duality

Types of Christ

1. Adam 43
2. Abel 45
3. Moses 46
4. Isaac 47
5. Joshua
        a. A Sabbath Remains..48
        b. The Sabbath's Millennial Typology.......................48
6. King Solomon 48
7. The Levite Priest 49
8. Christians.. 49
9. Joseph 50
10. Jeremiah 52
11. Cyrus... 52
12. Zerubbabel 55
13. Elisha 56
14. Jonah 57
15. Israel 59

Chapter Four
Types of the True Church

1. Eve... 61
2. Rebekah 63
3. Ruth 64
4. Samson.. 67
5. Haggar 68

Chapter Five
Types of Satan

1. Pharoah 71
3. Simon Magus... 72

4. King of Tyre 76
5. Uziah 77
6. Haman 78
7. Antiochus IV 81

Chapter Six
Types of Christ and Satan

1. Cain and Abel 85
2. Saul and David 87
3. Saul and Satan 88
4. Absalom and David 90
5. The "Three" Judas' 91
6. The "Man of Sin 97

Chapter Seven
Types of the Holy Spirit

1. The Tree of Life and Death 99
2. Water 101
3. Wine 104
4. Oil 104
5. Wind 104
6. Palm Tree 105
7. Manna 107
8. "Laying on of Hands" 108

Chapter Eight
Types of Baptism

1. Death and Ressurrection 111
2. Old Testament Types 113
3. The (3) Baptisms 115
4. Circumcision 117
5. Purity and Purification 119

Chapter Nine
Types of the Two Witnesses

1. Moses and Aaron 123
2. "Two Olive Trees" and "Two Candlesticks" 124
3. Zerubbabel and Joshua 125
4. John the Baptist 130
5. Clothed in Sackcloth 134
6. Not Moses and Elijah 135
7. Ezekiel's Message 136
8. Levitical Types 137

Chapter Ten
Types of Sin

1. Babylon, Egypt and Sodom 143
2. Nebuchadnezzar's Dream 144
3. Babylon the Great 147
4. Today's Babylon 151
5. The "Image of the Beast" 153
5. Satan's Fate 156

Chapter Eleven
God' Government of Numbers

1. Restoring the Government of God 162
2. God's "Fail-Safe" Government 163
3. Jesus was Born to Rule 164
4. A Pyramid Government 164
5. Christianity and Politics 166
6. Why Man's Government will Fail 169

Chapter Twelve
God's Plan of Names

1. Adam 178
2. Eve 178

3. Methuselah 179
4. Noah 179
5. Abraham 180
6. Nimrod 180
7. Semiramis 180
8. Tammuz 181
9. Isaac 182
10. Moses 183
11. Joshua 183
12. Aaron 183
13. Jacob 184
14. Judah 185
15. Jesus 185
16. Lucifer 186

Chapter Thirteen
God's many Names

1. Elohim 192
2. Jehovah 193
3. El Shaddai 196
4. Adonai 202
5. El Olam 205
6. Jehovah Sabaoth 208

Chapter Fourteen
The Seven Stages of Sonship

1. Carnal Adam 215
2. Cain and Abel——Two Ways of Life 217
3. Righteous Noah 219
4. Faithful Abraham 221
5. Isaac the Begotten Son 223
6. Jacob the Server 225
7. Joseph the Ruler 227

Chapter Fifteen
God's Plan in the Old Covenant

1. To Rule all Nations 234
2. To be Rejected by Israel 238
3. The Messiah's Sufferings 240
4. The Day of Atonement 243
5. The Feast of Tabernacles 243
6. God to Dwell with Us Forever 251

Chapter Sixteen
God's Plan in the First Five Books

1. Genesis 256
2. Exodus 256
3. Leviticus 257
4. Numbers 257
5. Deuteronomy 257
6. Freedom—a Process 259
7. God's 7,000 Plan 260
8. The Creation Week 265

Preface

How did we get the Bible?

Exactly how did a collection of many different manuscripts, letters, and narratives discovered in many different parts of the world become 27 books of the New Testament?

I began this study when I was 27 years old and became a Christian. It has been a never ending study of God's plan for mankind! I simply wasn't satisfied with just being saved—I wanted to what I was being saved for!

These 27 controversial books have come to change the course of history and the heat of many biblical studies by scholars who have examined historical artifacts and scrolls and fragmented papyrus.

Before we begin our study on the various agencies that God has revealed Himself, we must first realize why Christians may disagree on these various agencies especially typology. That is why we need to understand that even though various books, both accepted and not accepted as canon are quoted for the reader to decide truth from speculation and conjecture.

We must realize that there are no original manuscripts of early church writers such as Matthew, Mark, Luke, John, Peter and Paul. We have only copies of copies of the original. Modern translations have also muddied the waters of truth as we cannot even find the name Lucifer mentioned in any of the modern translations.

St. Catherine's Monastery in Egypt is the home of one of the most vast libraries of ancient manuscripts and books and has attracted researchers and scholars all over the world to find the truth of who said what and when.

Using modern scientific techniques, researchers have searched for the truth, but still cannot find common agreement. The Codex Sinaiticus or book of Sinai is believed to be the oldest book of the Bible. It dates from the middle of the fourth century. It contains two books (The Shepherd of Hermas and the Epistle of Barnabas) that are not in modern New Testament Bibles.

The second oldest Bible known as The Book of Alexandria, contains two additional books (1 and 11 Letters of Clement).

Why are these four books omitted from the 27 books recognized by most orthodox Christian scholars? There are many other books that have surfaced over the years such as the gospels of Thomas and Mary, and the book of Enoch to name a few.

Realize, during the first few hundred years of Christianity, there were no books written, only letters on papyrus but mostly oral tradition of Jesus' life and resurrection.

As Christianity spread, there were many false teachings being spread as noted by the apostle Paul and Peter's letters. Many of these false teachings were eventually written down in manuscripts and eventually deemed as heretical by church fathers because of obvious contradictions.

Other books, like the book of Maccabees, although historically accurate, were not included in the original 27 for other reasons. We must also realize that Scribes made copies of copies over the years since there were no printing presses—and it was their job to make copies of the existing manuscripts. They had to decide which manuscripts to make copies of and which were fraudulent.

The gospel of Mark is a perfect example as some manuscripts ended with Mark 16:18; while others ended with Mark 16:20. Which was correct? The Scribes had to decide! We also find that some Scribes were even writing comments in the margins, even adding to what we would call God's Word. Was that inspired?

A remarkable Discovery

In 1945 a remarkable discovery occurred in a cave in Egypt that contained a jar with many ancient manuscripts including the gospel of Thomas. Two Egyptian peasants stumbled upon a large jar, hidden by a boulder. Inside the jar was a collection of ancient leather-bound books which most likely were written by an early Christian monastery in Egypt near the village of Nag Hammadi.

The jar contained one of the earliest manuscripts on papyrus dating approximately A.D. 125. But how did it get into Egypt? Had the gospel gotten to Egypt in A.D. 125 and by whom? There certainly was a lot of commerce going on between Egypt and Jerusalem. But once again there is uncertainty among scholars in the dating.

The Nag Hammadi Library consists of fifty-two texts or "tractates" written in Coptic on papyrus and gathered in thirteen volumes, twelve of which have separate leather bindings. Most of the writings are of a Gnostic character (special knowledge) and why it is important to know the history of Gnosticism.

Toward the end of the century, heresy was spreading, especially in Alexandria Egypt. Alexandria is a port city located on the Mediterranean Sea in northern Egypt founded in 331 BCE by Alexander the Great, who conquered Egypt.

After he founded Alexandria, eventually Alexandria came under the rule of Alexander's general Ptolemy and the rule of the Ptolemaic Dynasty (332-30 BCE) which followed. The city became famous for its magnificent library, known as the Royal Library which was the largest in the known world at the time, and became a hub for attracting scholars, scientists, philosophers, mathematicians, artists, and historians.

It is thought that the Greek translation of the Bible (Septuagint) was composed in Alexandria, completed in 132 CE. Religious scholars from all over the known world came to the library attracting people of many different faiths.

Eventually this cultural city would also become a city of religious contention between the new faith of the Christians and the old faith of the pagan majority.

It has been estimated that the Library held over half a million documents from Assyria, Greece, Persia, Egypt, India and many other nations attracting the worlds best scholars to research, translate and copy documents.

The Didascalia, believed to be the oldest Christian school for studying theology was renowned for studying allegory. Because of its Greek and Roman influence, students of many faiths came to study other religions, as well as science, mathematics, physics, chemistry, astronomy, and medicine.

It was where the Arian heresy developed by Aruis (250-336) which held that Jesus, although divine, was not equal with the Father, and was finally settled by Athanasius (296 373) bishop of Alexandria who condemned heretics and their "apocryphal books. Alexandrian teachers believed that Christians could learn much from Greek Philosophy and thought differently from the church fathers Irenaeus and Tertullian.

It is suggested that monks in Nag Hammadi, instead of getting rid of heretical works by burying them, hid them in pottery jars, later to be discovered by a local farmer named Muhammed al-Samman.

Most writings of the Gnostics themselves had been destroyed or lost. Now and then a fragment would surface, but for the most part scholars trying to reconstruct Gnostic beliefs and texts had to rely on accounts given by Irenaeus, Tertullian, Hippolytus, Epiphanius, and other early church fathers hostile to the Gnostic systems that they were describing.

Much of the Gnosticism beliefs came from various writings in Judaism, Hellenistic philosophy, mystery religions, early Christianity, Greco-Egyptian religious movements, the religions of India, and Persian Zoroastrianism.

It will be the Christian's challenge to discern the truth from error as we examine many different concepts in this study from the various sources of controversy.

There are 27 accepted books of the New Testament, of which 21 are letters of warning. As Christianity spread, persecution of Christians began in A.D. 64 under the Roman Emperor Nero.

It is believed the apostle Paul and Peter were both martyred early on, but pastoral letters to Titus and Timothy began to surface believed to be written by Paul towards the end of the first century. Many of the second century church fathers questioned who wrote them, especially the book of Hebrews.

All of the apostle Paul's letters begin with similarities of "Paul an apostle of Jesus Christ", but the book of Hebrews starts without any name. There are other discrepancies that are not consistent with Paul's writings.

Using modern technology, scholars began to evaluate the age of the papyrus discovered in the caves. They compared the style of the characters and tried to verify the age of the manuscripts for authenticity, only to find disagreement. If they could verify the age of the book of Matthew for example prior to the Temple's destruction in A.D. 70—then it would legitimize its destruction as a true prophecy.

There is scholarship and then like most things, there is FAITH! At best, we Christians can only believe that God has given us His inspired Word—but we will most likely never be able to prove it to others!

There are copies of copies of early writings. There are letters and traditions—and then there is FAITH in them!

Over the years, orthodox Christians decided which of the many books were to be included in the Bible. If the gospel of Thomas or the book of Barnabas was to be included, Christian doctrine would certainly be different today.

In the end, it is not scholarship that determines what we believe—it's FAITH!

One man, probably had more bearing on deciding that the 27 books which most orthodox Christians accept as the inspired books of the Bible—his name is Athanasus!

Gnosticism, the belief in special knowledge to be saved was spreading throughout the Christian world. Books like the gospels of Philip and Mary Magdelene were being circulated, only to be deemed heretical by orthodox Christians.

All of the apostles had been martyred including Peter and Paul by the end of the first century. We know that the apostle Paul went to Rome to confront the false beliefs of the pagan gods of Rome. Christianity threatened the rule of the Caesars. Persecution of Christians followed until the reign of Constantine.

Religion was dividing the Roman Empire, but under Constantine, he saw how religion could also be a unifying force. But instead, it brought more contention as the question of Jesus' divinity by a priest named Aruis became a heated topic. To him there was only one God and Jesus was created by Him. This new heresy was called Arianism.

The nature of Christ was dividing the Empire. Constantine called for all of the bishops of the Church to settle this controversy of Aruis. Thus, the Nicean Creed was established that Christ was truly divine being one substance of the Father.

Eventually Constantine moved his Empire to Byzantium, modern-day Turkey and renamed it Constantinople. There he established many churches and chose his friend Eusibius to create a Bible. But which Bible would he choose?

It was Athanasus who branded many of the books of the New Testament at the end of the fourth century heretical—except the 27 that most orthodox Christians have accepted today, until the heretical books were discovered in a cave in the twentieth century!

Some of the controversial books being discussed as authoritative even to this day are 3Corinthians, the Shepherd of Hermas, the Didache, the first letter of Clement of Rome, the letters of Ignatius, Barnabas, the Apocalypse of Peter, the Acts of Paul, the Gospel of Peter, and the Gospel of Thomas.

Although these books are not part of the New Testament cannon as being inspired, many scholars feel that other books were inspired as well.

The Dead Sea Scrolls

In 1947 a Bedouin boy accidentally discovered these scrolls in a jar of pottery in a cave in Qumran. Would these scrolls be proof of the Bible or would they add to its mystery?

The Old Testament had been meticulously preserved faithfully by Jewish scholars known as Scribes who are mentioned many times in the New Testament. It was their sacred duty to preserve the canonized text of every jot and tittle of God's Word (Matt. 5:18).

The area of Qumran is where the Essene community dwelt, who had accepted and preserved more that one form of biblical text, and therefore did not have the blessing of the Jewish priesthood which they rejected.

The significance of the scrolls, which are about a thousand years older than any Hebrew text ever discovered is that they prove the antiquity and authority of the Masoretic text of the 10th century in which the King James Bible was based upon.

In all 40,000- fragments of leather and papyrus were discovered at Qumran, the most important of these is the book of Isaiah on 23 feet of leather.

Some of the fragmentary scrolls differ somewhat in the text of the official Hebrew Masoretic text preserved by the Jews and used in their synagogues from the time of Christ till now.

But Jesus didn't recognize the Essene community as He did the Scribes and Pharisees of the day as He said, "they sit in the seat of Moses" (Matt. 23:2). The heretical sect of the

Essenes centered near the Dead Sea and was never appointed by God for the purpose of preserving His truth!

Nor did they preserve with great care and accuracy the copies of the Hebrew Old Testament which they possessed which has minor spelling changes and misplaced words on the book of Isaiah from the Masoretic text.

Through the ages, church fathers disagreed on which books were inspired and should be in the cannon. Polycarp was one of the leaders in the Eastern Church and claimed to be loyal to the apostle John, often quoted from the New Testament!

The controversial Epistle of Barnabas

The Greek Epistle of Barnabas written between 70–132 A.D. is included in the fourth century Codex Sinaiticus. Polycarp's letter to the Philippians 1.1–9.2 continues with Barnabas 5.7a and following, without any indication of the transition, survives in twelve Greek manuscripts.

Researcher Bart D. Ehrman has stated that the Epistle of Barnabas is "more anti-Jewish than [any of the books] that [made] it into the New Testament".

"Although the work is not gnostic in a theological sense, the author, who considers himself to be a teacher to the unidentified audience to which he writes (see e.g. 9.9), intends to impart to his readers the perfect gnosis (knowledge), that they may perceive that the Christians are the only true covenant people, and that the Jewish people are no longer in covenant with God (3.7). His polemics are, above all, directed against Judaizing Christians (see Ebionites, Nazarenes, Judaizing teachers).

"In no other writing of that early time is the separation of the Gentile Christians from observant Jews so clearly insisted upon. The covenant promises, he maintains, belong only to the Christians (e.g. 4.6–8), and circumcision, and the entire Jewish sacrificial and ceremonial system have been abolished in favor of "the new law of our Lord Jesus Christ"

(2.8). According to the author's conception, Jewish scriptures, rightly understood, serve as a foretelling of Christ and its laws often contain allegorical meanings. He is a thorough opponent to Jewish legalism, but by no means an antinomist (rejects laws or morality). At some points the Epistle seems quite Pauline, as with its concept of atonement.

"It is likely that, due to the resurgence of Judaism in the early 2nd century, and the tolerance of the Roman emperor Hadrian, Christians, such as the text's author, felt a need to resist Jewish influences polemically. In this case, the author seems to aim to demonstrate that Jewish understanding of the Mosaic legislation (Torah) is completely incorrect and can now be considered superseded, since in the author's view the Jewish scriptures foreshadowed Jesus and Christianity when rightly understood.

"The author quotes liberally from the Old Testament, including the apocryphal books. He quotes from the New Testament gospels twice (4:14, 5:9),[5] and is in general agreement with the New Testament presentation of salvation-history. He quotes material resembling 4 Esdras (12.1) and 1 Enoch (4.3; 16.5), which did not become part of the Biblical canon except in some traditions (e.g. 1 Enoch is considered scriptural in the Ethiopian church). The closing Two Ways section (chapters 18–21), see also Didache, which contains a series of moral injunctions, presents "another gnosis and teaching" (18.1) in relation to the body of the epistle, and its connection to the latter has given rise to much discussion." Article, Epistle of Barnabas, *Wikepedia*).

Irenaeus, a follower of Polycarp quoted the New Testament more than 1,000 times. However, Irenaeus also called other books such as the Shepherd of Hermas scripture.

Conclusively, the proof of the Bible does not depend upon when or who wrote the manuscript. Ultimately it depends upon its message of hope and love.

Introduction

Guess what God has done? He has REVEALED HIS MASTER PLAN of salvation and the purpose for mankind's existence through a myriad of agencies of interrelated subject matter!

These different facets include types, symbols, analogies, dualities, parables, occupations, numerical values, food, astronomy, holy days, the great pyramid, the family; etc.

Each of these entities contain a complimentary piece of this fantastically intricate puzzle that will enable us to better understand God's highest creation.

Why has God placed mankind upon planet earth? *Why* did He make man out of matter—*How* does one receive salvation? All of these seemingly unanswerable questions are *revealed* by God through these many different vehicles!

As we view the different types, numbers, holy days, parables, etc. of the Bible as a whole—we will see how God's Master Plan for planet earth becomes magnified!

We will become as little children playing on the shore, splashing in the shallow waters—realizing there are more joys in the deeper waters of the ocean! And like a mighty ocean, fathomless and boundless—God's Word will become a Sea of great Pearls.

Through progressive revelation of the types, God's grand design for mankind will unfold—but this will be a step by step procedure. Each chapter will add an intricate piece to God's most complex puzzle—but when it is finally completed, it will resemble a beautiful mosaic.

Every word of God's Holy book is in its right and proper place. Sometimes it may appear to be out of order—but the *lock* and *key* are there. The lock may be in one place and the key in another. The key may be hidden in a *number, holy day, duality* or *parable*.

This only proves that no one person, group or organization could have planned such a marvelous work. Securing such uniformity in consistency of thought would have been absolutely impossible without a "guiding hand." Though many different writers *penned* the Bible—God Almighty was its Pen!

Evolutionists would have us look at the earth with blindfolds on—as though it all came into being through time and chance. But the spiritual man sees the *order* and *design* of a Master Builder. He sees the *harmony* of the animal and plant kingdom. He understands the relationship of the heavenly bodies to the earth—ALL DESIGNED FOR GOD'S HIGHEST CREATION—MAN!

After we see the harmony of God's written Word—it will be made crystal clear that neither Moses, Joshua, the prophets or the apostles could have conspired such an incredible book. To do so would have meant fifteen centuries of conspiracy. The final writer would have had to know to write or use a specific word, or number a certain number of times, to attain a particular meaning.

How absurd!

To the contrary—each writer was unaware of the final intent. Instead, he was guided by God through the Holy Spirit to contribute a portion of truth to this perfect ordinal design!

After analyzing God's "bread of life" we shall start to "digest it" instead of criticizing it!

Types, analogies, dualities or *symbols* of one age may convey a literal interpretation of some part of God's plan of the future. This is a spiritual tool to help us better understand and appreciate the plan of God, rather than an acting agency.

As we scrutinize God's word under a spiritual microscope—we shall see the *perfection* of God's wonderful work. The seemingly *insignificant* will become highly relevant.

In the *types* we will see a jig-saw puzzle of God. Each set of *pictures* or *emblems* forms a piece of this intricate and fantastic puzzle. It is God's kindergarten method of instructing His children in the understanding of salvation through Jesus Christ! God uses *types,* etc. like a cartoonist uses his imagination to express truth by a *picture.*

By a *type*, in a Biblical sense, is meant a *picture* or object lesson by which God taught His people concerning His grace and redemptive power. A *type* is a preordained person, event or thing that *prefigures* a future person or thing in such a way that their familiar earmarks authenticate them as a distinguishable group.

An *antitype* is that which is represented by the *type* or its fulfillment. The passover is a *type* of Jesus Christ, and Jesus Christ is the *antitype*, our true Passover fulfillment (1 Cor. 5:7).

Old Testament *types* are instructive of New Testament examples. It is imperative that we understand what is meant by a *type*. The apostle Paul presents a clear commentary of the meaning of a *type* in (1 Corinthians 10:11). Concerning the various wilderness experiences of the Israelites Paul says: **"All these things happened unto them for ensamples [Gr. *tupos,* marg. *types*]: and they are written for our admonition..."**

This identical Greek word *tupos* is used in (Hebrews 8:5) for "pattern" and "figure" in (Romans 5:14).

In order to convey truth concerning the spiritual realm, which we are not familiar, there must be instruction in a realm with which we are familiar with, so that, by a transference of what is literally true in the one realm, we may learn what is true in the other realm. There must be a parallelism between the *type* and the *antitype* for the type to be of any value.

God has also unveiled His GRAND DESIGN through *symbols*. A *symbol* is something which stands for or depicts an idea or quality of something else. It may be a visible sign or representation of an *object, occupation, animal,* etc. to portray a much deeper *spiritual lesson.*

Unlike a *type,* a *symbol* represents something already existent, rather, than something yet future. However, the Passover was *both* typical and symbolical.

The Old Testament ceremonies were but *types and symbols* or *shadows* (Gr. *skia)* of New Testament realities (Col. 2:17; Heb. 8:5; 10:1). These were merely God's "kindergarten" methods to teach His children deeper spiritual meanings!

Accordingly, we see that the *type* or "shadow" (Old Testament) became the *antitype* or reality in the New Testament. Clearly, the Old Testament object casts a "shadow" in the New Testament actuality. Consequently, what was concealed in the Old Testament, was revealed in the New Testament!

The Old Testament planted seeds to bear fruit in New Testament fulfillment. The nation of Israel kept the holy days, but didn't understand their spiritual implication.

Physical *types* help us understand spiritual realities. For example, we would not understand spiritual darkness unless we understood physical darkness. We would not understand how the Holy Spirit works unless we knew about physical water.

Through *symbolism,* our spiritual insights and perceptions are enlightened, enriched and deepened. The wisdom of the visible expression through them *enhances* our innermost convictions.

The Bible contains many *symbols* for our Christian edification and in fact interprets most of them for us. For example, the book of Revelation describes the "bowls of incense" as the "prayers of the saints" (5:8). Satan is described in *symbolic language* as a "great dragon" (12:9).

Revelation 17:15 depicts peoples, multitudes, nations and tongues *symbolically* as many "waters."

By letting God's Word interpret itself, we are always on the safe side. There are times however, when *symbols* in the Bible will have to be interpreted through God's Holy Spirit.

There are some *symbols* which even have a *dual* interpretation such as the lion. A lion is *symbolic* of both Christ ("the lion of the tribe of Judah"), and Satan (the "roaring lion"). Oftentimes one entity will have *several* symbols to represent it. Jesus is described through symbolism as a lion, lamb, and a branch, while Satan is seen as a serpent, lion and dragon. The Holy Spirit is represented by water, wine, dove, wind and oil.

Numbers, names, objects and colors are also *symbols* which have deep spiritual significance as we shall see.

This book will REVEAL why we humans were born—God's purpose for our existence upon planet earth. God's plan for mankind is revealed through many different relationships and each aspect will be explained in detail. Each phase will reveal more about God's intricate mind, His personality and character!

It is my hope that once you read about God's wonderful plan and comprehend it—you will no longer be confused. Your eyes will be opened, "knowing good from evil" (Gen. 3:5). Then you will understand that what has appeared to be a maze of confusion is in fact perfect, orderly and the greatest masterpiece ever designed. Gradually, as we separate the kernel of truth from the husk of seemingly utter nonsense, God's fantastic and intricate plan for mankind will be revealed because: "**The Foolishness of God,** is Wiser than Men" (1 Cor. 1:25).

What has been written here, should be regarded as suggestive and not authoritative expositions of the truth. In my quest for truth, it is my hope that I have not looked for more in the *types* than our Creator has intended.

I do not profess to be a prophet, nor have I received special revelation from God concerning the end-time. I am merely a student of the Bible and would like to share with you my research for your edification, enjoyment and consideration.

If these opinions are correct, it is because God inspired them. If wrong or misleading, I hope no one will judge me too harshly, for I, like you will ultimately be judged by Jesus Christ. Though I do not press points of speculation as doctrine, I do give my opinion for reproof, for correction and for instruction in righteousness (11 Tim. 3:16).

Chapter One

IN THE BEGINNING

To understand and comprehend God's wonderful plan for man and the whole picture of the universe in order of time and sequence, we must go all the way back into prehistory.

Most people would probably tell you that the beginning of prehistory of the Bible is found in (Genesis 1), but the event recorded in (John 1:1) reveals an existence perhaps long prior to the time God created the earth and the material universe. Let's read it: **"In the beginning was the Word, and the Word was with God, All things were made by him, and without him was not anything made that was made."**

The term "all things" is translated in (Hebrews 1:3) in the *Moffatt* translation as "the UNIVERSE." Therefore, the entire UNIVERSE was made by the WORD of God! But who was the Word?

The "Word" is also God

The fourteenth verse of (John 1) says, "

And the Word was made flesh, and dwelt among us, [and we beheld his glory, the glory as of the only begotten of the Father], full of grace and truth."

The Personage called the Word was the one who ultimately was born Jesus Christ. The name "the Word," is translated from the original Greek word "Logos" which means "Spokesman"

According to *An Expository Dictionary of New Testament Words*, by W.E. Vine, *Logos* denotes the personal Word, a title of the Son of God...His distinct and superfinite Personality, His relation in the Godhead...His Deity...His creative power...

In the *King James Authorized Version* of the Bible, the word "Lord" is frequently used, and is usually in small capital letters. Wherever this word appears in capital letters, it is translated from the Hebrew word "YHVH." In writing in Hebrew, the vowels are omitted. They are supplied only in speaking the language. Thus the precise pronunciation of "YHVH" is not definitely known. Today, it is commonly assumed to be Yahveh or Yahweh.

The YHVH when more correctly translated, implies "The Eternal" or the EVERLIVING ONE, rather than "Lord." This Hebrew word reveals that the LORD GOD OF THE OLD TESTAMENT IS THE CHRIST OF OUR DAY.

The Lord—Yahveh—was the active partner of the One we now know as the Father, in guiding Old Testament Israel. He was "God"—the divine Spokesman, or "Word" of the Godhead in Old Testament times. And it was Yahveh who spoke to Adam and Eve in the Garden of Eden! The "Lord" who spoke and was seen of men was always Jesus Christ, for no one has ever seen or heard the Father (Jn. 1:18, 5:37, 6:46; 4:10-12).

It was the One that ultimately became Jesus Christ that followed Israel (1 Cor. 10:4). It was the personage of Jesus Christ that created Adam and Eve, spoke the Commandments and showed His back to Moses!

Christ the Creator of the Universe

And so, we find Jesus Christ is the second person of the Godhead. God has eternally existed (Ps. 90:2). GOD IS ETERNAL. GOD HAS ALWAYS BEEN! Do you need a creator for a being that has always existed? Of course not!

The difficulty in understanding eternity lies in our human minds. We deal in finite things...dollars and cents, years, miles, acres, gallons, pounds. We measure, count and estimate in units, always arriving at a definite quantity.

But eternity is without beginning. It is without end! Eternity cannot be limited to a definite number of years. Even as numbers can go on forever, so does God's life into both the past and the future.

Those things which have not always existed require a Creator. But things which have always existed need no Creator!

The material universe was created at a definite time in the past. Both science and scripture are firm on this point. Therefore, the creation is temporal and had a Creator. Since all in existence except the Creator is temporal, then HE MUST BE ETERNAL! He could not have had a beginning of days!

The Godhead consisting of Father, Son and Holy Spirit had creative powers—they had perfect supreme minds—they possessed perfect, holy and righteous CHARACTER.

In the beginning there was nothing else! There was no matter—no material universe—YET! No other living being or thing.

Only these three, equal in mind with divine powers, except God the Father was supreme in authority, and the Word and Holy Spirit in perfect harmony under that authority. They were of one mind, in absolute agreement.

However, it was the personage that later became Jesus Christ that did the creating. In (Ephesians 3:9) we read:

> **God created all things by Jesus Christ...Whom he hath appointed heir of all things, by whom he also made the worlds (Heb. 1:2,10). For by him [Christ] were all things created, that are in heaven, and that are in earth, visible, and invisible, whether they be thrones or dominions or principalities or powers; all things were created by him, and for him (Col. 1: 16-17).**

Truly, ALL THINGS were made by "the Word" or the one who became the Savior of the world He created—Jesus Christ! (Jn. 1:3,10).

Was the Holy Spirit present at Creation?

In the beginning God created the heaven and the earth. And the earth was without form, and void; and darkness was upon the face of the deep. And the Spirit of God moved upon the face of the waters. And God said, Let there be light: and there was light (Genesis 1:1–3).

Exactly how did our universe come into being? We have just read how Jesus created all things as the scriptures testify. But where was the Father and the Holy Spirit, of the Triune God?

The Hebrew for "God" is the uni-plural Elohim, a plural noun (as noted by the "im" ending), yet normally represented by a singular pronoun "He." This is the first foreshadowing of the marvelous doctrine of the Trinity—only one Creator God, yet functioning as three divine Persons.

It is only conjecture, but it seems the Father planned the work of creation, the Son did the work as "all things were made by Him" (Jn 1:3), and the Spirit empowered it as "the Spirit of God moved".

The problem that we have as humans is that we cannot understand the Trinity as three Divine Persons as being "One in Being" because we don't have any physical examples! There are not three Gods in the Trinity, but One!

The Holy Spirit is not a separate God with His own mind, acting independent of the Father and Jesus. Instead, the Holy Spirit is joined with the Father and Son in unity. This means that the Holy Spirit is fully and completely divine and has from all eternity all the attributes of the Father and the Son. Like the Father and Son, the Holy Spirit is omniscient, holy, omnipotent and eternal.

The Triune God is ONE in being, and the three Divine Persons are one in act. Whether in creation, redemption or in the perfecting of the creation, the Persons act together as the one God. However, there are times when Scripture shows the Persons working in distinct ways. For example, the Son becomes incarnate in a way that is distinct from the Father and the Spirit. Also, at Pentecost, the Spirit descends and indwells the believing church in a way that is distinct from the Father and the Son.

The unique names of the Godhead also reveal unique relationships. The Father has a different relationship with the Son than the Son has with the Father. And the Spirit has a different relationship to the Father than does the Son. The names identify and reveal to us unique relationships.

To summarize, the doctrine of the Trinity is strange to humans because of its uniqueness that three Divine Persons eternally exist in absolutely unique relationships, and that is what is essential to their being distinct Persons. We don't know how to explain what all that means, because we don't have any human examples and at best can only use physical analogies like water (liquid, solid and gas) to describe these unique relationships. That's why we use unique words because they are unique relationships.

The perfect Creation of Elohim

The first four words of the Bible are, **"In the beginning God..."** The Hebrew word for "God" in (Genesis 1:1) and throughout the account of creation is "Elohim" which is a uniplural noun for the God of Israel but is also used to describe other gods as well. When used to describe the God of Israel, it is generally; but not always, found in the plural.

When God said in Genesis 1:26, "Let us make man in our image and our likeness," the plural form appears both in the verb "let us make" and in the possessive suffix "our." Elohim takes a singular verb here much the same as family or church which can also have a uniplural meaning. For example, a church can have a singular meaning but when composed of many members, a plural meaning. The same could be said of God as a family composed of an infinite number of children!

There are several Hebrew words translated with dual meaning. *"Adam"* is translated as *"man."* The word *"Adam"* can refer to the individual; it can refer to both man and woman; and it can even refer to "man-*kind*." That the Bible refers to man and woman as *"Adam"* because the Bible says that the two are to become "one" Jesus also explained this concept as He said on several occasions that the Father and He were "one". See also John 10:30. In fact, Jesus also explained that His disciples should also be "one," as the Father and He are "one" (John 17:20–22). Clearly, Christ was not saying that the Father and He are one *being*; rather, He was speaking about oneness of unity of purpose of their mindset.

When we examine other Hebrew words we can see their uniplural meaning as well. The word Cherub and *Cherubim* is another example.

It was "the Word" of this Godhead that is Creator of ALL...the entire UNIVERSE with its galaxies, its suns, planets and moons.

The King James Version renders the word "heaven" in (Genesis 1:1) in the singular, but the original Hebrew is in the plural, and should read: **"In the beginning God created the *heavens* and the earth."** Genesis 2:4 makes this clear: **"These are the generations of the *heavens* and the earth when they were created, in the day when the Lord God made the earth and heavens."** Genesis 1:1 is correct in the *Revised Standard* Version, *Moffatt* translation, and others. God reveals himself as Creator of perfection, light, and beauty. Every reference in the Bible describes the condition of any phase of God's creation as "very good"—PERFECT!

The words, **"In the beginning"** in (Genesis 1) are referring then to THE PHYSICAL UNIVERSE when God created the heavens and the earth!

Is God a Family?

In one short remarkable sentence, the Eternal Godhead summarizes the purpose for His highest creation—MAN! "Let us (God-Father-Son-Holy Spirit) make man in our (Father-Son-Holy Spirit) image, after our (Father-Son, Holy Spirit) likeness" (Gen. 1:26).

Notice also that the phrase "after its kind" is not applied to mankind as it is for other reproductive life such as plants and animals. Why is this? Because God created man for a special purpose—to reproduce after His kind!

Some believe this is only a metaphor, a figure of speech—but could God mean what He says? Could God be creating a family of individuals with His character? A point of clarification must be made here, lest anyone think we are saying that God is creating more Gods! What we are suggesting here is that the Godhead is creating children composed of the same spirit (DNA) that will have His holy and righteous character, each with their own individual personality. The apostle Paul states in the eighth chapter of Romans that Christians are literally "sons of God" and "children of God," having received "the spirit of Sonship whereby we cry, Abba Father."

We read in Revelation 21:7, "He that overcometh shall inherit all things; and I will be his God and he shall be MY SON." Thoughout the Bible we read of family terminology such as Father, Mother, Son, Wife, children, marriage, divorce, etc. Why does God use these family terms? The apostle Paul enlightens us concerning what the Godhead is doing in Romans 1:20: **"For the invisible things of Him from the creation of the world are clearly seen, being understood by the things that are made, even His eternal power and Godhead..."**

Notice that the apostle Paul says that the Godhead (Father-Son-Holy Spirit) can be understood by looking at the things that are made! Is the apostle Paul trying to tell us here that the human family is a reflection of heavenly things including a marriage of the Bride Elect? We have read the scriptures that teach us that the physical realm of types are a reflection of the spiritual world and not visa versa!

Some may think it a metaphor, but the Bible tells us that there will literally be a marriage between Christ and His Church, the Bride upon His return. Christians are being prepared to be that spotless Bride. This plan was set in motion for the Bride before the creation of Man (Eph. 1:4). In order to understand the relationship of this spiritual marriage, God gave us human marriage!

The Spirit in Man

The Bible talks in several places about a spirit in or of man. Job 32:8 says, "But there is a spirit in man, and the breath of the Almighty gives him understanding." *Zechariah 12:1 says that God "forms the spirit of man within him."*

The apostle Paul explains that our human mental abilities come through this spirit: *"For what man knows the things of a man except the spirit of the man which is in him?" (1 Corinthians 2:11).* Paul contrasts this with the Spirit of God that gives understanding of the things of God.

What happens to a person upon death?

Ecclesiastes 12:7 mentions the spirit in man in speaking of what happens to a person upon death: *"Then the dust will return to the earth as it was, and the spirit will return to God who gave it."*

Heirs of God

We read in Romans 8: 16-17, "The Spirit of God joins with our spirit in testifying that we are the children of God. And if children, then heirs; heirs of God."

It sounds incredible, but the Bible tells us that we were created to be the Father's true children, sons of God, joint heirs with Christ (Heb. 2:10-11). Jesus is called our elder brother, the firstborn among many brethren (Rom. 8:29). We are called the children of God (1 Jn. 3:1-2; Jn. 1:12-13); and son and daughters of God in (II Cor. 6:18).

We have just read that God is reproducing "His kind"—but how is that going to be done? The apostle Paul tells us in Romans that it is when God's Spirit unites with our spirit. Yes, humans have a spirit in them which is not the Holy spirit, but a non physical component that can unite with God's Holy Spirit!

Upon death, all spirits go back to God! To put it into a modern-day comprehension that we can understand—it's like a computer/hard drive system. The computer is like our body, and the information is stored on the hard-drive or disc, which is our memory or spirit! This spirit, like a flash-drive can be put into another computer (spiritual body) or not!

But being God's children, what are we going to inherit? Let God's word tell us, "He that overcometh shall inherit all things; and I will be his God and he shall be my son" (Rev. 21:7). Romans 8:32 also clarifies this point: "He who did not spare His own Son, but delivered Him up for us all, how shall He not with Him also freely give us all things?"

Notice again God's promise to His children in Revelation 22:5: "And they shall reign forever and ever." Notice God's children are to RULE with Him FOREVER! This will be a glorious time when the Godhead rules over the earth: "And there shall be no more curse, but the throne *of God and of the Lamb* shall be in it, and His servants shall serve Him. *They* shall see His face, and His name shall be on *their* foreheads. There shall be no light there: *They* need no lamp nor light of the sun, for the

IN THE BEGINNING

Lord God gives *them* light. And *they* shall reign forever and ever" (Rev. 21:3-5).

Predestinatiion of the "Elect"

I would be remiss if I didn't address the very controversial subject of Predestination and the "Elect." This is a highly controversial subject and to summarize the most widely held viewpoints: 1) God has decided before a person was born, that person would be saved and have eternal life, and 2) God had decided certain people will have eternal punishment before they were even born.

The word "predestinate" is found in only two passages in the *Authorized Version* of the Bible. These passages are found in Romans 8:29-30 and Ephesians 1:5,11. Each time the underlying Greek word is *proorizo*. It can be translated "ordain" or "decide upon beforehand."

Many people believe that God has already determined the good and the evil, the saved and the lost, the sheep and the goats! But is Christian life only a stage on which a prearranged farce is being played out according to parts chosen at random? Kind of like a puppet show with auto-controlled mannequins oblivious to true freedom of choice?

Are Christians robots who unerringly act according to a present pattern and speak only the words already recorded for them. Are they dumb figures on a chessboard to be manipulated unprotesting by the divine power?

Let's think about this concept very carefully and evaluate its credibility using the Word of God as our guide. Here are some scriptures to ponder:

God's plan is for all men to be saved and to come to the knowledge of the truth ((1 Tim. 2:4).

God is not wanting anyone to perish (cease to exist), but everyone to come to repentance (2 Pet. 3:9).

God did not spare his own Son, but gave him up for us all (Isaia 53:6; Rom. 5:18, 8:32; 1 Tim. 4:10; Titus 2:11).

Everyone who asks receives; he who seeks finds; and to him who knocks, the door will be opened (Matt.7:8; Rev. 3:20).

Now I ask you—Do these scriptures indicate that God wants everyone to be saved or not? It sounds to me that the Godhead's desire it for all individuals to come to repentance and be saved!

That's why the angels rejoice when one sinner comes to repentance (Luke 15:7, 10). Why would there be any rejoicing if the plan was set from the beginning?

As we venture into the types and parables we shall see that there are many scriptures that speak of the salvation process in which God encourages us to heed His warnings. These scriptures make no sense if God has already predetermined our fate. Instead He gives us free volition!

We have a choice to obey God and choose Jesus as our personal Savior or not! We have freedom to believe Jesus died on a cross for our sins and was resurrected or not! (Rom. 10:9). Jesus said that there are two gates and two roads that we can take. One road leads to eternal life and the other to destruction (Matt. 7:13-14). The only requirement is for us to choose which road we will take! God will not twist anyone's arm, He only demands that we choose! (Deut. 30:19).

There is a compelling argument that some have with Romans 9:18 in which God says that "God has mercy on whom he wants to have mercy, and he hardens whom he wants to harden." But does this mean that God's hardening of someone is predetermined?

The reference to this argument is when God hardened Pharaoh's heart when he refused to let the children of Israel leave Egypt. If we follow the story closely, we will notice that God did this when Pharaoh was the ruler of Egypt, who considered himself a god. God already knew his heart (Ex. 3:19; 4:21, 7:3).

Another scripture that is used to promote "predestination" is that of Romans 1:18-32 where the apostle Paul says of the rebellious, God "gave over to a depraved mind." But once again, this was done after God knew they had rejected Him by their deeds!

The writer of the book of Hebrews speaks of some whom it is "impossible" to bring to repentance (Heb. 6:4-6). Why is this? Is it because God knew their heart before they were born or because of what they did after knowing God's truth and refused to obey Him? The answer is they rejected God after they knew the truth!

We could argue these scriptures until we are blue in the face, but ultimately if we believe God is sovereign, we must accept the fact that He can do whatever he chooses to do, which may not be the way we as humans would rationalize. Ultimately, we must have FAITH that God is just and merciful!

God is Sovereign but does He know everything?

We have just examined the controversy of Predestination and now we will examine God's plan from His Sovereignty. From the scriptures we have learned many characteristics of God's plan for mankind including the fact that Jesus was destined to die on the cross for mankind's sins from the foundation of the world.

Clearly, the purpose of God's plan is God's glory as the apostle Paul explains in Ephesians 1:5-6: that God chose us in Christ and destined us "according to the purpose of his will, to the praise of his glorious grace." It's hard to fathom as humans, but God does things for his own name's sake (Isa. 48:11; Ezek 20:9).

Indeed, the Godhead has made decisions concerning their plan from eternity as God "chose us in [Christ] before the foundation of the world" ((Eph. 1:4; Isa.22:11).

We have viewed the concept of Predestination and how God does not force us to do his will but gives us free choice. Certainly God has a part in providing that free will as God must call individuals to do His will (Jn. 6:37, 44; 17:2, 6, 9).

But does God's plan allow for God to change His mind? Scripture tells us that God does not change His mind, but how then to we account for the seeming alterations of his intentions? For example, why didn't God foresee how people would act in the following illustrations:

- Adam and Eve (Genesis 3).
- Mankind's wickedness before the flood (Gen. 6:5-7). God said, "…for I am grieved that I have made them." God wanted to wipe them off the face of the earth because it pained him. God caused a cataclysmic flood that destroyed the inhabitants of the earth except for Noah and his family (2 Pet. 3:6).
- God was angry with the Israelites when they worshipped the golden calf and wanted to destroy them (Ex. 32:7-10). God wanted to destroy them as

well and start all over with Moses and his descendants. But Moses seems to talk God out of it.
- Again, God wanted to wipe out the unfaithful Israelites when they refused to enter the land of Canaan because of the adverse report of the ten spies and start all over with Moses (Lev. 14:34; Num. 13:2; 14). God was angry but kept his overall plan by stating that no Israelite over 20 years of age (except for Joshua and Caleb) could enter Canaan. Eventually their children would be able to enter (Num. 14:20-31).
- God tested Abraham by telling him to sacrifice his son Isaac on an altar to see if he would be faithful (Gen. 22). It doesn't appear that God knew what he would do until he actually was going to do it, and God intervened and the angel of the Lord said, "Now I know that you fear God, because you have not withheld from me your son, your only son" (vs. 12).
- Did God choose Jacob over Esau before they were even born to make choices as the scripture implies? (Rom. 9:11-13).
- Nineveh is another example what appears a change of God's mind after specific determinations. Nineveh hopes God may "turn and change (nacham) his mind" (Jonah 3:9) and indeed He did Jonah 3:10).
- It seems that God "turned" from one course of action to another course of action and God "changed his mind."
- Some Bibles say God "Repented," which is a misleading translation. Consequently, many translations use the concept of "relent" rather than "repent" when talking about God. When the people repented, God relented or showed mercy instead of bringing harsh judgment.
- This, according to the narrative, constitutes a "change of mind," which is the basic meaning of the Hebrew verb *nacham*. God has a change of mind in response to a new situation. Given Nineveh's repentance, God shows mercy whereas previously

God was determined to "overthrow" Nineveh if they persisted in their sin.
- There are many Prophecies that are often conditional based upon the response of the people. The classic example of this is Jeremiah 18:5-11 (NRSV; see also Jeremiah 26:3, 13, 16):
- God is in control of events of human history, and can change these events before they occur if it is His will. In 586 B.C. the kingdom of Judah was destroyed by King Nebuchadnezzar of Babylon because of their disobedience of His laws and idolatry (2 Chron. 36:17). Of God's will and character the prophet Jeremiah wrote: "I am about to hand this city over to the Babylonians, and to Nebuchadnezzar, King of Babylon, who will capture it" (Jer. 32:28). The prophet Isaiah also declared God's words:

"Remember the former things, those of long ago. I am God and there is no other; I am God and there is none like me. I make known the end from the beginning, from ancient times, what is still to come. I say: My purpose will stand, and I will do all that I please. From the east I summon a bird of prey; from a far-off land, a man to fulfill my purpose. What I have said, that will I bring about; what I have planned, that will I do" (Isa. 46:9-11; see also Isaiah 14:24, 27). God "works out everything in accordance with the purpose of his will" (Eph. 1:11) as He declared, "Surely the Sovereign Lord does nothing without revealing his plan to his servants the prophets" (Amos 3:7; see also Isa. 42:9). God is sovereign and controls everything that happens on earth: "He brings princes to naught and reduces the rulers of this world to nothing" (Isa.40:23). He tears down and destroys and builds up and plants nations and kingdoms (Jer.1:10). "There is no authority except that which God has established" (Rom.13:1). God declares, "With my great power and outstretched arm I made the earth and its people and the animals that are on it, and I give it to anyone I please" (Jer. 27:5).

• God is omnipotent as He declares, "There is no god besides me. I put to death and I bring to life, I have wounded and I will heal, and no one can deliver out of my hand" (Deut.32:39). "I am the Lord and there is no other. I form the light and create darkness, I bring prosperity and create disaster; I the Lord do all these things" (Isa.45:7; see also 1 Sam.2:6).

Summary

Based upon the many seemingly confusing scriptures, the Christian finds himself in a very unique role. He did not ask God to call him. But God did call him according to His plan and purpose (Rom. 9:10-21). Most theologians agree on this point. But then we have many differences of opinion. It is my personal belief that God intended to call a certain number of individuals even before the world began (Eph. 1:4). Those that He does call, He "foreknew" in a sense even though it is not implied that specific knowledge of specific persons was involved.

Christians are not robots who unerringly act according to a present pattern and speak only the words already recorded for them. Neither are they dumb figures on a chessboard to be manipulated unprotesting by the divine power.

Think about it! If God had predetermined everything that is to happen in this life as some suppose, does it really matter what humans do in this life? Our way of life becomes irrelevant! If we are one of the "Elect" we would be saved no matter what we do! Why bother to evangelize? Why bother to preach the gospel if a preselected number of fortunate individuals are going to be saved regardless! Why bother to pray for missionaries and our lost loved ones! Why would God commend us for doing good, or chastise us for doing wrong if we were not free to choose! This concept makes no sense to me!

The Greek word *proginosko* can mean "general expectations" of human beings, as in Acts 26:5. It does not mean that God caused specific spermatozoa to impregnate specific ova to produce specific individuals all down through the ages.

Once God calls a person, He gives that person His Holy Spirit upon the individual's repentance. This already requires certain decisions. At every turn in his Christian life, he must make decisions. He has the free will to reject God's Spirit, his calling, and even salvation completely.

Jeremiah was predestinated to be called (Jer. 1:4-8) as well as John the Baptist while yet in their mother's womb! Although God's plan is basically fixed, I believe the part of the individual—your part and mine—has not been predetermined.

I believe Predestination has only to do with being called (invited) NOW—the first to be called NOW as "firstftruits"! Others will be called or invited to understand God's plan and purpose later. Predestination, in my opinion has only to do with those being pre-called—not prejudged or precondemned. It has only to do with those called first—before the world in general, as explained in Romans 11. It has to do with the Father of the Godhead opening up a person's mind to the truth (Matt. 16:14-17, Jn. 6:44), and the Son choosing His disciples (Jn. 15:16). As we venture the parables and other examples in this study, perhaps this will be made more evident!

Creation of Angels

King David wrote in (Psalm 148:2,5), of angels, **"Praise ye Him, all His angels: praise ye Him, all His hosts. Let them praise the name of the Lord: for He commanded, and they were created."**

Yes, angels are created beings—perhaps there are millions of them that God created.

Angels are spirit beings, composed of spirit, immortal, with life inherent. Jesus, their Creator, said so in Luke 20:34,

> **...The children of this world marry, and are given in marriage; but they which shall be accounted worthy to obtain that world [age], and the resurrection from the dead, neither marry, nor are given in marriage NEITHER CAN THEY DIE ANY MORE, FOR THEY ARE EQUAL UNTO THE ANGELS.**

It seems apparent that three levels of angels were created: 1) Ordinary angels which do not have wings, 2) Seraphim which do have wings (Isa. 6:2,6) and 3) Cherubs who also have wings and are the supreme creation in angel life. There is indication that there are three Cherubs mentioned in the Bible—Michael, Gabriel, and Lucifer, all of which are also Arch-angels! Although the Bible does not mention this trinity of higher angels as arch-angels—the apocryphal book of Enoch does (chp. 9,20,40).

The prophet Ezekiel saw strange creatures covering God's throne and knew they were Cherubs (Ezek. 1). These Cherubs appeared to men in ancient times and were known from the time of Adam until Noah as the guardians of the garden of Eden. When God placed two cherubim with "flaming swords" there to guard the way to the tree of life, they remained there from that day until the destruction of Eden in the Flood (Gen. 3:4). That was a considerable amount of time since that was about one-sixth of all recorded history.

There was a time when Michael the Archangel contested with Satan over the body of Moses (Jude 9). Michael came to help Daniel (Dan. 10:13). Michael will help God's people in the last days (Dan. 12:1). Michael and his angels will cast the devil and his angels out of heaven in the last days (Rev. 12:7).

Gabriel appeared to Daniel and gave him understanding of prophecy (Dan. 8:16, 9:21). Gabriel appeared to Zacharias (Lk. 1:11-20) and Mary (Lk. 1:26) to tell them of their new offspring.

Cherubim were able to manifest themselves as lions, oxen, men, and eagles—or as an aggregate of all four. These huge spirit creatures were preserved in stone as the "winged bulls of Baashan" on ancient Assyrian kings' palaces. Search the great museums of Britain, France, Germany, and Egypt, and you will see hundreds of examples of worship of "the host of heaven" as gods in the form of men with eagles' heads [common in the inscriptions of ancient Egypt, and in Egyptian tombs], winged bulls featuring the heads of men and lions' claws, and other assorted mixtures of these four.

The tales of the children of Noah, all of whom had seen those cherubim, repeated down through time gave rise to the mythologies about winged dragons, flying serpents whose mouths breathed fire, which guarded mysterious castles filled with fabulously valuable treasures at the top of craggy mountains. These all undoubtedly are mythological tales endlessly repeated and embellished, stemming from human encounters with Cherubim.

Earth originally populated by Angels

The inspired Job wrote of the angels in Job 38:4,7: **"All the angels shouted for joy at the creation of the earth."** This reveals that the angels were created before the creation of the earth and the material universe!

Based on certain scriptures it seems evident, although we can only speculate that the earth was originally intended to be the dwelling place of a third of the angels to prepare the earth for God's highest intended creation—MAN.

It is very likely the entire physical universe was created at the same time as the earth.

Lucifer Covered God's Throne

When God told Moses to decorate the interior of the Tabernacle in the wilderness with "cherubim" (Ex. 25:18), Moses didn't ask God, "What do they look like?" He knew, especially since he had come from a background of the royal courts of Egypt.

The apostle Paul enlightens us to the meaning of the earthly Tabernacle in (Hebrews 8:2; 9:1,2; 13:11). The earthly Tabernacle was a *type* of the true heavenly throne of God of which Christ is our High Priest (Heb. 10:1-18).

But notice that God told Moses to make only TWO cherubim. Why only two if there were originally THREE cherubim that covered God's heavenly throne? The answer is astounding!

God placed the great cherub Lucifer on the newly created, perfect earth, in charge of apparently a third of the angels.

This Lucifer was a super being of awesome, majestic beauty, dazzling brightness, supreme knowledge, wisdom and power—perfect as God created him. Now God created Lucifer with the power of free volition—FREE CHOICE to make decisions or he could not have been of individuality and character.

The name "Lucifer" comes from the Latin. It is translated from the Hebrew word *Nelel* which means "light-bringer" or "truth bringer."

Lucifer rebels against God

God's prophet Isaiah wrote of what happened to Lucifer, the great archangel that once covered God's throne in (Isaiah 14:12-14). Starting in verse four, we read of the physical king of Babylon who is pictured as a grasping, conquering tyrant, who is the lesser or *type* of the *antitype* who controlled him, Satan the devil. You will notice that things are said of the great former Cherub, Lucifer, who now becomes Satan the devil!

"How are you fallen from heaven, O Lucifer, son of the mourning... who did weaken the nations?" The name Lucifer means "shining one" or "shining star" [angel], Rev. 1:20) of the "dawn." He was the *light bringer*—the one who had tremendous truth, knowledge and understanding. Apparently, he had been given authority over many angels and it was his responsibility to teach and to educate them. He was the Illuminator of his day! He personified God's Holy Spirit!

But what was his attitude towards the responsibilities and power he had been given by his Creator? HE WANTED MORE POWER! He became filled with jealousy, vanity, lust and greed. He wanted to take over the whole universe! He said:

> **I will ascend into heaven [where God's throne is located]. I will exalt my throne [position of rulership] above the stars [angels] of God. I will sit upon the mount of the congregation in the sides of the north. I will ascend above the heights of the clouds, I will be like the most High (Isa. 14:13-14).**

In the original Hebrew the words should read "I WILL BE THE MOST HIGH" (vs. 14). Lucifer wanted to be God! The total boss of the universe!

This is how Lucifer became Satan the Devil. It was God who changed his name when Lucifer changed his character. Lucifer literally became a "Frankenstein Monster"!

More insight into this amazing truth is found in (Ezekiel 28). Here again we see a human despot [this time it is the prince of Tyre] who is a human instrument in the hands of Satan, the real ruler of this world. (Verses 2-6) plainly reveal that the prince of Tyre was an "insidious operator" who had accumulated a tremendous amount of wealth and power. In (verses 12-16) we see the real power behind the throne—Satan. Please realize, once again, just as in (Isaiah 14), that these words can in no way apply to a mere mortal human being, Notice:

> **Thou hast been in Eden, the garden of God...thy tabrets and of thy pipes was prepared in thee in the day that thou wast created. Thou art the anointed cherub that covereth; and I have set thee so: thou wast upon the holy mountain of God; thou hast walked up and down in the midst of the stones of fire. Thou wast perfect in thy ways from the day that thou wast created, till iniquity [sin] was found in thee. By the multitude of thy merchandise they have filled the midst of thee with violence, and thou hast sinned: therefore, I will cast thee as profane out of the mountain of God: and I will destroy thee, O covering cherub, from the midst of the stones of fire (Ezek. 14:13-16).**

This verse could not be speaking of the human king of Tyre, for he was never *created*. The only individuals that could possibly fulfill being created were Adam, Eve or Lucifer! *All were created*, and in the Garden, and all sinned! But the only one of these that was ever a *cherub* was Lucifer!

This Lucifer, then, had been stationed at the very throne of God in heaven, He was trained and experienced in the administration of the government of God. God chose such a being, well experienced and trained, to be the king ruling the government of God over the angels who inhabited the whole earth.

The Sin of the Angels

Incredible as it may seem, the first sin, even before man's, was made by the angels. Lucifer sinned (Ezek. 28:16) and apparently convinced one-third of the angels to rebel with him against the very throne of God (Rev. 12:4). Stars are *symbolic* for angels in the Bible (notice Rev. 1:20). In (11 Peter 2:4) we read,

> **For if God spared not the angels that sinned, but cast them down to hell [Gr. *Tartaros*—a condition of restraint], and delivered them into chains [restraint] of darkness, to be reserved unto judgment.**

Jude 6 sheds more light on this:

> **And the angels which kept not their first estate [earth], but left their own habitation, he hath reserved in everlasting chains under darkness unto the judgment of the great day.**

What caused the angels on earth to sin, to turn to lawlessness? Certainly, the ordinary angels did not persuade Lucifer, this great super being, to turn from God. No, most likely it was Lucifer that rebelled first and convinced one-third of the angels to plan a coup de tat with him. How long did this take after the angels were created is not known. God does not reveal this. It could have been one year or less to millions of years!

Lucifer becomes Satan the Devil

Isaiah continues Satan's revolution in Isaiah 14:12: **"How art thou fallen from heaven, O Lucifer, son of the morning? How art thou cut down to the ground, which didst weaken the nations?"** Jesus answers this disturbing question in Luke 10:18: **"And he said unto them, I beheld Satan as lightning fall from heaven."** Jesus, remember, was there in His glorified form as God! The account of round one of this great angelic fight continues in the Book of Revelation:

> **And there was war in heaven: Michael and his angels fought against the dragon; [another name for Satan—Rev. 12:9] and the dragon fought and his angels. And prevailed not; neither was their place found any more in heaven. And the great dragon was cast out, that old serpent, called the Devil, and Satan, which deceiveth the whole world: he was cast**

into the earth, and his angels were cast out with him (Rev. 12:8-9).

The power of the Creator was loosed upon Lucifer and his angels with such terrible destructive force that he and his regiment were blasted out of heaven and back to earth (Jude 6; 11 Pet. 2:4; Isa. 14:15). At this time, Lucifer's name was changed to Satan, which means enemy or *adversary* (Rev. 12:9).

Earth in chaotic Confusion

In (Genesis 1:1-2) we read, **"In *the* [Hebrew 'a'] beginning God [Heb. 'Elohim'—the God family] created the *heaven* [Heb. 'heavens']—same word used in (Genesis 2:1; Psa1m 8:3), correct in *RSV*, and *Moffatt*. And the earth *was* [Heb. 'became'] without form and void."** A big debate took place over 300 years ago concerning the word "was" in (Genesis 1:2) as to whether this word should be in italics or not. It is not in the original Hebrew manuscripts.

All words in italics in the *King James Version* of the Bible [translated from the original Hebrew and Greek manuscripts into King James English in 1611] are not in the original manuscripts, but were added by the King James translators.

However, the translators decided to make an exception of the word "was" in (Genesis 1:2) and did not put it in italics. This has only caused confusion to the true meaning of the context. **"Without form"** [Heb. "tohu"—means chaotic] **"and void"** [Heb. "bohu"—means confused]: **"and darkness was upon the face of the deep. And the Spirit of God moved upon the face of the waters."**

In (Jeremiah 4:23; Isaiah 24:10, 34:11) and other places in the Bible, you find the Hebrew words "tohu" and "bohu"; the words used in the original Hebrew in (Genesis 1:2) translated to mean "chaotic" and "confusion." The *Rotherham* and *Companion Bible* translations have these meanings correct. The correct rendering of (Genesis 1:1-2) should be:

In a beginning the God Family created the heavens and the earth by the "Word" or personage that ultimately became Jesus Christ. And the earth became chaotic and

confused as a result of Lucifer's rebellion: and darkness was upon the face of the deep. And the Spirit of God moved upon the face of the waters.

Yes, even before Adam was created, the world was in *chaotic confusion*. This is the period of time when Lucifer, and his angels, rebelled against the throne of God and became Satan the Devil! This is the time period when dinosaurs roamed the earth.

The earth turned into a cosmic wreck. Probably nothing lived through that terrible time. Animal and vegetable life was crushed out (Psalm 104:29).

For a time our planet stayed buried in a deep sea of gases, smoke and water vapor. There was no longer any dry land. Oceans covered the whole earth. The gases and smoke and vapor were so thick that no light could reach the seas that covered the planet. How long this condition existed the Bible does not reveal!

The seven days of creation then, were a *re-creation* of the earth by the personage of Jesus Christ!

Notice Psalm 104:30: **"Thou sendest forth thy spirit, they are created and thou RENEWEST THE FACE OF THE EARTH!"**

In order for the earth to be renewed or made new again, it would have to have been destroyed at some time. This was the time of Lucifer's rebellion.

Did God Create the Devil?

The Bible tells us a lot about the Devil— that he is a great deceiver, a murderer, a liar, the god of this world; etc. Why then would our great omniscient "all-knowing" (Job 37:16; Psalm 139:2–4, 147:5; Proverbs 5:21; Isaiah 46:9-10; and 1 John 3:19–20), God create such a being?

Because God is "all knowing" we must assume one of two things, 1) God knew that Lucifer, would rebel and become the Devil, or 2) Even though God can know all things if he chooses, did not choose to know Lucifer's fate. This concept can also be applied to Christians, as God may not choose to know our outcome as the theory of predestination suggests. This would mean that God would know the outcome of all things from the very beginning.

IN THE BEGINNING

To continue these two concepts, if God knew that Satan would rebel and fall from heaven, why did God create him? Obviously, it would mean that God would use Satan to further his ultimate plan, which was to create man in His "image" and "likeness."

As we continue the study of the types, we can only speculate what may have happened prior to the creation of man. The earth was a perfect creation as the created angels shouted for joy.

Lucifer, an archangel, a cherub, sat on a throne (a position of rulership) until sin (rebellion against his Creator) entered his mind and became Satan, God's Adversary.

No, God did not create a Devil—Lucifer became the Devil through his own volition (choice). It is not certain why God has allowed the Devil to cause deception, pain and suffering on this earth until Christ returns. But we must have faith to believe God has an ultimate purpose.

And the ultimate purpose of all things is for the glory of His Son, by whom and for whom all things were created.

Chapter Two

SATAN BECOMES GOD OF THIS WORLD

God instructed man in the garden of Eden the way that would lead to eternal life. Then He told man that doing the wrong thing—eating the fruit of the tree which God had forbidden—would lead to death (Gen. 2:17).

But Satan, the FATHER of all lies (Jn. 8:44), told the woman, **"Ye shall not surely die" (Gen. 3:4).** Satan deceived Eve through *subtlety*. Then God allowed Satan to confront Adam. Satan got to Adam through his wife. Satan subtly deceived Eve into DISBELIEVING what God had taught them. Adam followed her in choosing rebellion and rejecting God's rule and government over them.

When Adam and Eve disobeyed God's instruction and ate of the fruit of the knowledge of good and evil, THEY SINNED!

What is "sin"? According to the Bible definition: **"Whosoever committeth sin transgresseth also the law: For sin is the transgression of the law" (1 Jn. 3:4).** This law is defined as the 10 Commandments, for the apostle Paul says in (Romans 7:7) that he did not know sin , "but by the law: for I had not known lust, except the law had said, Thou shalt not covet."

The only law that contains the words, "Thou shalt not Covet" is God's 10 commandments. In (Romans 4:15) we read, **"Where no law is, there is no transgression." "For by the law is knowledge of sin" (Rom. 3:20).** This is exactly what the apostle Paul said in (Romans 7:7) as to how he knew what sin was, for: **"Sin is not imputed where there is no law" (Rom. 5:13)**. James 4:17 reads, **"To him that knows to do good and does it not, to him it is sin."** Adam and Eve knew what was right and good! Therefore they sinned!

Adam and Eve sinned! They broke three of God's Commandments. They dishonored their only parent...and thereby broke the fifth Commandment. They stole something, which wasn't theirs. They stole something, which didn't belong to them (coveting).

Paul writes of Adam's transgression: **"Wherefore as by one man [Adam] sin entered into the world and death by sin..." (Rom. 5:12).** Death is the penalty for sin as (Romans 6:23) declares: **"For the wages [something you earn] of sin is death; but the gift of God is eternal life through Jesus Christ our Lord."**

God placed the great Cherub, Lucifer, to carry out His government on the earth. But Lucifer *refused* to carry out God's will, God's commands, God's government. He wanted to substitute his own. So Lucifer disqualified himself. Adam had the chance to supplant him.

In the contest to see if Adam would conquer, if he would obey God—he failed. He obeyed the Devil instead, and the man became the property of the Devil ever since. Satan became the god of this world. Notice (11 Corinthians 4:4) in referring to Satan Paul says: **"In whom the god of this world [Greek meaning 'age' or dispensation of time] hath blinded the minds of them which believe not..."**

Christ conquers Satan

Jesus Christ came 4,000 years after Adam sinned to replace Satan as ruler over God's government. God had made a "fail safe" plan realizing that man would yield to Satan even before he was created. Notice: **"...Jesus Christ was slain from the foundation [casting down] of the world [age]" (Jn. 17:5,24 and I Pet.1:19-20).**

SATAN BECOMES GOD

God planned that Jesus Christ would die for the sins of the world even before man was created! The Father had said in effect, long before man was created, "We will create mankind in our image. But since they will have the power of choice, yet will lack godly character, *they will choose* the way of sin. They will, therefore, need a Savior. And since you [the one who later became Christ] will create man and be my Spokesman in dealing with humanity, it will be necessary for you to give your life for erring, sinning mankind." Before the ages of this world began, Christ voluntarily agreed to lay down His life for these yet uncreated sons of God.

We read of the great contest between Jesus and Satan—the great temptation of the devil in (Matthew 4:1-11). The story continues in verse 8:

> **Again, the devil taketh him up into an exceeding high mountain, and sheweth him all the kingdoms of the world, and the glory of them; And said unto him, All these things will I give thee, if thou wilt fall down and worship me.**

Notice, Satan offered Christ ALL THE KINGDOMS OF THE WORLD—they were His to give (Lk. 4:61)—if only Christ would *obey* him then. But Christ would not submit to Satan like Adam did and instead deposed him as ruler over God's Government!

However, it was not a part of God's plan that Jesus was to take over as ruler of this earth from Satan at that time. God has a time limit on His plan and Jesus will take over Satan's office upon His return. Satan will still be in control of this age until that time. But that time is short, and Satan knows he only has a little time left (Rev. 12:12). Then Jesus will take over with authority and take away the power of the prince of the air [Satan], and become the Prince of Peace (Isa. 9:6). This situation is like that of our government offices. Even though a man is newly elected, he doesn't take office immediately.

Eve was tempted by Satan in the same manner as Christ: Satan suggested an act contrary to God's command, then twisted God's word to make it appear the right thing to do. God said in Genesis 2:17:

> **But of the tree of knowledge of good and evil, thou shalt not eat of it: for in the day that thou eatest thereof thou shalt surely die.**

But the Devil twisted this and said, **"Ye shall not surely die" (Gen. 1:4-5).**

Thus mankind came under Satan's rule for,

> **Know ye not that to whom ye yield yourselves servants to obey, his servants ye are to whom ye obey, whether of sin unto death, or of obedience unto righteousness (Rom. 6:16).**

Had Adam and Eve obeyed God they would have ruled the earth.

A merciful God, He immediately revealed to Adam and Eve that One was to come who would again make it possible for mankind to have the opportunity of obtaining eternal life, for God said to Satan:

> **I will put enmity between thee and the woman and between thy seed and her seed, it shall bruise thy head, and thou shalt bruise His heel (Gen. 3:15).**

This verse has spiritual significance to that of Christ's Church and Satan's counterfeit system thoughout the ages. A male offspring born of a woman [Christ]—by a super-natural conception was going to make it possible once again for mankind to come under God's rule and obtain eternal life.

Proof of this is in (verse 20) of the same chapter. Adam named his wife "Eve" which means, according to *Strong's Exhaustive Concordance*, "life giver." This referred to some special life-giving property which would be imparted to mankind through woman alone [as represented by Eve]—eternal life through her divinely begotten Son Christ: for both Adam and Eve shared equally in the giving of mortal life to their offspring. This is the first mention given by the Bible to the coming of Christ as Savior.

Pagans knew of promise of Eternal Life

From this point on to the flood the records prove that the Devil was very active in deceiving mankind. The earth became full of sin as, **"All flesh had corrupted his way upon the earth" (Gen. 6:12).** This brought on the flood to show us the terrible results of disobedience.

Did Satan cease to deceive mankind after the flood? No! The Bible speaks of a man that many scholars believe had a profound impact on the existing world—his name was Nimrod!

Noah's son Ham begat Cush (Gen. 10:6). Cush was the father of Nimrod (Gen. 10:8). Cush in Hebrew means "Black" or "Burnt" according to *Young's Concordance.* Nimrod, the son of Cush, became a great hunter. Egyptian tradition shows that their god Osiris [Nimrod] was black (*Plutarch's De Isid,* et. Os; vol ii, p.359). Egypt is the land where the color of the skin is only slightly dusky. This then suggests that the man they worshipped was not of their own nationality.

Nimrod's fame spread to many nations and may even have been China's first king as Buddahs are black.

The *Jewish Encyclopedia* says Nimrod was the one who made all the people rebellious against God.

The land was overrun with wild animals which were a constant threat to the safety of the inhabitants (Ex. 23:29-30).

Because scripture tells us that Nimrod **"was a mighty hunter before the Eternal" (Gen. 10:8-9),** we can only speculate that it was Nimrod who gathered the people together and organized them to fight the wild beasts!

Cush and Nimrod build first city—Babylon

There was a better way to protect the people from the wild animals that roamed the earth than by constantly fighting them. Nimrod built a city of houses and surrounded this city with a high wall and gathered the people therein. Thus, the people were protected and Nimrod was able to rule over them. This arrangement was agreeable to the people, for **"They said...let us build us a city and make us a name, lest we be scattered abroad" (Gen. 11:4).**

The people not only protected themselves from the wild animals by building a walled city but also established authority of their own—**"let us make us a name."** This was to be a central place of mankind's authority—the necessity of their obedience to God was not going to be recognized! Nimrod was their leader. They built a tower whose top was to **"reach unto heaven".**

With a tower this high they could do as they wished—disobey God and still be safe from His punishment which had drowned the inhabitants of the earth once before. This was mankind's first act of open REBELLION against God after the flood! They thought they had placed themselves out of God's reach if they wished to disobey Him. They, like Satan, thought that if they could "ascend above the heights of the clouds," they "could be like the most High" (Isa. 14:14).

Josephus tells us Nimrod built the tower of Babel so God could never again destroy the people by a flood *(The Life of Flavius Josephus.* p.39).

Then it was that Nimrod **"began to be a mighty one"** and a **"mighty hunter before the Eternal"** in a ruling sense (the Hebrew word for "mighty" is "gibbor" which means "tyrant," *(Strong's Concordance).* Nimrod became a TYRANT over the people. He made the laws. Not only was he "mighty.. before the Eternal" (The Hebrew word "paniym" translated "before" here, should be translated "against"—*Strong's Concordance).* The Bible says Nimrod was AGAINST God! Conspiracy and sedition were carried on by him *(Epiphanius,* Book 1 vol.i p.7).

Like most despots, perhaps Nimrod wanted to be worshipped and turned the people against God as the apostle Paul writes in Romans 1:23: **"they changed the glory of the incorruptible God into an image made like... corruptible man" (Rom. 1:23)**, forgetting that God needed to be worshipped in spirit and truth, instead of through idols (Jn. 4:24 and Ex. 20:4-5).

Nimrod and Semiramis

Although it may be difficult to attempt who Nimrod and his supposed wife Semiramis were and did historically—we will try to piece together what we do know about them.

Very possibly, Nimrod may not represent any one person known to history, as archaeologists and historians have provided a great deal of clues from discoveries in Mesopotamian antiquity, including the Mesopotamian god Ninurta, the Akkadian kings Sargon and his grandson Naram-Sin (2254–2218

BCE), and Tukulti-Ninurta I (1243–1207 BC) of the Middle Assyrian Empire.

We must also believe that the Jews have been given a special calling to preserve ancient biblical history as Scribes.

From the Hebrew, the name Nimrod may derive from the verbs *marad*, meaning "rebel" or 'nimrodh' which is translated, "Let us revolt."

We know that names have meaning in the Bible and the name "Nimrod" may be representative of his character. Perhaps he represents a system that he started that rebelled against God soon after the Flood? Another Hebrew word describes him as a "tyrant."

The Bible informs us that Nimrod established a kingdom (Genesis 10:8-11). One would think anyone who has established a kingdom in history, especially in the ancient Near East should have something written about them. There appears to be much written about two individuals who have different names in various parts of the Near East, but with the same character as the biblical Nimrod. Coincidence or fact—you be the judge?

One commentator renders the biblical account thusly: "Cush begat Nimrod; he began to be a mighty despot in the land. He was an arrogant tyrant, defiant before the face of the Lord; wherefore it is said, Even as Nimrod, the mighty despot, haughty before the face of the Lord. And the homeland of his empire was Babel, then Erech, and Accad, and Calneh, in the land of Shinar. From this base he invaded the kingdom of Asshur, and built Nineveh, and Rehoboth-Ir, and Calah, and Resin between Nineveh and Calah. These make up one great City." (Barnhouse, *The Invisible War*).

The Jewish historian of the first century, Josephus wrote:

"Now it was Nimrod who excited them to such an affront and contempt of God. He was the grandson of Ham, the son of Noah—a bold man, and of great strength of hand. He persuaded them not to ascribe to God as if it was through his means they were happy, but to believe that is was their own courage which procured that happiness.

"He also gradually changed the government into tyranny—seeing no other way of turning men from the fear of God, but to bring them into a constant dependence upon his power. He also said he would be revenged on God, if he should have a mind to drown the world again; for that he would build a tower too high for the waters to be able to reach and that he would avenge himself on God for destroying their forefathers.

"Now the multitude were very ready to follow the determination of Nimrod, and to esteem it a piece of cowardice to submit to God; and they built a tower, neither sparing any pains nor being in any degree negligent about the work; and, by reason of the multitude of hands employed in it grew very high sooner than anyone could expect; but the thickness of it was so great, and it was so strongly built, that thereby its great height seemed, upon the view, to be less that it really was. It was built of burnt brick cemented together with mortar, made of bitumen, that it might not be liable to admit water.

"When God saw that they acted so madly he did not resolve to destroy them utterly, since they were not growing wiser by the destruction of the former sinners; but he caused a tumult among them, by producing in them divers languages; and causing that, through the multitude of those languages, they should not be able to understand one another.

"The place where in they built the tower is now called Babylon; because of the confusion of that language which they readily understood before; for the Hebrews mean by the word Babel, Confusion." Quotes from: "Antiquities of the Jews" pp 79-80 (Vol II of *Works of Josephus*).

Semiramis—"Queen of Heaven?"

We can only speculate as to the historical figure Semiramis, believed by some to be the wife of Nimrod and where goddess worship began. Historically, she is believed to be queen of Babylon, and where the concept of goddess/planet Venus originated.

Once again we must learn as much as we can from scripture, before we let unproven theories become fact instead of legend.

The Bible tells us that the Israelites were warned against offering sacrifices to "the Queen of Heaven" (Jer. 7:18). But was Semiramis this "Queen of Heaven?" Several prophetic writers including Alexander Hisslop has linked her to the harlot of Revelation 17, a type of the false church.

In 1858, Scottish minister Alexander Hislop wrote a book which has become a best seller among enquiring Christians titled,

The Two Babylons. The book's traces the pagan ritualistic practices of Nimrod and Semiramis of ancient Babylon to Roman Catholicism. The book has been highly criticized as being fraudulent by most orthodox Christians.

Here is what *Wikipedia* says under the article, Alexander Hislop regarding the books criticism:

"For example, when one tries to find the ancient history of Babylon, one account says that Semiramis is the mother of Nimrod. Another account says that Semiramis is the sister of Nimrod. One says it was Nimrod who married his mother. Another account says that that Tammuz not Nimrod married his mother.

"The book has been severely criticized for its lack of evidence, and in many cases its contradiction of the existing evidence: for instance, the Roman state religion before Christianity did not worship a central Mother Goddess, and Jupiter was never called 'Jupiter-Puer.' Likewise, Semiramis lived centuries after Nimrod, and could neither have been his mother, nor married him.

"Hislop also makes unacceptable linguistic connections and fanciful word plays, e.g. the letters IHS on Catholic Holy Communion wafers are alleged to stand for Egyptian deities Isis, Horus and Seth, but in reality they are an abbreviation for Ihsous, the Latin spelling of Jesus's name in Greek (Ιησους), although popularly, they stand for the Latin Iesus Hominum Salvator meaning Jesus, Savior of Mankind (which also fits the teaching of Transubstantiation, where the wafer and wine are said to become the body and blood of Christ)."

Unquestionably, there is ample historical proof of a mother and child worship in various parts of the earth long before Christianity, that many prophetic writers have linked to ancient Babylon. But did mother and child worship stem from Sermiramis?

Bible archaeologist Dr. David P. Livingston, has linked Nimrod to the Gilgamesh Epic:

"The person we are referring to found in extra-Biblical literature was Gilgamesh. The first clay tablets naming him were found among the ruins of the temple library of the god Nabu

(Biblical Nebo) and the palace library of Ashurbanipal in Nineveh. Many others have been found since in a number of excavations....

"The date of the composition of the Gilgamesh Epic can therefore be fixed at about 2000 BC. But the material contained on these tablets is undoubtedly much older, as we can infer from the mere fact that the epic consists of numerous originally independent episodes, which, of course, did not spring into existence at the time of the composition of our poem but must have been current long before they were compiled and woven together to form our epic" (Alexander Heidel, 1963: 15).

Livingston compares what the Jewish historian Josephus says of Nimrod,'and Gilgamesh:

"What Josephus says here is precisely what is found in the Gilgamesh epics. Gilgamesh set up tyranny, he opposed YHWH and did his utmost to get people to forsake Him. Two of the premiere commentators on the Bible in Hebrew have this to say about Genesis 10:9,

"Nimrod was mighty in hunting, and that in opposition to YHWH; not 'before YHWH' in the sense of according to the will and purpose of YHWH, still less,... in a simply superlative sense... The name itself, 'Nimrod' from marad, 'We will revolt,' points to some violent resistance to God... Nimrod as a mighty hunter founded a powerful kingdom; and the founding of this kingdom is shown by the verb with consecutive to have been the consequence or result of his strength in hunting, so that hunting was intimately connected with the establishing of the kingdom. Hence, if the expression 'a mighty hunter' relates primarily to hunting in the literal sense, we must add to the literal meaning the figurative signification of a 'hunter of men' (a trapper of men by stratagem and force); Nimrod the hunter became a tyrant, a powerful hunter of men.

"Likewise, Gilgamesh was a man who took control by his own strength. In Genesis 10 Nimrod is presented as a type of him. Nimrod's descendents were the ones who began building the tower in Babel where the tongues were changed. Gilgamesh is a type of early city founders..." (Keil and Delitzsch 1975: 165).

There are still other parallels between the Bible and the Gilgamesh epic:

- "YaHWeH" has a somewhat similar sound to "Huwawa." Gilgamesh did just as the "sons of god" in Genesis 6 did.
- The "sons of god" forcibly took men's wives. The Epic says that is precisely what Gilgamesh did.
- The Bible calls Nimrod a tyrant, and Gilgamesh was a tyrant.
- There was a flood in the Bible; there is a flood in the Epic.
- Cush is mentioned in the Bible, Kish in the Epic.
- Erech is mentioned in Scripture; Uruk was Gilgamesh's city.
- Gilgamesh made a trip to see the survivor of the Flood. This was more likely Ham than Noah, since "Nimrod" was Ham's grandson!
- References and Bibliography
- Brown, F., Driver, S.R., and Briggs, C.A. (abbreviated to BDB), *A Hebrew and English Lexicon of the Old Testament.Oxford* (Clarendon Press, 1962).
- Cassuto, U., *A Commentary on the Book of Genesis*, 2 vols. (Jerusalem: Magnes, 1964).
- Frankfort, H., *Kingship and the Gods* (Chicago: University Press, 1948).
- Heidel, Alexander, *The Gilgamesh Epic and Old Testament Parallels* (Chicago: University Press, 1963).
- Jacobsen, T., *The Sumerian Kinglist* (Chicago: University Press, 1939).
- Josephus, Jewish Antiquities. Books IIII (Cambridge MA: Harvard University Press, Loeb Classics, 1998).
- Kautzsch, E., editor, *Genesius' Hebrew Grammar* (Oxford: Clarendon, 1910).
- Kramer, S. N., editor, *History Begins at Sumer* (Garden City NY: Doubleday, 1959).
- Keil, C. F., and Delitzsch, P. *Commentary on the Old Testament*, vol. 1 (Grand Rapids: Eerdmans, 1975).
- Pritchard, J., *Ancient Near Eastern Texts and the Old Testament*, 3rd edition (Princeton: University Press, 1969).
- Roux, G., *Ancient Iraq*, 3rd edition (Harmondsworth, Middlesex, UK: Penguin, 1992).
- Thomas, D.W., Documents From Old Testament Times (New York: Thomas Nelson and Sons, 1958).

Serpent-Sun Worshippers

It seems that even after the flood mankind would not put himself in subjection to God's laws. Their carnal minds still *rebelled* against His ways.

Men turned once again to the Serpent of the Garden of Eden. Had it not been through the Serpent that they had learned the knowledge of good and evil? The Serpent did not pose any restrictions on man, so before long this great deceiver of mankind [Satan] became the "Enlightener of mankind".

Another object of worship was the sun. Did not the sun provide light and heat, as well as life to plants, animals and man? Since the sun provided life, it was natural to *associate* the sun as God, replacing the true Creator God as the life bringer. The sun in all of its brilliance is still not as bright as the great God (Rev. 21:23), and Satan desires so much to be like God in all of that glory and to be worshipped "as God" (Ezek. 28:12-19). Thus, by associating himself with the sun, he deceived people to worship him.

Therefore, these two *"enlighteners,"* the Serpent of the spiritual world, and the Sun of the physical world, became associated together. One of the most common symbols was a sun-god with a serpent encircling it (*Bursen's Hieroglyphics*), vol. i, p.497). *Davie's Druids* (p.437) also shows that the Serpent became universally known as the symbol of the sun.

Now we can see how ancient sun-worship is, in reality became Devil-worship! Mankind, at this early date, did not want to obey God's laws even though they knew them, so they worshipped objects suited to their own lusts. Objects that Satan himself had deceived mankind to worship and to submit.

Paul referred to this time period when he said to the Romans:

> **When they knew God, they...changed the glory of the incorruptible God into an image made like to corruptible man, and to birds, and four-footed beasts and creeping things...and worshipped the creature [thing created] more than the Creator (Rom. 1:21-25).**

SATAN BECOMES GOD

People were worshipping the serpent, a creeping thing and the sun! To prevent sun worship, the Eternal God had originally called it "shemesh", meaning servant.

These were some of the false beliefs that the people worshipped in Nimrod's time. They had rejected the one true God and worshipped in their own desires.

The Ammonites called their heathen god Moloch to which they sacrificed little ones. At some places an image of the god was heated and the bodies of children who had just been slain were placed in its arms. The worship of Moloch was known to the children of Israel before they entered Canaan, for Moses very sternly forbade its worship (Lev. 18:21;20:1-5).

In spite of this prohibition, King Solomon, to please his numerous heathen wives, set up high places for chemosh and for Moloch on Mount Olivet (1 Kings 11:7), though its principal place of worship in and after Manasseh' time was the valley of the son of Hinnom (11 Chron. 33:6), a place of such ill repute that "Gehenna", i.e; "the valley of Hinnom" became a type of hell (Matt. 5:29-30). The words "Moloch", "Molech", "Milcom" (1 Kings 11:5), "Malcam" (Zeph. 1:5) are all variants of Hebrew words meaning "the reigning one" (*The Zondervan Pictorial Bible Dictionary, p.* 550, "MOLOCH").

Confusion of Tongues

This open rebellion of God was an outrage to Him, so:

> **The Eternal came down to see the city and tower which the children of men had built. And the Eternal said, Behold, the people is one, and this they begin to do: and now nothing will be restrained from them which they have imagined to do...let us go down and confound their language, that they may not understand one another's speech. So the Eternal scattered them ...upon the face of all the earth: and they left off to build the city. Therefore the name of it is called Babel because the Eternal did confound the language...and...did scatter them abroad (Gen. 11:5-9).**

A city by the name of "Babel" was where God confused the languages of man. Interestingly enough, the word "Babel" means "confusion." God did not destroy the city, but, by confusing the language, He did slow down the growth of the city to enable man to have time to learn how to govern himself. Because of the separation of languages, groups of people had to separate as well, thus causing the beginning of nations as (Genesis 10:5,20,31) shows. At that time people migrated from Babel and took their pagan Sun-Fire-Serpent worship with them, and their memory of Nimrod and Babylon.

Apostasy Spreads

Apparently, this confusion of languages did not stop Nimrod's quest for power, even though it was increasingly more difficult. With increased zeal he continued construction work on the city of Babel and also built three other cities [Erech, Accad, and Calneh], which he subsequently ruled. These cities, mentioned in (Genesis 10:10), became the foundation of his empire that later expanded to include all of the known world of that time. This was land that God had intended for rule by Shem (Ex. 23:31).

According to *Bryant,* Vol. ii, p.377, Nimrod conquered all of the nations from Babylon to Lybia, which included Egypt as well. This area included the majority of the populated world. It appears that Nimrod's religion and government was placed on these peoples, thus making Nimrod the first person to impose any form of army, economic, political, social and civil system other than God's system of government.

Semiramis expands Apostasy

There is a legend that Nimrod was killed by Shem and the pieces of Nimrod's body were sent out as a warning to the cities throughout the country, the counterfeit pagan worship seemed to stop (*Wilkinson's Egyptians*, Vol. V, p. 17).

This evil apostatizing system became known as the ancient "Mysteries." The ones who became associated with the "mysteries" knew that in reality they were worshipping the forbidden SUN or SERPENT when they worshipped these new symbols. The outsider would not know, so it was a "mystery" to him.

The False Messiah

According to an early Roman historian, Semiramis was a very beautiful woman. Once her beauty was said to have ended a rising rebellion among her subjects by her sudden appearance among them. She fully intended to use her beauty to aid her scheme (*Valeriu Maximu*m, lib. ix, chap. 3, p.2).

Nimrod was known as the first to invent magic. To impress his convert he used tricks of magic (*Justinius Historia*, lib, i, Vol. ii, p. 615). Some early writers have speculated that Semiramis continued to use these tricks of magic or deceptions after Nimrod's death for the same purpose of impressing converts to her "Mystery" of the imaginary gods she had concocted.

It was thought that Nimrod was deified, then herself, and then her son. Due to the opposition, she gave them secret forms that were only known to the initiated and these were worshipped. These were the "Mysteries"! Outsiders from this new religious practice did not see the symbols, such as a calf or tree, were actually the same as the worship of Nimrod and Semiramis. These symbols represented the Sun and Serpent [Satan] and were the same as the actual Sun-Serpent worship which Shem had tried to destroy!

Those who wanted to take part in these Mysteries in Semiramis' day had to have it explained to them. The title of the priest that explained the Mysteries was called "Peter." In the primitive Chaldee, the language *(Parkhurst's Hebrew Lexicon*, p. 602).

Idolatry Spreads Everywhere

BABYLON WAS THE PRIMEVAL SOURCE FROM WHICH ALL SYSTEMS OF IDOLATRY FLOWED (*Herodotus' History*, book ii, p. 109). Layard in his *Nineveh and Its Remains*, vol. ii, p. 440, speaks of this Babylonian system of worship. He writes that we have the united testimony of sacred and profane history that idolatry originated in the Assyrian [Babylonian] area and is believed to be the most ancient of religious systems!

One has to wonder how mother and child worship has spread all over the world from Babylon the mother of civilization, after the scattering of Babel.

Why are there statues of the same mother and child found with different names all through ancient civilizations, dating before the time of Christ? Diana was worshipped all through Asia in Paul's time (Acts 19:27). The names varied in different countries and languages. In Egypt it was Isis and Osiris. In Asia, Cybele and Deoius. In pagan Rome, Fortuna and Jupiterpuer. Even in Greece, China, Japan, and Tibet is to be found the counterpart of the Madonna, long before the birth of Christ!

Chapter Three

GOD'S PLAN REVEALED BY DUALITY

There is a *duality* or contrast between the *physical* and *spiritual* in almost everything in God's plan in working out *His* purpose here below. This *duality* runs through the entire plan of God. It also runs through the prophecies. That means prophecy is fulfilled twice. Once in a small way, then in a big way.

In almost every case, the physical comes first, then the spiritual. There is usually a former *typical,* and then a final *antitypical* fulfillment of the many prophecies. God has revealed the spiritual to us through the physical (Rom. 1:20).

This is a method God uses to teach us His spiritual plan of salvation. But Satan is a great counterfeiter, as we have shown through the Babylon "Mysteries", and has tried to confuse everyone by his demoniacle system. This will be made more evident in the *dualities*!

The Old Covenant and New Testament bring out this *dual* relationship. Abraham was chosen of God to be the "father of the faithful" *spiritually*, and God's plan began with Abraham, the patriarch of the Old Testament nation of Israel, which became known as "the church [Gr. *ekklesia,* 'called out ones'] in the wilderness" (Acts 7:38).

The Old Covenant was purely material in the sense that it dealt with the physical nation of Israel, a *carnal* minded materialistic people, the *seed* of Abraham to whom the promised *seed* was to culminate in the Messiah, as well as materialistic promises of wealth, land and protection were made by God. In return for these physical blessings, the Israelites were to carry out physical rituals and keep the letter of God's 10 Commandments. These were temporal promises and did not offer eternal life.

The New Testament deals with Jesus Christ also the seed of Abraham. The followers of Jesus Christ [Christians] will have better *spiritual* promises (Heb. 8:6). Promises of eternal life! Ancient Israel was the physical *forerunner* or *type* of the New Testament "Church"—called out of Satan's world! All through the pages of your Bible, this principle of *duality* is interwoven into a beautiful embroidery which eventually reveals God's transcendental purpose for mankind!

On page 405 of his book, *Biblical Hermeneutics*, Milton R. Terry, defines what is a *type*: "In the science of theology it properly signifies the preordained representative relation which certain persons, events and institutions of the Old Testament bear to corresponding persons, events and institutions in the New."

Charles T. Fritsch, provides us with a brief definition of a *type,* and its difference between an *allegory:*

> **The definition which I propose for the word "type" in its theological sense is as follows: A type is an institution, historical event or person, ordained by God, which effectively prefigures some truth connected with Christianity...Firstly, by defining the type as an institution, historical event or person we are emphasizing the fact that the type must be meaningful and real in its own right...In this respect a type differs from an allegory...For an allegory is a fictitious narrative, or to put it less bluntly, in an allegory the historical truth of the narrative dealt with may or may not be accepted, whereas in typology, the fulfillment of an antitype can only be understood in the light of the reality of the original type (*Biblical Typology, Bibliotheca Sacra,* 104:214).**

A *type* then is a *figure* or *pattern* of something yet to come in the future. A *figure* is something that *prefigures* or is an emblem, image, or imitation of something yet to come in the future—a *type*. A *type* is a literal representation, illustration, image, example or symbol of a spiritual reality!

Baptism is a *figure* or emblem of the resurrection (1 Pet. 3:21). Adam was a *figure* or image of our Savior Jesus Christ, who was yet to come in the future (Rom. 5:14). The earthly sanctuary and Temple services with priestly functions was but a *figure* of the heavenly sanctuary and ministry of Jesus Christ (Heb. 9:8,9,24).

We will see through the dualities, that everything in the Old Testament worship was *symbolical* of spiritual realities, conveyed through physical people and emblems. Every physical emblem will have a spiritual counterpart!

Oftentimes, figures of speech appear which quite obviously are not meant to be and cannot be understood literally. The consistent theme of the Bible is God and His redemptive plan for mankind. Therefore, the main thrust of the Bible is spiritual, and these heavenly realities are often set forth under the form of earthly objects and human relationships. We will study these early experiences of the physical nation of Israel such as the deliverance out of Egyptian bondage, their passage through the Red Sea, the wilderness sojourn and entrance into Canaan as they relate to Christian experiences.

In studying the *types* we must be cautious in realizing that eventually every analogy breaks down, and we should therefore look for the main point the Holy Spirit is trying to teach us. Types and antitypes are never completely identical but only similar. For example, the Holy Spirit is described as "oil" yet it cannot lubricate your car. Christians are described as "sheep", yet we do not need to be sheered once a year! I think get the point?

TYPES OF CHRIST

Adam—A Type of Christ

There was the first Adam, who was *material* and carnal [in nature] (1 Cor. 15:45), just as the ancient Israelites. He was of the earth, earthly, but the second Adam [Christ] is *spiritual* and divine [in nature] and eternal (1 Cor. 15:45-48) just as will be the New Testament Church of God.

Satan *tempted* both Adam and Christ with *food!* (Gen. 3; Matt. 4:1-11). What Adam lost for mankind, Christ regained!

God made man mortal, physical, of the ground and of the human kingdom; but through Christ he may be begotten of God to become immortal, spiritual, and of the Kingdom of God!

The earliest *foreshadowing* of our Lord's death appears to be given in the *deep sleep* that God caused Adam to have. It was then that God formed [margin—builded] Eve out of one of Adam's ribs! This was a *type* of Christ *building* His Church through the deep sleep [death] of Christ! Only through Christ's death [shed blood] could the Church be built!

That is why the Church is Christ's body—for it was taken out of Him as "bone of His bone, and flesh of His flesh"! The life of Eve did not come from God breathing into her nostrils as was Adam—her life, like the Church, came from her husband! That's why Eve was called woman (Heb. isha or female man).

What a glorious *type* of the Church we have here in that it was fashioned out of Christ's death!

So at this point, notice the system of *duality* in this ultimate creation of God. Physically, man was made complete in two stages; first *male*, then the addition of *female*. Spiritually and mentally he was to be made complete in two stages; first a *human mind* empowered by a human spirit. Even as God had supreme mind, man was made with human mind. But in mind and spirit man was not yet complete. This is also the similarity between the Old Testament Church and the New Testament Church.

To complete His physical creation, once the female was added to the male, they became ONE as a human family. So, in the spiritual creation, the addition of the Holy Spirit of God must be added to the *human spirit*. This makes the man spiritually AT ONE with God. But even at this stage the principle of *duality* is still in force.

Once the Holy Spirit is joined with his human spirit, his human mind is complete, but he is still a human—now begotten as God's child. He is only an *heir* of God, not an *inheritor* of the God kingdom. He is only begotten, not yet born immortal as he will be at the ressurection. The *duality* principle continues as human birth is the precise *type* of spiritual birth. We will learn more of this in volume 4.

Abel—A Type of Christ

The sacrifice of righteous Abel is a *reflection* of the sacrifice of Jesus Christ, our High Priest for the sins of mankind! Abel's sacrifice was well *pleasing* to God, while his brother Cain's [symbolic of mankind's] was an abomination to God.

Mankind's first sin resulted in the slaying of an innocent animal to shed its blood. From the very beginning, our Lord taught our first parents that the penalty for sin required the sacrifice of Jesus Chirst for the remission of sins. This knowledge was passed down to Adam and Eve's offspring, and therefore Cain was without excuse for not sacrificing properly.

Abel was a keeper of sheep, but Cain was a tiller of the ground. In the process of time, Cain brought an offering of the fruit of the ground unto the LORD, but Abel brought of the firstlings of his flock and of the fat thereof. And the LORD had respect unto Abel, but unto Cain and to his offering he had not respect (Gen. 4:2-5).

When Cain slew his brother—he should have received the death penalty! But because of Abel's righteous blood, God intervened and spoke to Cain (Gen. 4:10). Cain received a *curse* instead of the death penalty (vss. 11-12).

This ancient event was but a *type* of intercession on behalf of our High Priest Jesus Christ for the sins of the world?

In this sacrifice, as in the sacrifices of the high priests of Israel, who were also *types* of Christ—was established the pattern of forgiveness of sin through INTERCESSION for others!

Of course the ultimate *intercessor* for sins is our elder brother and High Priest Jesus Christ! Because of His righteous blood, the death penalty has been nullified on our behalf!

Abel was the first *type* of high priest, followed by Melchizedek and then the Levitical priesthood. All were *types* of Jesus Christ, who we now emulate, as Christian priests!

Christian priests can *intercede* for their brothers and sisters because we have been made righteous through the shed blood of our Savior Jesus Christ! We then become a "living sacrifice" and pleasing to God. When we are righteous, God hears our prayers and can intervene in the lives of others on our behalf!

Thank God for such wonderful *parallels* to comprehend His wonderful plan of salvation!

Moses—A Type of Christ

Moses was a physical *type* of Christ and there were many similarities (Deut. 18:15). The Messiah would be a Prophet like Moses from the midst of his brethren Israel (Deut. 18:18). Moses appointed seventy rulers over Israel, Jesus anointed seventy disciples to teach the nations. Both confronted demonic powers and were successful in overpowering them. Moses and Christ fasted for forty days and faced a spiritual crises on the top of a mountain. Both quieted the waters. Moses the Red Sea, Jesus the Sea of Galilee. The glory of God was reflected in both of their faces, Moses on mount Sinai, Jesus in the transfiguration on the mount. Moses lifted up the brazen serpent in the wilderness, Jesus, the antitype, was lifted up on the cross to heal our sins.

Moses was a *lawgiver* like Christ. The Old Covenant was *mediated* by Moses, the New Covenant by Jesus Christ (Heb. 9:15; 8:6-10; Jn. 1:7, 7:19). Both performed *miracles.* Moses *led Israel out of* physical *bondage* during the first Exodus and Passover, Jesus will lead them out of *captivity* after He returns in fulfillment of a future Passover (Ezek. 39:25-28). Christ of course is leading His Church out of spiritual bondage to sin. Moses led his people to drink *physical water* in the wilder-ness— Jesus is leading His people to drink *spiritual water* (the Holy Spirit). These *prophets* of God were *nearly killed by Satan* when they were mere *babes* (Ex. 2:1-10; Matt. 2:16).

Both *bring plagues* to a sin filled and rebellious world! Moses and Christ were *prophets of God*, sent with His message (Lk. 1:76). Both leaders take "Israel" to a place of safety (Ex. 3:1-4; Rev. 12), and bring them out of the tribulation of this world (Ex. 12:31-36). The children of Israel would not hearken unto Moses (Ex. 6:9), just as their modern descendants [the Pharisees] would not listen to Christ!

Isaac—A Type of Christ

The offering of Isaac was a *picture prophecy* of the death of Christ—a father offering his only begotten son. Abraham was the *human type* of God the Father. There are many parallels. **"And if ye be Christ's, are ye Abraham's seed, and heirs according to the promise" (Gal. 3:29).** Abraham is the father of all the faithful (Gal. 3:7). Abraham was called on even as God gave His only begotten Son, Jesus Christ, for the sins of the world (Heb. 11:17; Gal. 22:2).

The son dead for three days [in Abraham's mind] is a vision of Christ being dead three days (Gen. 22:4). A *substitution*—a ram was offered instead of Isaac (Gen. 22:13), and Jesus Christ [the Lamb of God] was *substituted* for the sins of mankind. Both required an actual sacrifice. Even the wood laid upon the back of Isaac, was a *picture* of the Cross! (Gen. 22:6). And it was on Mt Moriah, the very same place where 2,000 years later God's own Son was offered. This was also a *forepicture* of Christ's resurrection from the dead (Heb. 11:17-19).

There is also the possibility that Isaac was about the same age [33] as Jesus Christ. Notice the words "the lad" in (verse 12 of Genesis 22).

Joshua—A Type of Christ

The apostle Paul says in (Colossians 2:16-17), that the **"Sabbath days are a *shadow* of things to come."** Notice, it does not say *were,* but *are!* Exactly what was yet to come is revealed in (Hebrews 3 and 4).

In (Hebrews 4) Jesus Christ's 1,000 year reign (Rev. 20:4-7) is depicted by the 7th day of *rest*—God's Sabbath!

Joshua is a *type* of Christ. Joshua brought the ancient Israelites into Palestine [the physical promised land]. Notice: **"If Jesus [Gr. Joshua—see R.S.V.] had given them *rest*..." (Heb. 4:8).**

Joshua did give the Israelites rest in the land of Canaan, or Palestine (Joshua 11:23). **"The Children of Israel assembled together at Shiloh"** [Heb. 'Place of Rest'] **(Joshua 18:1).** Those who failed to believe in God [except for the faithful spies] could not enter into the physical rest of Canaan, under Joshua (Heb. 3:16).

Notice how God compares *this physical rest* with *His spiritual rest* in (Hebrews 4:11). God's *rest* [through Jesus Christ] is going to be "The Kingdom of God" for 1,000 years of no war, disease, famine; etc. (Isa. 14:3,7). "His rest" shall be glorious, speaking of God's Kingdom (Isa. 11:10). The center column reference in (Isaiah 11:10) in many Bibles refers you to (Hebrews 4:1), speaking of the *rest* we can enter into with Jesus Christ.

"Therefore there remains a *rest* [or *keeping of the Sabbath*—see center margin of the K.J.V. and R.S.V.] to the people of God " (Heb. 4:9).

A Sabbath Remains

This chapter tells of the *millennial rest* to come for God's people who are faithful and inherit the promises of God. A "rest" is mentioned several times prior to verse nine. The Greek word for "rest" in the first part of this chapter is *katapausin;* however, in verse nine the word "rest" comes from an entirely different Greek word, *sabbatismos.* This word literally means, as most margins show, "keeping of a sabbath." The *Sabbath rest* is a MEMORIAL OF CREATION and a picture of the future Millennial "rest."

The fourth commandment given to the nation of Israel mentions the seventh day of creation as a picture of the *rest* that God had on creation week and therefore honors the fact that He is Creator. It also *foreshadows* the fact that He is going to bring a Millennium of peace to this world!

King Solomon—A Type of Christ

King Solomon was a *type* of Jesus Christ RULING over the nation of Israel, and his reign of *beauty* and *luxury* is a *type* of the Millennial setting!

Solomon had *wisdom* and wealth that exceeded all men and was the most powerful man of all time (1 Kings 10:4,7).

His reign of abundance and prosperity in which every man will have his own fig tree is a beautiful *type* of the Millennium (Micah 4:1,4; 1 Kings 4:20-25).

During this time, Jesus Christ will *rule* with His resurrected Church in a pristine environment truly fit for a King!

The Levite Priest—A Type of Christ

The 21st chapter of the book of Leviticus describes the Levitical priestly qualifications. Here we find the Levite priest, who was functioning as a *type* of Christ, could not take a wife who was a WHORE (vs. 7), but only a VIRGIN (vs. 13).

This qualification was representative of the "spotless" nature and character of the future spiritual Bride of Jesus Christ—the resurrected Church!

Levitical priests could not take a divorced woman, and only a woman from their own people (vs. 14).

Like our spiritual High Priest, no Levite who had a blemish [physical defect] could be a priest. Those who were blind, lame, flat-nosed, dwarfed, or had a broken foot or hand did not qualify to be a priest (vss. 18-20). Even the offering of the priest had to be without blemish (Lev. 22:24-25).

Thus, in the Levitical priesthood and it's detailed offerings—a beautiful portrait of the sinless, perfect life of Christ is painted!

Realize, the Levitical priesthood was a *type* of the Church. Everything that the Levites performed, Christ reenacted!

The nation of Israel, like it's counterpart in the New Testament Church was to be a kingdom of priests...an holy nation (Ex. 19:6; 1 Pet. 2:9).

God will bless mankind through the Church, even as the Levitical priesthood was commanded to bless the people! We will study the significance of the Levitical priesthood, and it's fuller implications to Christian principles under the Tabernacle in volume 3.

Christians—Types of Christ

Through the *types* we shall see how every prophet who preached the gospel and gave warnings of destruction for failure to repent, was a *type* of Jesus Christ! Whether it was Adam,

Enoch, Noah, Abraham, Isaac, Jacob, Isaiah, Ezekiel or David—it was a form of Christ!

When Jesus Christ came and was crucified—He started a Church through the apostles who continued this very same work. Each of them individually carried on the very same commission as did Jesus Christ. They formed a spiritual Body, replacing His physical body to do the very same work Jesus was given by His Father in heaven.

Christians throughout the ages, and today, led by the very same spirit, or mind of God have done the very same work! Ultimately it is God the Father who is carrying on His work in us through His Holy Spirit!

Every trial we face, every time we are persecuted for righteousness sake, every time we set a good example in marriage or in our family—we are emulating the life of Jesus Christ and the mind of God Almighty!

Truly, Christians are *types* of Jesus Christ individually—as well as a collective Body to do the work of the living God!

Joseph—A Type of Christ

The life and treatment of Joseph by his brothers is but another *type* of the life of Jesus Christ. Several incidents in Joseph's life are a *perfect portrait* of the animosity Christ received from the Jews of His day.

You will recall the story of how Joseph's brothers *hated* him because he was his father's favorite—and especially for his dreams of *rulership* over them!

This should immediately call our attention to the parable in which our Lord describes His fate at the hands of the Jews: **"But his citizens *hated* him, and sent a message after him, saying, we will not have this man to reign over us"** (Lk. 19:14).

We are also reminded of the parable of "The Wicked Husbandman," as Joseph's father sent his "beloved son" to his brethren only to find them conspire to kill him. They said of both Jesus and Joseph: **"...Come, let us kill him..."** (Matt. 21:37-38).

Joseph's dream of *ruling* over his brethren in which the sun and moon and eleven stars *obeyed* him [the eleven stars, himself being the twelfth—Gen. 37:9], was a *picture* of Jesus Christ RULING over Israel on the screen of prophecy.

PLAN OF DUALITY

The first verse in the twelfth chapter of Revelation records an almost identical description of Jesus, the manchild ruling over the nations, being born of a *woman* [Israel] clothed with the sun, and the moon under her feet, and upon her head a crown of twelve stars (symbolic of the 12 tribes of Israel).

Joseph as well as Christ the *antitype,* was loved and clothed by his father, and sent on a mission of mercy towards his brethren. But they hated him and conspired to kill him by delivering him into the hands of the Gentiles!

The price paid for Joseph when he was sold into slavery was twenty pieces of *silver* (Ex. 21:32), while Christ the *anti-type* was betrayed for thirty pieces of *silver!*

Clearly, the REJECTION and JEALOUSY of Joseph's brothers was a *mirror* of our Lords treatment of His own people! The story of Joseph also parallels Christ's life in that both were stripped of their robe and became servants to their brethren—but both were then EXALTED above measure as every knee was to "bow" before them!

Like Joseph whose brothers finally acknowledged him as their Savior during the seven years of famine—Israel will very soon hail Christ as their personal Savior and King, after He delivers them personally from famine and captivity!

Joseph was Israel's deliverer from famine; Moses from Egyptian slavery; David from the power of the adversary—and all were *types* of Christ!

Joseph's *coat of many colors* given him by his father was a *symbol* of his prophesied sovereignty (Gen. 37:3). Most likely, Joseph's coat was made up of twelve colors, each representing one of the twelve tribes of Israel—and Joseph was wearing all twelve of them! His brothers grew envious of him, for this *symbol* declared his *supremacy* over them.

The sun in Joseph's vision represented his father Jacob, the moon was Rachel, and the eleven stars (eleven zodiacsigns) represented Joseph's brothers. Jacob interpreted this vision for Joseph as he said: **"Shall I and thy mother and thy brethren indeed come to bow ourselves down to thee to the earth?" (Gen. 37:10).** Indeed, they all did as Joseph ascended the throne of Egypt several years later.

Joseph's Egyptian wife Asenath is a *type* of the Gentile Wife of the Lamb—who will also comprise a part as Jesus reveals

Himself to His Family! God's spiritual family will be comprised of both Jew and Gentile!

The whole, a *type* of God the Father [the sun], and Jesus Christ [the moon reflecting the sun]—ruling over the tribes of Israel! We will study more of the Zodiac signs and their relationship to the twelve tribes of Israel—as well as the colors of the high priest's breastplate in a Vol. 2!

Jeremiah—A Type of Christ

Jeremiah was a prophet of God who lived approximately 100 years after Isaiah. Isaiah had spared Jerusalem from Assyrian captivity, and Jeremiah tried to save it from Babylonian captivity, but was unsuccessful.

Jerusalem, was partly destroyed in 606 B.C. and finally burned in 586 B.C. as the nation of Judah went into captivity to Babylon.

Like the life of our Savior, there are many similarities to the life of Jeremiah. Jeremiah, like Christ was called in his mother's womb, before he was even born, **"to be a prophet unto the nations" (Jer. 1:5).**

Jeremiah began preaching when he was a young man as the hebrew word *child* is translated young man in (11 Sam. 18:5). Our Lord and Savior was around 30 when He began His public ministry Lk. 3:23).

Jeremiah's heart-rending pleas for the nation of Judah to repent are merely echoes of the many times Jesus warned them of the destruction of their city if they would not repent (Jer. 7:5-7).

Just as Jesus was a man of sorrows, so was Jeremiah as he implored the nation of Judah to turn from their wicked ways (Jer. 8:6; 9:2-9) and lamented their destruction (Lamentations).

It was God's will that neither Christ nor Jeremiah take a wife (Jer. 16:2).

Cyrus—A Type of Christ

It is difficult to imagine that God would use a Gentile king as a *type* of Christ—but as we examine the prophecy given to Cyrus the Persian king in (Isaiah 45), that is the only conclusion we can reach!

PLAN OF DUALITY

Cyrus, like Jesus Christ was named and prophesied to come even before he was born, notice: **"I am the LORD, and there is none else, there is no God beside me; I girded thee, though thou hast not known me" (vs. 5)**.

It is very possible that Cyrus may have been the son of Astyages and Queen Esther. This is confirmed by recent deciphering of the ancient inscriptions of the kings of Persia written by Herodotus, Xenophon, Ctesias, and Nicolas of Damascus who lived before Christ.

According to the Persian king genealogy, Astyages was the husband of Esther and the father of Cyrus. He was the Ahasuerus of (Esther 1:1) and Darius the Mede of (Daniel 5:31).

Astyages is listed by Herodotus as the 8th of a succession of Lydian kings, called Aryenis the husband of Vashti who gave up the queenship to Esther (*Dakes* p. 490, 868).

Herodotus says Cyrus was the son of Mandone, the daughter of Astyages who sought to kill the child because of dreams he had of his own defeat at his hands (*History* 1.107-130). Xenophan says he was the son of Cambyses, king of Persia.

Cyrus was the subject of many prophecies of Isaiah concerning the restoration of the nation of Judah from Babylon, and the rebuilding of Jerusalem and the Jewish Temple after the captivities (Isa. 44:28; 45:1).

His name was prophesied 175 years before his birth, the prediction to liberate the Jew and rebuilding of Jerusalem (2 Chron. 36:22-23; Ezra 1:1-8; 3:7; 4:3-5; 5:13-17; 6:3,14).

The story of Cyrus' birth is told by Herodutus who lived in 484 B.C. and is recorded in *Rawlinson's*. Cyrus was born approximately 600 B.C. Herodutus, a Greek, wrote about the Persian Wars, (see *The Persian Wars* Bk. L Rawlinson).

The story goes like this. Ostiago, the King of the Medes had a daughter named Mandon about 600 B.C. Ostiago had her married outside his country to Cambysis a Persian, and they had a son named Cyrus. It was Ostiago's dream of uniting the empire through marriage!

One night, Ostiago had a dream that the baby Cyrus was going to take over his empire when he died and therefore told his servant Harpagus to have the baby killed. Recall how Satan tried to disrupt God's plan by killing the baby Moses and Jesus when they were mere babes.

However, Harpagus didn't want to do this abominable act himself, for he realized that if he killed Mandon's baby, once the King died, she would inherit the throne and have him killed immediately for killing her son.

Instead, Harpagus gave the baby to a shepherd to do the job. But because the herdsman's wife was with child, and her baby was born still birth, he decided to keep Cyrus as his own, and tell Harpagus that he had killed Cyrus.

In (Isaiah 44), God called "Cyrus My Shepherd"—because he grew up as a shepherd. One day Ostiago met his grandson after finding out the circumstances of his birth. As fate would have it, Cyrus got the Persians to rebel against him and then became King of Persia himself.

To set the Captives Free

In verse one of (Isaiah 45), we read of Cyrus: **"Thus saith the LORD** *to his anointed,* **to Cyrus, whose right hand I have holden, to subdue nations before him, and I will loose the loins of kings..."** This verse should immediately ring a bell in connecting Christ as *God's anointed*, who will subdue all nations as King of Kings upon His return!

Continuing in verse two: **"I will go before thee, and make the crooked places straight: I will break in pieces the gates of brass, and cut in sunder the bars of iron."** The typical fulfillment of this verse occurred in 538 B.C. when Cyrus broke through the brass gates of the impregnable city of Babylon, and shortly afterwards set "the crooked places straight" by allowing the Jews to return to their homeland. Jesus Christ will fulfill this verse as God's "anointed Shepherd" when He returns to *set the captives of Israel free*, and straighten out this crooked world!

Again, the *duality* between Cyrus and Christ surfaces in verse 13:

> **I have raised him up in righteousness, and I will direct all his ways: he shall build my city, and he shall** *let go my captives,* **not for price nor reward, saith the LORD of hosts.**

The book of Jeremiah explained that the captivity would last 70 years, and then the Jews would be allowed to return. Other details about this deliverance were given in the book of Isaiah, which was probably among the "books" that Daniel studied. The prophecy in Isaiah is especially significant in this connection, for it revealed the *name* of the man that would set the captives free and cause Jerusalem to be built again. His name would be CYRUS.

It was Cyrus who led the armies that overthrew the Babylonian empire on the night the mysterious "handwriting on the wall" appeared. The 70 "weeks" prophecy of Daniel 9 was to begin with **"the going forth of the commandment to restore and to build Jerusalem."** The evidence is clear from secular history that it was Cyrus who gave the decree [although not the actual commandment] which restored the people to Jerusalem so that it could be built—both city and the Temple!

According to Bible prophecy, Cyrus was to be the one that would speak the word which would cause the city of Jerusalem to be built, as well as the Temple:

> **He [Cyrus] is my shepherd, and shall perform all my pleasure: even saying to Jerusalem, Thou shalt be built; and to the Temple, Thy foundation shall be laid (Isa. 44:28).**

Continuing Isaiah's prophecy of Cyrus: **"I have raised him up in righteousness, and I will direct all his ways: HE SHALL BUILD MY CITY, and shall let go my captives, not for price nor reward"** (Isa. 45:14).

As we journey through more of the *types* and *antitypes* throughout the remainder of this book, these verses and the *parallels* between Christ and Cyrus will become more apparent.

Zerubbabel—A Type of Christ

The book of Haggai contains several prophecies concerning Zerubbabel that very few are indeed familiar with. Some prophetic interpreters go so far as to say that the entire book has already been fulfilled—but based on sound scripture and history, we shall prove that these prophecies are yet future.

Zerubbabel was in fact a *type* of a spiritual leader to arise in the last days, *both* of which will be *types* of Christ! To understand these end-time prophecies, let's go back to the days of

Zerubbabel, and review what occurred to him and the nation of Judah.

Cyrus, the king of Persia had conquered the Babylonian empire in 539 B.C. Previously, Babylon had taken captive the Jewish nation in 606 B.C. God had declared 70 years of national punishment before the nation of Judah would be released for it's sins! This ties in with Daniel's "Seventy Weeks Prophecy" concerning Judah's *seven times* punishment in the desolations of Jerusalem.

Cyrus, being a wise king, always endeavored to secure peace and cooperation of conquered nations by granting them religious freedom. It was to this humanitarian aspect, that the spirit of God led Cyrus to grant the Jewish exiles their return to Zion, *to rebuild their Temple* (Jer. 29:10 14; Isa. 44:28; 45:1).

However, approximately 50,000 persons took advantage of Cyrus' generosity (Ezra 2:64-65). Only seventy-four Levites heeded this opportunity, along with four of the twenty-four orders of the priests [4,289] (1 Chron. 24:3; Ezra. 2:40; 7:13,14; 8:15).

Why did so few Jews want to leave Babylon?—because it offered them material prosperity and security of new homes and jobs. They were afraid of the long and dangerous journey back to a land that laid desolate. In other words, they chose to live in exile as rich slaves, rather than as free men in a poor country!

Do you see the parallel to today's Christian experience? Are the majority of people desirous of coming out of the MENTAL SLAVERY of spiritual Babylon in favor of worldly riches—or do they seek the spiritual truths and blessings contained in another country (heaven)? As we continue our explanation of the *types,* the parallels between ancient Judah under Zerubbabel, and today's Church age under Christ will become more apparent.

To faithful Israelites, the rebuilding of the Temple was the *symbol* of God's presence in their midst, the outward expression of faith, and a manifestation of true repentance towards the service of God.

Elisha—A Type of Christ

Elijah and Elisha, as a pair, in their personal lives and in public work, are *prototypes* of John the Baptist and Jesus Christ. The life of Elijah was a *fore-picture* of John the Baptist (Matt.

11:14). Jesus' ministry of kindness was an extension and expansion of Elisha's ministry.

The life styles of Elijah and Elisha were very different, demonstrating that many different kinds of men are called to do the work of God.

Elisha was flint-like; Elijah, gentle, gracious, diplomatic. Elijah was a man of the wilderness, with a cloak of camel's hair [as was his *type* in John]; where Elisha lived in cities, and dressed like society.

As Elijah went up to heaven in a chariot, his mantle [a *symbol* of authority] fell on Elisha. Elisha began to perform miracles immediately.

Taking the mantle of Elijah, he used it to make a dry path over Jordan, just as Elijah had previously done (1 Kings 2:8, 14) and what Jesus will do as He leads the nation of Israel out of captivity on their journey back to the "promised land."

When a present of twenty loaves of barley bread was given him, Elisha set it before 100 men, and the Lord increased the supply to feed them (11 Kings 4:42-44).

Immediately, we are reminded of the two incidences that our Savior fed five thousand people on five loaves of bread (Matt. 14:17-21), and four thousand on seven loaves (Matt. 15:32-37).

Elisha's ministry was filled with miracles, many relieving private needs such as feeding the hungry, raising the Shunammite's son from the dead, and healing poisonous pottage (11 Kings 4,5,6,7).

Jesus took the healing of Naaman the Syrian, as predictive that He would also be sent to heal other nations (Lk. 4:25-27).

When idolatrous lads from Bethel, the seat of Baal worship, mocked his bald head, Elisha called upon God, and they were torn apart by two she bears (11 Kings 2:23-24).

Elisha finished the work of Elijah by destroying the system of Baal worship—a *type* of what Jesus Christ, their ultimate fulfillment, will do!

Jonah—A Type of Christ

Through the very amusing and graphic story of Jonah in the belly of a great fish, there is a blending together of both Old and New Testament teaching to show a harmonious account of spiritual lessons.

Jonah's unbelievable and unprecedented experience is a *portrait* of the manner in which Jesus was buried and RESURRECTED from the dead! After all, it was Jesus Himself that made the direct analogy, and He said that the example of Jonah was the *only* SIGN the world would be given that He was indeed the Messiah!

This is why the *resurrection* of Christ after three days in the heart of the earth is vital to Christians. For it is the only SIGN which proves that Jesus was the *only* begotten Son of God the Father and Savior of the world!

Let us now notice some interesting *parallels* between the life of Jonah and Jesus Christ.

First of all, the Greek [as well as the Hebrew from which it was translated] word "whale" in the *King James Version* should be rendered "a great" or "huge" fish. This huge fish was undoubtedly specially created by God as the book of Jonah said the Lord "prepared" a great fish to swallow up Jonah (Jonah 1:17).

The text also says that Christ would be in the heart of the earth just as Jonah was in the fish's belly for the duration of three days and three nights.

Notice the comparison to Christ being dead for three days in the grave, **"out of the belly of hell [Heb. *Sheol* meaning grave] cried I, and thou heardest my voice" (Jonah 2:2).** Because Jesus was actually dead for three days and nights, it appears to have also been Jonah's fate as he reckoned that "the waters compassed me about even to the soul" (Jonah 2:5).

When God told Jonah to go to Nineveh, the capital of Assyria, and proclaim repentance—he wanted to run away from this commission. Jonah knew by neglecting their repentance, God would destroy them who were going to be used in destroying the nation of Israel for their disobedience. In other words, Jonah was willing to die in the ocean, rather than see his people Israel suffer for their sins. Likewise, Jesus expressed the attitude of being willing to die for His people.

Now here is another SIGN of Jonah that corresponds to our Lord's ministry. Prophesying the destruction of the nation of Israel by the Assyrians, Jonah **"...cried, and said, Yet, forty days, and Nineveh shall be overthrown" (Jonah 3:3).** This was a *dual* prophecy to the nation of Israel, as occurred in A.D. 70.

Using God's day for a year principle, each day (40) would correspond with forty years. It was precisely 40 years between the time our Savior warned the nation of Israel to REPENT in His day [beginning in A.D. 30] to their destruction of their city by the invading Roman armies of Titus in A.D. 70.

Another comparison between Jonah and Christ was in their burying. Jonah's head was *wrapped* in weeds (Jonah 2:5) as Christ's body was *wrapped* around with pieces of linen cloth (Jn. 19:40). At Jonah's "resurrection" he left the weeds that encompassed him behind, just as Jesus left his graveclothes in the tomb when He came forth from the dead!

What a wonderful *analogy* between Jonah and Christ!

Israel—A Type of Christ

There is a most fascinating *typology* between the experience of the nation of Israel and the life of Jesus the Messiah as prophesied by the prophet Hosea, **"When Israel was a child, then I loved him, and called my son out of Egypt"** (Hos. 11:1).

Here we find a most interesting parallel to the happenings of the nation of Israel to that of the baby Jesus as foretold by Matthew,

"When he arose, he took the young child and his mother by night, and departed into Egypt: And was there until the death of Herod: that it might be fulfilled which was spoken of the Lord by the prophet [Hosea], saying, Out of Egypt have I called my son" (Matt. 2:14-15).

These verses clearly verify the nature of *typology* in the Word of God. Both Jesus and the nation of Israel were called God's "son" and as such were entitled to very special blessings. Both were led out of Egypt, Israel during the exodus, and Jesus after the death of Herod.

Therefore, Jesus becomes the *antitype* or fulfillment of Hosea's prophecy and becomes the embodiment of the nation of Israel—or in fact *personifies* the nation of Israel!

In other words, Jesus relived what the nation of Israel did, [or should have done in lifestyle], by going back into Egypt, and fulfilled the exodus deliverance. Jesus' personal deliverance from Herod was the *antitypical* fulfillment of Hosea's prophecy and demonstrates the typological relationship between Jesus and the nation of Israel, both of whom were "sons" called out of Egypt.

In another typological relationship, Christian "sons of God", are also *types* of Christ and Israel coming out of spiritual Egypt or sin. In all three "son" relationships we find 1) Israel came out of Egypt, a type of sin, 2) Jesus lived a sin-free life, and 3) Christians are to follow in Jesus' footsteps. Becoming God's "Son" entitles Christians to special blessings. By following in Christ's footsteps, when He died we died (spiritually). When He was resurrected, we were resurrected (spiritually, Rom. 6). When He was "accepted" of the Father, we were accepted as righteous! What He inherits, we inherit. This relationship will be more fully explained as we continue our study of typology.

Chapter Four

TYPES OF THE CHURCH

The Church—A Mother

The Bible uses the physical *analogy* of a mother in describing the responsibilities of the Church. That's why the Church is called the mother of us all spiritually. Notice Galations 4:26: **"But Jerusalem which is above is free, which is the mother of us all."** See also (Heb. 12:22-23). Just as a physical mother must provide for and protect her children; so the Church must do likewise for its members. The minister must provide its members with [spiritual] food to keep them healthy and growing spiritually strong.

Eve—A Type of The Church

Eve means "life giver" and mother Eve literally gave *birth* to all the races. She is the *mother of us all* physically and a *prototype* of the true Church who will give us all birth spiritually. Mother Eve's seed produced Christ who will eventually give us all eternal life! Likewise, the Church [woman] that Christ is the head (Eph. 5:23) will teach people how to attain eternal life.

God says in (Genesis 3:15) He will put enmity [hostility] between the serpent [Satan] and the woman's [Eve's] seed—Christ and His Church. This hatred has existed since the inception of the Church and was prophesied to continue on down through the ages, until Christ smashes the head of the serpent! The "false church" of Satan and the true Church of Jesus Christ will come "head to head" in a final confrontation in the last days! The true Church will be victorious—and Satan's head will be bruised permanently!

The very first chapter of the book of Genesis contains the very express purpose of life itself, notice:

> **And God said, Let us make man in our image, after our likeness: and let them have dominion over the fish of the sea, and over the fowl of the air, and over the cattle, and over every creeping thing that creepeth upon the earth.... So God created man in his own image, in the image of God created he him; male and female created he them. And God blessed them, and God said unto them, Be fruitful and multiply, and replenish the earth, and subdue it: and have dominion over the fish of the sea, and over the fowl of the air, and over every living thing that moveth upon the earth (Gen. 1:26-28).**

Notice carefully God's twofold purpose for the human race: 1) to let them have dominion or RULERSHIP over the earth, and 2) to MULTIPLY their race.

God made the first Adam and Eve to assist Him in this masterful plan. We, the Church are the finished product of the Church (the 2nd Eve), and Jesus Christ (the 2nd Adam)! Eve was created to reproduce the human kind—and the Church is to help her Husband, Jesus Christ to reproduce the Christ kind! (Gen. 2:18).

It is through marriage that ONE FLESH is produced (Gen. 2:24). The actual act of intercourse *typifies* this relationship, and on a spiritual plane, that's why the Church is called both the Bride and Body of Christ!

The Hebrew name for Eve is "Chavah" and means "Mother of all living", and she is a *type* of the spiritual Church who is the Mother of us all spiritually (Gal. 4:26; Heb. 12:22-23). The Bible uses the physical analogy of a mother in describing the responsibilities of the Church, such as providing for and protecting her children.

These future spiritual children of the Millennium will be forced to obey God's laws, as it will not be a free-will society! (Zech. 14:16-17).

Here's what the *Revised Standard Version* says about God's future creation: **"For the creation waits with eager longing for the revealing of the sons of God; for the creation [the Universe] was subjected to futility..."(Rom. 8:19-23).** Yes, the entire Universe is waiting for Christ's Bride so it can produce LIFE like the earth. It is now in bondage (vs. 21), but then, Christ's Bride will give it LIFE, even as Christ gave the earth life in seven days!

Rebekah—A Type of Christ's Church

Through the marriage of Isaac to Rebekah, is a beautiful *type* of the calling and marriage of the Church to Jesus Christ! The 24th chapter of the book of Genesis portrays how Isaac's wife was chosen for him by his father! Isaac was to find a wife from his own people (vs. 4). Notice also that Rebekah was given an opportunity to refuse this offer (vs. 8). A suitable dowry was then paid to the Bride to be by the father [precious jewels] (vs. 53).

The *parallels* to the calling of a Christian and eventually marriage to Jesus Christ are apparent. Realize that no man can come to the Father [through marriage of His Son] except that God the Father call that person (Jn. 6:44). Recall, Abraham, as a *type* of God the Father was the one who made the decision to select Isaac's wife!

Finally, once the Bride accepts the calling, [invitation] to the marriage, a crown of jewels is given her (Mal. 3:17; Rev. 3:11: 12:1). In Volume 2, we will cover the exact sequence of the physical marriage of Isaac and Rebekah, as it will also apply to the sequence of the betrothal and marriage of Jesus Christ and His Church!

Isaac's wife Rebekah is a *type* of the true Church, and had to fall in love with him and *accept him* as her husband [as will the Church] before she saw him with her own eyes (Gal. 4:22-31). Both Isaac and Jesus Christ were *born by promise* and by a divine miracle from God. Isaac being born when his father was 100 years old, and Jesus being born of a virgin.

Rebekah was a *virgin* [Heb. *bethulah*, "whom no man had known"] (Gen. 24:16) as will be Christ's *spotless Bride* (11 Cor. 11:2-3). Even as Rebekah drew *physical water* out of a well (Gen. 24:19, the Church must draw *living water* [the Holy Spirit] from God (Jn. 7:38).

Ruth—A Type of The Gentile True Church

The book of Ruth is a wonderful story of a converted heathen maiden who won the heart of her earthly lord. This is a powerful prophetic message for us today, for we win Christ in the same way that Ruth won Boaz!

The story of Ruth begins with these words: **"There was a famine in the land" (Ruth 1:1).** Thus, the Israelite Elimelech, his wife Naomi and their two sons, Mahlon and Chilion, flee Judah for Moab. Elimelech dies there, and Naomi's two sons marry heathen wives, Orpah and Ruth. They remain in Moab for another ten years where Naomi's sons die. Moab is a place of idolatry. In fact, the name "Moab" stands for fornication. The Eternal forbade the Israelites to marry Moabite women, notice: **"…for surely they will turn away your heart after their gods" (1 Kings 11:2).**

Back in Judah, "the Lord had visited his people in giving them bread" (Ruth 1:6). The word came to Naomi that the famine in Judah was over—that once again God had visited His people with plenty of bread and blessings.

Naomi tried to discourage her two daughters in-law from going with her, but rather to remain with their families (Ruth 1:8-9). Orpah remains in the land of idolatry, but Ruth desires to leave with Naomi.

Ruth, a widowed gentile of the land of Moab, *typified* the Gentile New Testament Church. Ruth followed her mother in-law, Naomi, back to Israel (Ruth 1:6-7). Naomi could be considered a *type* of the Holy Spirit. When Ruth and Naomi arrived, the firstfruits harvest was underway (Ruth 1:22).

Ruth is penniless, with no future in sight; yet she is a virtuous woman and has committed everything to the Lord. She says, **"Let me now go to the field, and glean" (Ruth 2:2).** Only the very poor do such work, for the law demanded the owners not harvest the four corners of their fields and not glean the remains, so that the poor could have them (Lev. 19:9-10).

Ruth and Naomi were poor and destitute, but Naomi pointed Ruth to her husband Elimelech's kin, the rich landowner Boaz whose field they were gleaning (Ruth 2:3-5). Boaz is a *type* of Jesus Christ and grew to love Ruth and married her. This true story *pictures* Christ's future marriage to the Gentile Church. The commentary suggesting that the True Church is composed of all peoples!

From the moment Ruth crossed the border and trusted her life to be protected under God's wing, she was supernaturally led by God's Spirit to her ultimate destiny. Do you see the parallel to Christians?

Commitment brought Blessings

What attracted Boaz to Ruth? She asks him that question herself: **"Why have I found grace in thine eyes, that thou shouldest take knowledge of me, seeing I am a stranger"?** And Boaz answered and said unto her, **"It hath fully been shewed me, all that thou hast done unto thy mother in law...and how thou hast left thy father and thy mother, and the land of thy nativity" (Ruth 2:10-11).**

Boaz was first attracted to Ruth because she wanted to leave Moab, the land of sin, and live a righteous life!

Can you see the bigger picture? Ruth's Boaz is a *type* of Jesus Christ! From the moment we begin to walk in RIGHTEOUSNESS and forsake the Moab in our lives—the former idols, old friends and old ways—is when the eyes of Christ fall upon us! That is when, like Ruth, we will never hunger [spiritually] again!

Boaz did this for Ruth, and these words of Boaz were the clincher for her: **"Inasmuch as thou followedst not young men, whether poor or rich."** Think of what Boaz said: **"I will do for you all that you have desired."** Every desire of her heart would be granted because she was faithful—because she did not have roving eyes! She had not looked for wealth, success or glamour. She wanted only Boaz!

So, at the gate of Bethlehem, before ten witnesses, Boaz redeems Ruth's inheritance. He satisfies all claims to her and her possessions:

> **Boaz said unto the elders, and unto all the people, Ye are witnesses this day, that I have bought all that was...of the hand of Naomi. Moreover Ruth...have I purchased to be my wife, to raise up the name of the dead upon his inheritance, that the name of the dead be not cut off (Ruth 4:9).**

The book of Ruth clearly illustrates God's plan of *redemption* for mankind! After Naomi's husband and two sons died, she returns to Bethlehem with no property [Naomi's husband had previously sold their property], no sons and no grandsons! According to the Levirate law, a kinsman of her husband could legally marry her and reclaim her sold property. However, the only one who came to her rescue was Boaz, a near relative, who bought back Naomi's possessions and also married Ruth! Like Jesus Christ, Boaz came forth to claim what was legally lost!

This is the work of the Cross! Jesus has cleared all claims of the devil on us or our inheritance. We are now free to be espoused to Christ!

Interestingly enough, the promised Seed, Jesus Christ, came from this marriage between a Jew and a gentile (Ruth 4:18-22). Today, instead of calling only one nation, God calls, **"...out of every tribe and tongue and people and nation" (Rev. 5:9).** This time God's spiritual nation—God's firstfruits—will not fail! Through physical Israel, God showed the creation of a peaceful, abundant society cannot be accomplished by man alone. It requires God's Holy Spirit, the very power of God.

Even as Ruth's transcendental purpose was accomplished, God has planted the seeds of His Kingdom, and those seeds are going to bear abundant fruit. Every physical seed carries the genetic codes required to produce the type of plant the seed produces. The Creator works the same way with His spiritual seed (1 Cor. 15:37-38). The Master's skillful hand is creating the qualities needed for His Kingdom inside His spiritual firstfruits.

Ezekiel 16 is discussing two marriages. First, an old covenant marriage with ancient Israel. The second is the new covenant marriage with Jesus and His Church bound by the Holy Spirit! The Church in the wilderness as it was called was not led by the Holy Spirit, but this is the main focus of the new covenant marriage. The Bible tells us there are two Israels, one physical and one spiritual! The Church in the wilderness could not even keep the letter of the law because they did not have God's Holy Spirit.

Now here is something interesting in describing Ancient Israel as recorded in Ezekiel 16:8, **"Now when I passed by thee, and looked upon thee, behold, thy time was the time of love; and I spread my skirt over thee, and covered thy nakedness: yea, I sware unto thee, and entered into a covenant with thee, saith the Lord God, and thou becamest mine."**

The expression "spread my skirt over you" is a sign of marriage. The best explanation is in Ruth 3:8-11 where Ruth meets Boaz. It is at the time of the firstfruit harvest in Israel. The firstfruits of the new testament marriage began on Pentecost, and will most likely climax in a marriage on a future day of Pentecost. The day of Pentecost pictures God marrying His wife. The marriage of Boaz and Ruth was a *type* of Christ marrying His Church!

Samson—A Type of The True Church

The love story between Judge Samson and the insidious Delilah, is a beautiful *parallel* between the Christ's Church, and Satan's COUNTERFEIT system during the last days.

As you will recollect, Samson's miraculous strength was proportional to his lengthy uncut hair which *symbolized* God's Holy Spirit. After being betrayed by Delilah, Samson's source of power was revealed to the Philistines, who took him captive, after which his hair was shorn and his eyes were poked out.

Samson cried out to God for vengeance upon these wicked Philistines who had taken away his eyesight. Samson's hair eventually grew back, and one day a "lad" led the spiritually restored Samson between two supporting pillars of the temple Dagon—where he brought the entire temple down with him!

In these last days before our Savior returns, many "lukewarm Christians" are going to go through a *refining process* to reawaken their conscience out of *spiritual slumber* and *blindness.*

During the Tribulation, these lukewarm Christians will cry out to God like Samson to take vengeance upon their wicked Philistine oppressors of the "Beast" power! Many will be martyred at this time—only to be delivered by a "lad" who will in *antitype* place the two hands of the Church upon the two supporting pillars of Satan's domain (the Beast and his image).

Then the kingdom of the "powers of darkness" will come crashing down like a house of cards—and the prince of the powers of evil will be smitten like the idol of Dagon *under the feet* of all the Church—by the Seed of the Woman (Christ)!

Haggar—A Type of The Old Testament Church

Haggar, Abraham's bondwoman, is yet another *type* of the Old Testament Church, known as "The Church in the Wilderness" (Acts 7:38). Recall the Old Covenant was based upon physical promises such as provision for food and protection in return for obedience to God's 10 Commandments.

The 10 Commandments were the basis of the civil and religious government in the nation of Israel. Certain rituals and ceremonies were performed, accompanied by animal sacrifices for disobeying God's divine laws!

These carnal-minded people, without God's Holy Spirit were only required to keep the "letter" of God's law—not the "spirit."

However, they were held in *bondage* to their human nature and to sin. This analogy is described as an "allegory" or *type* of Haggar, who was Abraham's *slave* woman that conceived Abraham's first son Ishmael, as outlined in (Galatians 4:22-31).

Contrariwise, Isaac was born by *promise* of God when he was 100 years old, and represents the New Covenant promise of God's Holy Spirit to Christians!

The apostle Paul writes of this allegory between Sarah's son Isaac and Haggar's son Ishmael and the two covenants in Galatians 4:24-26:

> **Which things are *an allegory:* for these are the two covenants; the one from the mount Sinai, which gendereth to *bondage,* which is [represents] Agar [Haggar]. For this Agar is mount Sinai in Arabia, [on earth] and answereth to Jerusalem which now is [on earth], and is in bondage with her children.**

TYPES OF THE CHURCH

But Jerusalem which is above [in heaven] is free, which is the mother of us [Christians] all.

Physical Jerusalem was under the spirit of BONDAGE because it didn't have God's Holy Spirit. But Jerusalem above, [whose citizens are New Testament Saints] are FREE—because they have God's Holy Spirit and are not controlled by, or in *bondage* to their human nature!

Hebrews 8:6-13 tells us that the old covenant is obsolete and the new covenant has been established. The old covenant, known as "the law of Moses" contained laws such as the Ten Commandments, Feast days, and sacrifices for sin. These laws were appropriate for the nation of Israel but they are not all the requirements for Christians today (Gal. 3:19; Heb. 9:10). This has been a supreme controversy in Christian circles, especially regarding the sabbath as to which specific practices that are required today.

The author of Hebrews informs us that when Jesus died as a ransom for sin, He set us free from the obligation of offering animal sacrifices of the old covenant. The old covenant is no longer the standard of righteousness and sin. Christ forgives sin, but he sets us free from the rituals of the old covenant.

Chapter three of the book of Galatians is one of the most confusing to interpret among Christians. The apostle Paul was astounded that they were being influenced by Jewish proselytes to go back to a system of observing "the law of Moses" to be saved after accepting the sacrifice of Jesus by "faith." Paul was telling them that their human effort of keeping the law is not what saves them, but their faith in what Jesus did for them! That Christians cannot be saved through human effort and that Jesus died for our sins on the cross! Whatever work had to be done to be accepted of God for our sins, was done by Jesus!

The law that was introduced 430 years after the promise to Abraham does not set aside the covenant previously established by God and thus do away with the promise (Gal. 3:17). That is, the "law of Moses" cannot change the fact that God accepts people as righteous on the basis of faith, not human efforts. The "Law of Moses" was not designed to give us eternal life!

It should be pointed out that many Christians continue to keep all 10 of the Commandments, including the fourth in obedience to our Savior's command, **"If you love me, keep my**

Commandments" (Jn. 14:15). Such Christians believe they are not saved by keeping the sabbath or feast days, and argue that because they have been accepted by God through the sacrifice of Jesus—keep these days because of their spiritual meaning and out of love for what He did on the cross.

Chapter Five

TYPES OF SATAN

Pharaoh—A Type of Satan

We read in (Revelation 12:9) of a great red dragon, that is clearly defined as none other than Satan the devil! Chapter 20, verse 2, confirms this identification. But we may ask, why is the dragon used as a *symbol* of Satan?

Pharaoh, king of Egypt, in his cruelty to God's people, and in proud and haughty independence of God, was termed "the dragon" (Ezek. 29:3,4). Nebuchadnezzar, also a *type* of Satan, is similarly spoken of in respect to his violence and cruelty (Jer. 51:34).

Satan is described in terms of the physical King of Babylon in (Isaiah 14:12-14) as already mentioned in chapter one. After reading this account, it is quite apparent that this could not be speaking of any physical human being. This wicked despot is only a *type* of Satan the Devil!

The Egyptians regarded the crocodile or dragon, as the source and author of all evil, according to their hieroglyphics.

The hardened Pharaoh of Egypt is clearly a *type* of Satan as he dealt deceitfully with the people of God (Ex. 8:29). God's Word describes Satan as a cunning being who DECEIVES the whole world (Rev. 12:9).

Like Satan, Pharaoh went after Israel *immediately* after they were out of Egypt [a type of sin] prior to being *baptized* in the Red Sea. Pharaoh's armies chasing God's people is a beautiful *cameo* of Satan's demons going after Christians!

This is also a *type* of what will happen in the end times (Rev. 12:15). But like the *type*—these armies will be destroyed by the Almighty God. Pharaoh's armies were engulfed by the mighty flood waters, and the armies of the "Beast" power will be swallowed up by the earth (earthquake)!

The crossing of the Red Sea, as well as the river Jordan, are *pictures* of God's people being REDEEMED by the baptismal waters in Christ! Both bridges were necessary to enter into the "promised" land! The crossing of the Red Sea *foreshadowed* Israel's **past sins forgiven,** while the crossing of the Jordan pointed to their **continual forgiveness** in Christ!

The Ark of the Covenant [symbolic of Jesus Christ's power and mercy] was placed in the river Jordan first, and remained there until all the people crossed over dryshod (Isa. 11:15)! This was *reminiscent* of Christ going down into *death* for us so we could receive salvation!

The *twelve stones* placed in the dried up river bed of theJordan, over which the river flowed immediately after the Israelites crossed over—was a *shadow* of baptism in Christ for the 12 tribes of Israel (Josh. 4:3,9). To the believer, these stones are a *portrayal* of our being dead and resurrected in Christ! Because there are "twelve"—this is also a *foretaste* into the future, when the nation of Israel will accept Christ and be baptized!

Simon Magus—A Type of Satan

Religion determined the sexual morals of the people. Normally, when a country was overthrown, and a new government came to power, a new religion was introduced. But when Nebuchadnezzar's Babylonian Empire was overthrown, their Assyrian Babylonian Mystery religion did not die!

By the time of Christ, the prevailing religion throughout the Roman Empire was Roman Paganism...a religion of Emperor worship. It was in Samaria, the northern capital of Israel, prior to their captivity by Assyria in 721 B.C. that the old Babylonian Mystery Religion was transferred and flourishing under a man named Simon Magus.

Some historians believe that Nimrod, the King and founder of Babylon, was not only its political leader, but he stood as the priest king, or its religious leader as well. It is believed that from

TYPES OF THE SATAN

Nimrod descended a line of priest-kings—each standing at the *head* of the occult Babylonian Mystery Religion.

In 33 A.D; the apostles encountered a Samaritan, a priest...a sorcerer, named Simon (Acts 8:9). When Philip came to Samaria, performing real miracles, many of the people accepted Christ and were baptized (Acts 8:5-24). Simon, may have been the leader of the "Mystery of Iniquity" spoken of by the apostle Paul in (11 Thessalonians 2:7). Iniquity, means Lawlessness... opposed to God's Law. This "Mystery" religion was the same Old Babylonian Mysteries. It is called, in (Revelation 17:5) by its true name, which is not "Christian," but MYSTERY, BABYLON THE GREAT."

This Simon the Magician, leader of the priests of the Babylonian Mystery religion, had gone along and been baptized with the other converts, when Philip preached at Samaria. He pretended to be a Christian!

It was shortly after this juncture that Simon, under the influence of his master, Satan, began to see the awesome potential of Christianity as a tool for his own advancement.

Without repenting, changing his whole life and giving up all of his pagan idolatry, Simon tried to purchase an apostleship in the Church. He wanted "this power" (verses 18 and 19) or official endorsement to go out and preach in the name of, or as if by the authority of, Jesus Christ!

It need not be supposed that when Simon broke with the Christians, he renounced all he had learned. It is more probable that he carried some of the Christian ideas with him and that he wove them into a system of his own (or Satan's). Thus, he became the leader of a retrograde sect, perhaps nominally Christian, and exalting Simon himself to the central position which Christianity was giving to Jesus Christ (*Hasting Dictionary of the Apostolic Church,* Vol. 1, p. 497).

"The amalgam of paganism and Christianity...(that) was especially obvious in the Simonian system, is readily explicable in the teaching of Simon Magus who...was brought into intimate contact with Christian teaching without becoming a genuine member" (*Ibid;* p. 496).

Simon starts Universal Church at Rome

"The author or first representative of this baptized heathenism...is Simon Magus, who unquestionably adulterated Christianity with pagan ideas and practices" (*Apostolic Christianity*, Vol.2, p. 566). He "subsequently attempted, with the aid and with the sanction of Christianity [so-called] to set up a rival universal [or Catholic] religion" (p. 514).

When Simon Magus went to Rome, he bewitched the inhabitants with his "magical" [demoniac] powers and soon became known as Simon Peter—Simon the Interpreter (of the Babylonian Mysteries).

Simon, as we read earlier, had taken the name of Jesus Christ and much of the terminology of Christianity and was using these tools to expand his own sphere of influence.

Peter of Pethor worship can be traced back to Mesopotamia where idolatry had its beginning and where Nimrod built the Tower of Babel. In (Deuteronomy 23:4) we read that Balaam "of Pethor of Mesopotamia" was hired to put a curse on the nation of Israel. History tells us that this Pethor was a sacred high place "where there was an oracle temple, and hence called Pethor, and here was, no doubt, a college of priests of whom Balaam had been appointed chief."

Balaam was the chief Patora [Peter] of the Pethor [Peter-temple] of Mesopotamia, the very home of idolatry and false religion.

In post-apostolic Christian literature, Simon Magus plays a prominent role. He was thought by Irenaeus to be the founder of Gnosticism and the infamous leader of the sect of the Simonians *(Against Heresies, I,23).*

Justin Martyr wrote he went to Rome during the reign of Claudius (*Apology*, I, 26). The *Acts of Peter* relates how Simon Magus led the Christians at Rome astray by his false teachings.

In the *Dictionary of Christian Biography*, vol. 4. 682, we read that when Justin Martyr wrote his *Apology* (152 A.D.), the sect of the Simonians appears to have been formidable, for he speaks four times of their founder, Simon...and tells that he came to Rome in the day of Claudius Caesar (45 A.D.), and made such an impression by his magical powers, that he was honored as a god, a statue being erected to him on the Tiber, between the two bridges, bearing the inscription "Simoni deo Sancto" (i.e; the holy god Simon).

Simon Magus is a *forerunner* to a great "False Prophet" who is yet to come and perform similar miraculous feats!

To perform Satanic Miracles

The "False Prophet" will use his deceptive miracle-working power as a supposed "proof" that he is God. This will undoubtedly bring the churches of the world together very quickly.

But the apostle Paul warned:

> **...Even him, whose coming is AFTER THE WORKING OF SATAN with all power and signs and LYING wonders, and with all deceivableness of unrighteousness in them that perish (are perishing); because they receive not the love of the truth, that they might be saved (11 Thess. 2:9-10).**

Here is pictured, in prophesy, the head of a vast ecclesiastical empire. Through Satan's power, he will perform *false miracles* and *lying wonders* to *deliberately deceive* the world into believing he is GOD on earth and that the returning Christ is the Antichrist!

This "False Prophet" will even call down fire from the sky!

> **And he doeth great wonders, so that he maketh fire come down from heaven on the earth in the sight of men, And DECEIVETH them that dwell on the earth *by means of those miracles* which he had power to do... (Rev. 13:13-14).**

Millions will be swept off their feet by his mighty signs. They will worship him "as [very] God" because of these spectacular, attention-getting, satanic miracles!

Nimrod, was the founder of the "Babylonian Mystery Religion" that brought paganism into the church at Rome. He was the valentine of his people and protected them from wild animals with his bow according to secular history. That is why cupid is found with a bow! The "False Prophet" comes riding on a *white horse* (as champion of the people *symbolically)*, and carrying a bow (Rev. 6:2). These are *symbolic emblems* of SATAN'S DECEPTION!

The true deliverer and Savior of the people [Jesus Christ] does not come to the earth until the start of the 7th Seal (Rev. 14:14; 15:1). Jesus Christ comes to smite the rebellious inhabitants of the earth with a sword (The Word of God) and bring everlasting righteous rule with a rod of iron! (Rev. 19:15).

Satan's *counterfeit* false prophet will come before this [the first Seal in time sequence] to deceive the world!

The King of Tyre—A Type of Satan

The 28th chapter of the book of Ezekiel contains a picture prophecy concerning the King of Tyre, who is another physical *type* of the fallen Lucifer.

The *proud* and *boasting* King of Tyre had gained an incredible empire and thought he was secure in his earthly citadel. He felt immune from any outside danger and took pride in all his newly accrued fortune.

With the king's fortune and superior merchant fleet—he vaunted himself above all the kingdoms of the earth. He thought in heart, *he was God*! (vss. 2-8).

Because of this nefarious monarch's overwhelming arrogance—the Eternal God would smite his kingdom down in the presence of other kings!

In the last days, the "False Prophet", *antitype* of the king of Tyre, will lift up his heart declaring himself as God (11 Thess. 2:4). Because everything that came through the then known world came through Tyre, this king controlled the world's economy! The "False Prophet," working closely with the "Beast" will once again, be involved in controlling the world's economy (Rev. 18). Starting in (Ezekiel 28:11), this prophecy then skips to the great cherub who *covered* God's throne in the garden of Eden. This cherub had *wisdom* and *beauty* above all the heavenly host. Then INIQUITY [sin] was found in his ways (verses 15,16).

This cherub was none other than the magnificent archangel Lucifer who *rebelled* against the administration of God! He,

TYPES OF THE SATAN

along with Michael and Gabriel *covered* or watched over the government of God.

Lucifer's *beauty* and *brightness* [intelligence] was eventually to become his achilles heel. Through pride, Lucifer's wisdom became perverted and eventually the sin of vanity set in (vs. 17). It now became apparent to the Eternal, that Lucifer's empire, like the King of Tyre must be brought to an end!

The King of Tyre is also a *type* of the end-time demi-god who will deceive and rule over the nations in the last days. This "Anti-christ" will be the epitome of Satan in the flesh (Dan. 7:25; 11;36; 11 Thess. 2:4; Rev. 13:6).

The Bible does not say that the King of Tyre was actually "demon possessed" or controlled by the devil. However, we know this to be true of the "False Prophet" to come (Rev. 16:13). Therefore, being a *type,* we can only speculate that the King of Tyre was also possessed by Satan!

Both of these human despots are actually vessels for Satan as he lived and worked through them!

Uziah—A Type of Satan

Uziah, was Israel's youngest king, and reigned from age 16 to 52 (11 Chron. 26:1).

As long as he sought the Lord, God made him to prosper (vs. 5). And as long as Uziah obeyed God, the nation of Israel prospered (vs. 8).

Now Uziah loved husbandry and followed God's agricultural laws (vs. 10). However, when he was strong his heart was *lifted up to* his destruction (vs. 16).

In other words, Uziah became full of vanity like Lucifer because of his *beauty* and *intelligence* (Ezek. 28).

He went into the Temple of God and offered incense, which was forbidden by everyone except the high priest of Israel. The high priest rebuked him and he was *cast out* (11 Chron. 26:20).

This "casting out" of the Temple of Uziah, is a *type* of the "Casting out" of heaven of Lucifer once he rebelled, as he was "cut off" from the house of the Lord (Rev. 12:21).

Let's take warning from these *types*—realizing that pride kills eternally!

Haman—A Type of Satan

Not long after the birth of Jesus in Bethlehem, Satan inspired King Herod to slay all the male children in the surrounding areas. But Mary and Joseph had been warned by God and escaped (Matt. 2:13-18).

Later, Satan attempted to get Jesus to submit to him and to reject the commandments of God. Had Jesus succumbed, He, too, would have been rejected as future ruler of the earth. Again, however, the devil was unsuccessful (Matt. 4:1-11).

But Satan's attempts were not limited to Jesus as a human. In an incident some 500 years before Jesus' physical birth, Satan tried to eliminate a whole tribe of Israel to thwart God's purpose to send a Savior.

If he'd been successful, there would have been no birth of Christ.

Because of their disobedience to God, the Jews had been taken captive by Babylon. Later, Persia conquered Babylon. Part of the Persian prize was the sizable Jewish slave community.

King Ahasuerus was the Persian king at this time of Jewish exile. During a particularly heavy drinking session, he summoned his queen, Vashti, to appear before the assembled male guests:

> **On the seventh day when the heart of the king was merry with wine, he commanded...to bring Queen Vashti before the king, wearing her royal crown, in order to show her beauty to the people and the officials, for she was beautiful to behold (Esther 1:10-11).**

Tradition says the queen was ordered to appear wearing *nothing but* the crown. She refused, and was banished from the royal court.

During the following months, a number of women were groomed to replace the deposed queen. Among them was a young Jewess called Esther (Esther 2:7). As things worked out, Esther became the king's favorite and was made queen (vs. 17).

Meanwhile, Esther's guardian, Mordecai, was having problems with a man named Haman, a leading official of the country. Haman expected those who came into his presence to bow before him, but Mordecai refused (Esther 3:2-5). As a result, Haman decided to make life as difficult as possible for the Jews in general and Mordecai in particular.

Haman's deceitful Plot

Haman managed to persuade King Ahasuerus to approve a decree that stated all Jews were to be annihilated on a certain day (vss. 8-15). What Haman didn't know was that he was, in effect, moving against the queen—and, by implication, against the king himself.

When Mordecai heard the news he was, understandably, distraught. Queen Esther soon learned of the matter and sent a servant to Mordecai to find out more (Esther 4:4-6). Mordecai requested that the queen plead with the Persian king for the lives of the Jewish population.

Esther agreed to help, provided the Jews joined her in a three-day fast. At the end of that period she would attempt to plead the cause. This was a delicate matter, as no one was allowed to approach the king without being summoned. To enter the court without permission could result in death (vs. 11).

However, God was working out a plan that would ensure His Son would be born of Jewish stock. Esther was received by the king. She explained that she wished the king and Haman to attend a banquet later that day (Esther 5:4). Later, the invitation was extended to another feast the following day (vs. 8).

These invitations swelled the head of Haman, but the sight of Mordecai refusing to pay homage marred his enjoyment of the situation. Acting on advice from his wife and friends, Haman had a gallows made on which he planned to hang the defiant Jew (vs. 14).

Coincidentally, that night the king suffered from an attack of insomnia. To help pass the hours of darkness, Ahasuerus demanded that the country's history be read to him. Contained within those records was an account of an incident when Mordecai had disclosed a plot against the king. Ahasuerus was surprised to learn that Mordecai had not been honored for this service.

Haman, who had just come into the palace to make arrangements for Mordecai's execution, was summoned into the king's presence. **"What shall be done for the man whom the king delights to honor?"** the monarch asked (Esther 6:6).

Haman immediately jumped to the wrong conclusion. Whom would the king delight to honor more than me? he thought. Believing that the blessings would come his way, Haman listed a number of honors suitable for a favorite of the king (vss. 8-9).

The king agreed with the assessment, and, much to Haman's chagrin, told him to arrange the suggested honors for Mordecai (vss. 10-11). Haman was devastated by this humiliating turn of events, but took some comfort in the thought that all the Jewish people would soon be eliminated.

Judah Saved

But the worse was yet to come. At the banquet that night, Esther made her request to the king. She explained that a proclamation had been made to annihilate all her people (Esther 7:3-4). The king was incensed and demanded to know who was responsible for such an act. **"And Esther said, `The adversary and enemy is this wicked Haman!" (vs. 6).**

In an ironic twist of fate, and act of justice, Haman was hanged on the very gallows he had prepared for Mordecai! But the problem of the proposed destruction of the Jewish people remained. According to the Persian law, no proclamation that was made by the king could be reversed.

At Esther's request, the king issued a decree stating that the Jewish people should prepare themselves for the day set aside for the slaughter. The Jews were instructed to arm themselves, and were given permission to kill anyone who attempted to destroy them (Esther 8:5-11).

The Jews successfully defended themselves (Esther 9:5) and celebrated with much feasting (vs. 17). Mordecai was later placed second in command of the country (Esther 10:3).

The Jewish nation had been saved! Jesus Christ could be born of a Jewish woman!

Although Haman was the human instrument planning the destruction of the Jewish people, Satan was the real force behind the plot. But Satan never seems to learn that God is very much in charge of the world's affairs.

In this intriguing story, Haman is a *type* of Satan who tried to destroy the Jews [Christ] but like Satan was destroyed! Esther is a *type* of the Church who is to TRIUMPH and RULE with Christ as the King!

What a tremendous lesson and story!

Antiochus—A Type of The False Prophet

Antiochus IV (Epiphanes), whose name means "God Manifest" ruled the Seleucid dynasty of Syria from 175-163 B.C. Antiochus made a covenant with apostate Jews, who favored him politically, and encouraged them to forsake God's laws. Even the high priest acquiesced to his demands. This *rebellion* began around 171 B.C. In his attempt to Hellenize the Jews, he stopped the sacrifices, and sacrificed a pig instead. Then this ruthless king committed a most abominable act by sprinkling pigs blood on the Holy of Holies in the Temple.

This "swine" forbade circumcision, observance of the holy Sabbath, and destroyed all of the Old Testament books he laid his hands on (*The Pictorial Bible,* Tenney, p. 421).

Anyone found possessing a copy of the holy scriptures was killed by decree! A great slaughter followed! As a result of these repugnant acts by this insolent monarch, these Syrian armies were eventually defeated by the gallant Judas Maccabeus (1 Macc. 1:10; 6:16).

This intriguing story is found in the first two books of the Maccabees in the Apocrapha. The Jewish uprising began in 168 B.C. when Mattathias, an aged priest, struck down a royal commissioner and an apostate Jew, who were about to offer heathen sacrifice in the town. Mattathias leveled the altar, and fled to the hills with his sons Eleazor, John, Judas, Jonathan and Simon.

Therefore, we may only conclude that Antiochus Epiphanes is only a *archetype* of the being known as the "Beast" who will perform similar heresies.

After a few months of guerrilla warfare, Mattathias died and his sons Eleazor and John were killed. Mattathias' other three sons continued the insurrection as Judas became the leader and was nicknamed Maccabee, meaning "the Hammerer."

Being a fine soldier and loyal patriot for Jewish independence—Judas organized a battalion consisting of Galieans that defeated major Syrian militia sent against them in 166-165 B.C. Finally, in December of 165 B.C. Judas formally "cleansed the temple" of Syrian pollution and celebrated the event with a great festival. This celebration became a permanent commemoration, falling on December 25, and lasting eight days (1 Macc. 4:52-59; 11 Macc. 10:6; Jn. 10:22). The descendants of the Maccabees became known as the Hasmonian Dynasty and ruled Israel for one hundred years with a strong measure of independence and peace.

The Cleansing of The Temple

This event also had been prophesied in the book of Daniel. In (Daniel 8:13 14), *New International Version,* God revealed:

> **Then I heard a holy one speaking, and another holy one said to him, 'How long will it take for the vision to be fulfilled—the vision concerning the daily sacrifice, the rebellion that causes desolation, and the surrender of the sanctuary and of the host that will be trampled underfoot'? He said to me, 'It will take 2,300 evenings and mornings; then the sanctuary will be reconsecrated.'**

In other words, there would be 2,300 evening and morning sacrifices that would not be offered—a period of 1,150 days or just a little more than three years till God would permit restoration of the sacrifices.

Those three years were to be among the most trying in Jewish history. Jews were forced to eat pork and worship pagan gods. Those who refused were mercilessly killed. Many of them therefore acquiesced to adopting Hellenistic customs, notice: **"Many also of the Israelites consented to his [Antiochus'] religion, and sacrificed unto idols, and profaned the sabbath" (I Macc. 1:20-53).** But when the Maccabees liberated Jerusalem, they tore down the pagan gods from the Temple Mount and relit the lights of the Menorah.

To this day, the Jewish eight day winter festival of Hanukkah, or Festival of Lights, recalls the cleansing of the Temple in the days of the Maccabees.

In all probability it had been 1,150 days or 2,300 evenings and mornings since Antiochus had forbidden Jewish sacrifices. What

TYPES OF THE SATAN

happened to the Jews in the days of the Maccabees was merely a *type* of what is yet to happen to them once again in the last days. The *Critical, Experimental Commentary* provides additional information concerning this travesty:

> **This horn is explained (vs.23) to be a 'king of fierce countenance,' etc. Antiochus Epiphanes is meant. Greece, with all its refinement, produces the first--ie., the Old Testament ANTICHRIST.** Antiochus had an extraordinary love of art, which expressed itself in grand temples. He wished to substitute Zeus Olympius for Jehovah at Jerusalem. Thus, first, heathen civilization from below and revealed religion from above came into collision. Identifying himself with Jupiter, his air was to make his own worship universal (cf. v.25 with ch. 11:36): so mad was he in this that he was called Epimanes (maniac) instead of Epiphanes (illustrious). None of the previous world rulers...had systematically opposed the Jews' religious worship...He is the forerunner of the final Antichrist, standing in the same relation to the first advent of Christ that Antichrist does to His second coming...He not only opposes God's ancient people, but God Himself. *The daily sacrifice*—one lamb was offered in the morning and another in the evening (Exo. 29:38,39). *was taken away*—by Antiochus (*Critical Experimental Commentary*, by Jamieson, Fausett and Brown, vol. 1, p. 427).

The Jews thought that the *Abomination of Desolation* in (Daniel 11:31) was fulfilled in 186 B.C. by Antiochus Epiphanes. This detestable king erected an idolatrous altar on the altar of the Temple in Jerusalem and sacrificed a pig to the heathen god Jupiter Olympus (1 Macc. 1:54; 6:7; 11 Macc. 6:2; Josephus *Antiquities,* 12:5,4; 7,6).

But Jesus said in 31 A.D. that the Abomination of Desolation spoken by Daniel had not yet occurred (Matt. 24:15)!

Today, there are many religious observers watching Europe believing that a future leader will emerge out of a "United States of Europe" and fulfill the prophecy in Daniel. If Antiochus Epiphanes is a *type* of the "Beast" to come, such an individual would have to be *contemptible*, who comes without *warning!* (Dan. 11:21,24).

Recall also that the kingdom was already formed when Antiochus came on the scene—as will occur when the already formed 10 nations give their power to the "Beast" (Rev. 17:12-13). Such a man will come with *flatteries* and without *warning* to take the kingdom! He will be the least likely man! The "Beast" will be someone who wouldn't offend anyone and is a satanic individual!

Chapter Six

TYPES OF CHRIST AND SATAN

Cain and Abel—Types of Satan and Christ

The Bible tells us there is a relationship between the lives of Cain and Abel to that of Christ and Satan. This *duality* of Adam's two sons to that of God's two spiritual sons [Christ and Satan] can only be understood by the relationship between Adam and Christ first.

The relationship between Christ and Adam is recorded by the apostle Paul in the fifteenth chapter of 1 Corinthians:

> **For in Adam all die, even so in Christ shall all be made alive (vs. 22). And so it is written, the first Adam was made a living soul; the last Adam [Christ] was made a quickening spirit. Howbeit that was not first which is spiritual, but that which is natural; and afterward that which is spiritual. The first man [Adam] is of the earth, earthy: the second man [Christ] is the Lord from heaven (verses 45:47).**

Adam, the first man was of a CARNAL MINDED physical nature who yielded to the temptations of Satan. Jesus was just the opposite, that is—SPIRITUALLY MINDED and divine in nature who overcame the devil's lures.

God's Word reveals more of the nature of Cain [carnal] and of Abel [righteous] in (Genesis 4). The very name Cain means "gotten from the Lord—acquisition, taking," while the name Abel implies "exaltation."

Starting in (Genesis 4:2-5) we read of the significance of their sacrifices to God as indicative of their character:

> **...Abel was a keeper of sheep [like Christ, a spiritual shepherd]; but Cain was a tiller of the ground, And in the process of time it came to pass, that Cain brought of the fruit of the ground an offering unto the Lord. And Abel, he also brought of the firstlings of his flock and of the fat thereof. And the Lord had respect unto Abel and to his offering. But unto Cain and to his offering he had not respect...**

The writer of Hebrews, explains *why* God respected Abel's offering and not Cain's: **"By *faith* Abel offered unto God *a more excellent sacrifice* than Cain, by which he obtained witness that he was righteous, God testifying of his gifts: and by it he being dead yet speaketh" (Heb. 11:4).**

In these two offerings we have two divergent ways of life. One had *faith* in God and the other in himself!

When God instituted the sacrificial system to Israel under Moses, they were required to make a Burnt-offering of a *male* animal without blemish as an atonement for sin. The high priest was then to sprinkle it's blood about the altar by the door of the Tabernacle (Lev. 1:1-5).

If a man did not have an animal to sacrifice, then an offering of grain [flour mixed with oil] could be used instead (Lev. 2:1-2).

Both, the blood of the animal and oil mixed in the flour were *superficial* of FAITH in the cleansing blood of Jesus Christ for sin! We will study this concept in more detail under "The Offerings"! Cain got his blood by killing his brother Abel! This offering of Cain's was *symbolic* of his very nature as recorded in 1 John 3:11-12:

> **For this is the message that ye heard from the beginning, that we should love one another. Not as *Cain, who was of that wicked one [Satan]* and slew his brother, And wherefore slew he him? because his own works were evil, and his brother's righteous.**

Truly, in these two ways of life we have the way of Christ and of Satan—we all must choose?

Saul and David—Types of Satan and Christ

The lives of King David as a *type* of Christ and Saul as a *type* of Satan is a most fascinating revelation. God inspired King David to write in Psalm 89:18-20:

> **For the Lord is our defense; and the Holy one of Israel is our King. Then thou spokest in vision to the holy one, and saidst, I have laid help upon one that is mighty; I have exalted one chosen out of the people. I have found David my servant; with my holy oil have I anointed him.**

Although part of this Psalm is a *picture* prophecy concerning Jesus Christ; it also applies to King David. Notice verses 27-29: **"Also I will make him *my firstborn*, higher than the kings of the earth. ...my covenant shall stand fast with him. His seed also will I make to endure *for ever*, and his throne as the days of heaven."**

This prophecy is *dual* and also refers to Jesus Christ who was God's "firstborn" from the dead and who will be King over all the Kings of the earth. David was the "firstborn" spiritually of Israel—not of his household physically.

The anointing of King David had many *similarities* to that of our Savior as well. These likenesses are recorded in 1 Samuel 16:

> (Vs. 1)...**I will send thee to Jesse [David's father]**, *the Bethlehemite*: **for I have provided me a king among his sons. (Vs. 4). And Samuel did that which the Lord spake, and came to Bethlehem**...**(Vs. 11) And Samuel said unto Jesse, are here all thy children? And he said, there remaineth yet the youngest, and behold,** *he keepeth the sheep*... **(Vs. 13) Then Samuel took the horn of oil,** *and anointed him* **in the midst of his brethren;** *and the Spirit of the Lord came upon* **David from that day forward...**

The similarities to our Lord should be obvious as Jesus and His physical father were *born in Bethlehem*. After being *anointed* through the "laying on of hands" in baptism, the Holy Spirit came upon Jesus in the form of a dove. Both David and Christ were *anointed* before their actual coronation into office. David, like Christ was a *shepherd* over sheep—Jesus over the Church or God's spiritual flock.

Saul and Satan

When David was anointed, **"the spirit of the Lord departed from Saul, and an evil spirit [demon] from the Lord troubled him" (1 Samuel 16:14).**

Saul's life is *typical* of Satan, notice his physical features:

> **And he had a son, whose name was Saul,** *a choice* **young man, and goodly: And there was not among the children of Israel a goodlier person than he: from his shoulders and upward he was higher than any of the people (1 Sam. 9:2).**

Of Satan's physical and spiritual character we read in Ezekiel 28:11:

> **...Thou sealest up the sum, full of wisdom, and** *perfect* **in beauty. (Vs. 15) Thou was perfect in thy ways from the day that thou wast created,**

TYPES OF CHRIST AND SATAN

till iniquity was found in thee. (Vs. 17) Thine heart was lifted up because of thy beauty...

Both Saul and Satan were choice beings—*handsome, beautiful, wise*; but both REBELLED against the throne and exalted position God gave them!

Because of REBELLION, God removed Saul's throne (1 Sam. 15:23) as He did Satan's (Lucifer).

Now focus your eyes on (1 Samuel 21:10) where David fled from Saul as he tried to kill him. Because Saul couldn't kill David, he went after the people that associated with David (1 Sam. 22:17). This is very similar to what Satan did to Christ and His Church. When Satan couldn't kill Christ, he tried to destroy His Church!

Continuing the analogy between David and Christ we read in (1 Samuel 24:1) where David fled into...**"the wilderness of Engedi"** from Saul. This again parallels the *fleeing of the Church from Satan* into the wilderness for protection (Rev. 12:14).

Saul's suicidal death as recorded in (1 Samuel 31) is also reminiscent of the fate of Satan and the sinful angels. All of these beings went from an anointed position of exaltation to a state of degeneracy. Like Saul, God says the angels who sinned will not be spared (11 peter 2:4).

Thus, even as David stood triumphant over Goliath [also a *type* of Satan] and Saul—so will Christ and His Church be *victorious* over Satan and his legions!

Forty days had the enemy been tormenting the people when David, the shepherd boy went forth to conquer him. This temptation of Goliath *parallels* the temptation of Christ in the wilderness for *forty days*! David obliterated the menacing giant with a smooth stone from a brook, even as Christ conquered Satan by quoting a scripture from Deuteronomy, one of the five books of Moses!

Goliath the giant had been compared to a lion taking a lamb out of David's flock, and had roared against himself—just as Satan the *antitype,* is pictured as our adversary walking about as a roaring lion, "seeking whom he may devour."

THE FOOLISHNESS GOD

Absalom and David
Types of Satan and Christ

Absalom was David's third son, by Maacah, daughter of Talmai, king of Geshur (11 Sam. 3:3; 1 Chron. 3:2). He was the *only* son of David that was born of *royalty*!

One day Absalom's sister Tamar was ravished by his half brother Amnon (11 Sam. 13:1-19). Although this malicious act greatly angered David, he did not punish his eldest son (vs. 21). As a result, Absalom became furious and after two years of harboring his hatred—he procured Amnon's assassination (verses 22-29).

After Amnon's death, Absalom fled to his grandfather for three years in exile (verses 37-39). Even after three years of hiding, David refused to see his son, although comforted after Amnon's death for two additional years (14:1-24). Then Absalom contrived a plan to have his father's friend Joab intercede for him, and Absalom was restored to favor before the king (14:28-33).

Meanwhile, Absalom had become a favorite son of the people of Israel, for **"...in all Israel there was none to be much praised as Absalom for his *beauty*, and for the abundance of his hair" (14:25-27).**

Because of his *beauty* and popularity, Absalom began to act like a candidate for the kingship (15:1-6). David at once perceived the scheming intentions of his young and ambitious, but rebellious son. He began making plans for Absalom's deportation from the holy city (15:13-18).

Realizing his empire was about to crumble—Ahithophel advised Absalom to attack his father David before he could regroup his forces (17:1-4). But Absalom's soldiers were disastrously defeated, as he was killed by Joab in the battle (18:1-8).

King David's grief over the death of his ungrateful son was so exorbitant, it almost cost him the loyalty of his subjects (18:33; 19:8).

One can hardly read this fascinating, yet remorseful story without seeing the *parallels* to Christ and Satan. David is a *type* of Christ as already demonstrated. Here we find Absalom, full of *beauty* coming from a family of *royalty* trying to usurp his father's throne! Surely, he is a *type* of Satan the devil! Lucifer was also a son of royalty who was the most beautiful being ever created! Then he tried to take over his Father's throne as well!

Satan's fate, like Absalom, will come to total defeat!

The "Three Judas'"

The name "Judas" has commonly been used in modern vernacular to connotate a *traitor*—and rightly so. Certainly everyone is familiar with the account in which Judas Iscariot, one of the original twelve apostles betrayed our Lord on the night of the Passover.

What you may not know however, is that there is a *duality* to this betrayal in the Old Covenant.

We have already revealed the duality of King David to that of Christ—but there is more. Jesus said of His betrayer:

> **I speak not of you all: I know whom I have chosen: but that the scripture may be fulfilled,** *He that eateth bread with me* **hath lifted up his heel against me (Jn. 13:18).**

This is practically a direct quote from (Psalm 41:9) which was written by King David. Let's read it: **"Yea, mine own familiar friend, in whom I trusted, which did eat of my bread, hath lifted up his heel against me."** This Old Testament Judas actually ate at David's table and later betrayed him. David reveals more about this individuals personality in Psalm 55: 12-14:

> **For it was not an enemy that reproached me; then I could have borne it: neither was it he that hated me that did magnify himself against me: then I would have hid myself from him: But it was thou, a man mine equal,** *my guide, and mine acquaintance.* **We took sweet council together, and walked unto the house of God in company.**

Who was this ancient Benedict Arnold that was David's trusted friend, counselor and adviser? His name was Ahithophel which means "foolishness." The entire account is found in (11 Samuel 17 through 19).

THE FOOLISHNESS GOD

The Bible does not reveal *why* Ahithophel turned on King David—but by understanding human nature, perhaps we can speculate. The following facts may give us a clue to this ancient turn coat. From (11 Samuel 23:34; 11:3) it can be determined that Ahithophel was Bathsheba's grandfather.

Very possibly, Ahithophel plotted a way in which he could become part of David's royal family through the seduction of Bathsheba. Perhaps he persuaded her to take a bath on her rooftop so David would see her and be enticed. Bathsheba may have been innocent of all this herself.

When David gazed upon the voluptuous Bathsheba—his heart was filled with passion. David eventually conspired to have Bathsheba's husband Uriah killed in battle. David wanted to marry Bathsheba more than anything in the world.

But finaly, David's sanity returned to him and he deeply repented of his heinous sins. When Ahithophel saw this, he threw in his lot with David's ambitious son Absalom. Recall how Absalom desired to usurp his father's throne. Perhaps Ahithophel thought, "Maybe Absalom will give me a high office in his new government?" Whatever Ahithophel's reasoning was—one thing is for sure—these two were in cahoots! More of this conspiracy is found in 11 Samuel 15:12:

> **And Absalom went for Ahithophel the Gillonite, David's counsellor, from his city, even from Giloh, while he offered sacrifices. And the *conspiracy* was strong; for the people increased continually with Absalom.**

Absalom had stolen the hearts of the people, probably with the advice of Ahithophel (verse 6). When Absalom moved against Jerusalem with an army, David fled for his life (verses 13-14).

The story continues in verse 31:

> **And one told David, saying, Ahithophel is among the conspirators with Absalom. And David said, O Lord, I pray thee, turn the counsel of Ahithophel into foolishness.**

Upon fleeing Jerusalem, David met his long time friend and adviser Hushsi (11 Sam. 15:32). These two began a plot of their own to regain the throne. David asked Hushai to return to Jerusalem instead of fleeing into the wilderness with him. David said to Hushai:

But if thou return to the city, and say unto Absalom, I will be thy servant, O king; as I have been thy father's servant hitherto, so will I now also be thy servant: then mayest thou for me defeat the counsel of Ahithophel (verse 34).

Faithful Hushai did as David requested and gave Absalom counsel diametrically opposite that of Ahithophel's. Absalom heeded the advice of Hushai and this eventually led to David's return to power.

Ahithophel foresaw the "handwriting on the wall" for Absalom—as David's forces began regrouping because of Absalom's procrastination of attack. If Absalom was defeated—Ahithophel knew he would be revealed as a traitor and punished severely. The thought of disgrace and shame to his family was too much for Ahithophel to cope with. Ahithopel realized his rope had run out for him—and went home and hanged himself (11 Sam. 17:23).

Here is an amazing *duality* that vividly parallels "the last supper." This account portrays Ahithophel as a traitor like Judas. And like Judas, he committed suicide when he became mentally depressed.

But this story also *parallels* Hushai as a true friend—even as the apostles were true and loyal friends of Jesus.

The "Son of Perdition"

Were you aware that the term "son of perdition" is only used *twice* in all the Bible? Most are aware that Judas Iscariot was called "son of perdition" (Jn. 17:12). It was this infamous character who betrayed our Lord during the night of the Passover.

But did you know that this phrase is also used in describing the "man of sin" in the last days? This account is found in (11 Thessalonians 2:3), notice:

Let no man deceive you by any means: for that day shall not come, except there come a falling away first, and that *man of sin* be revealed, the *son of perdition.*

There are two ways that people have interpreted this scripture: 1) the "man of sin" comes from an apostate system that never was a part of God's true Church, and 2) the "man of sin" would be a deceiver within the Church, and would cause a "falling away" of true believers.

We shall now view the most generally accepted and most logical explanation. First, we must understand *who* the apostle Paul was addressing this prophecy to, and the conditions that then existed.

Although his assessment of the end-time is correct, Paul thought these events would happen in his life time (vs. 2). Now, if we know what events were happening in Paul's lifetime, we can relate it to the end-time.

Paul said there would, **"come a falling away [Gr. *apostasia*], first"**—notice it does not say as some suppose, "A GREAT FALLING AWAY!"

The Greek word *apostasia* means "rebellion," "forsaking," "defection from the truth," "apostacy," (*Thayers Greek-English, Lexicon*). The International Bible Commentary says *apostasia* means "revolt" or rebellion against God. It is not stated whether the rebellion occurs among Jews, in the Church, or is a general refusal by men to acknowledge the Creators authority.

The word "apostasy" as used in the Septuagint and NT points to a deliberate abandonment of a former professed position (Thomas, *New Commentary on the Whole Bible*, by Tyndale).

The "man of sin" or "man doomed to destruction", or "man of lawlessness", or "man of rebellion" (NIV), is identical with "Antichrist", and like Antiochus will make claim to divine authority, as he takes over the rebuilt Temple. The "man of lawlessness" will supplement true Christian teaching just as Antiochus was a type.

Next, realize Paul said that this event was already existent, and referred to it as **"the mystery of iniquity" (vs. 7)**. As we have already read, Simon Magus, was chief leader of the "Babylonian Mysteries," an *apostate* system beginning in 33

TYPES OF CHRIST AND SATAN

A.D. Paul wrote this letter in 51 A.D. Iniquity means "lawlessness" or "opposed to God's law."

This false Babylonian system turned people away from God's laws by substituting pagan counterfeits!

Now notice what else Paul says this "son of perdition" will do during the end of the age: **"Who opposeth and exalteth himself above all that is called God, or that is worshipped; so that he as God sitteth in the temple God, shewing himself that he is God" (vs. 4).**

During the apostle Paul's day, the Temple in Jerusalem was still in existence, and wasn't destroyed until 70 A.D. That is why Paul thought that an individual would fulfill this event in *antitype* of what Antiochus Epiphanes did some 100 years previously. Paul was very familiar with the Old Testament prophecies and what Jesus said in regards to the "Abomination of Desolation."

Jesus indicated that the "Abomination of Desolation" spoken of by Daniel the prophet had not yet occurred in His day, and had something to do with the "holy place" [possibly the holy of holies in the Temple] (Matt. 24:15). Paul realized that the fulfillment of this prophecy would be similar to what occurred during Antiochus' reign.

Realize also, that the very name Epiphanes means "God manifest," from which the Catholic "Feast of Epiphany" is derived. Epiphany, is a festival held on January 6th commemorating Christ to the Gentiles as represented by the Magi. Truly, to commit the abominable acts of Antiochus, one would have to think he was God!

Paul was well acquainted with the prophecies in Daniel that spoke of a time in which and individual would come described by Daniel as "a Little Horn" who would "wear out the saints of the most high," and "change times and laws" (Dan. 7:25). Paul also knew this individual would plant his palace [Temple] in the glorious land of Palestine (Dan. 11:45), and come to his end when he stood against the Prince of Peace [Jesus Christ] after "magnifying himself in his heart" [proclaimed himself as God] (Dan. 8:25).

Notice that the fate of the "man of sin" is the same as that of Daniel's prophecy (11 Thess. 2:3-8). Most likely, Paul believed these Beings to be one and the same!

"The son of destruction" (i.e., destined to destruction), a title given only one other person—Judas, the traitor! The Antichrist will come up out of the earth "with two little horns like those of a lamb but have a fearsome voice like the Dragon's" (Rev. 13:11. TLB). In other words, he will be an imposter!

Realize also the *parallels* between the book of Daniel and the book of Revelation that describes the "False Prophet," or "Image of the Beast" to the "Man of Sin" and "Little Horn." The "Little Horn," "Image of the Beast," and "False Prophet," have power for 3 1/2 years prior to Christ's return (Dan. 7:25; Rev. 11:2; 13:5,14,16).

To Deceive The Elect?

The "Little Horn" comes by "flatteries" (Dan. 11:21,32,34), while the "Man of Sin," "Image of the Beast," and "False Prophet," all perform "false miracles" to deceive people (11 Thess. 2:9; Rev. 13:14; 19:19). But this deception is to deceive them that are in the world, not a wholesale deception of the Church of God! They make war with the Saints (Dan. 7:25; Rev. 13:15-16; 19:29). All come to their end by Christ's return (Dan. 8:25; 11:45; 11 Thess. 2:3-8; Rev. 13:16; 14:9-10; 16:14; 17:14; 19:19-20).

Now let us take a closer look at a very interesting Greek word that describes those that are to be "deceived" by the "lying wonders" or "false miracles" of the "Man of Sin" whose working is after Satan the devil (11 Thess. 2:9-10). These individuals are to "perish" [Gr. *apollumi*] because they received not the love of the truth that they might be saved, and for this cause God sent them strong delusion that they should believe a lie (11 Thess. 2:10-11).

Realize that in most instances, the Greek word *apollumi* refers to people who have never been converted and are lost until they receive the knowledge of our Savior! These are people who have been deceived by Satan, who deceives the whole world (Rev. 12:9). This same Greek word is used in (1 Cor. 1:18 and 11 Cor. 2:15) in describing two groups of people, 1) those that are in the process of being saved, and 2) those that are *deceived* and are *perishing*.

These "lying wonders" will cause "strong delusion" to those in the world to be deceived—not the Elect or Church! God has never purposely sent His people a deception [God does not tempt His people with evil] (Jas. 1:13).

TYPES OF CHRIST AND SATAN

Some have applied this coming deception to the true Church, quoting (Matthew 24:24) and believing this verse pertains to a "select special group" within the Church. Here's how (Matthew 24:24) reads: **"For there shall arise false Christs...and shall shew great signs and wonders; insomuch that if it were possible, they shall deceive the [very] elect."**

However, we must realize that the word "very" [Gr. *kai*] is a poor translation, and is translated as "even" in the *King James Revised Standard Version, The New King James Version, Phillips, and Interlinear Bibles*. In Vines, *An Expository Dictionary of New Testament Words*, under "very" it says regarding (Matthew 24:24): Sometimes it translates the conjunction *kai*, in the sense of "even," e.g. Matt. 10:30; in 24:24, A.V., "very" (R.V., "even"; Luke 12:59). Clearly, this verse is not referring to a "select group" of God's true Church that will not be deceived during the end-time by the "lying wonders" of the "man of sin"—but that it is not going to be possible to deceive [even] the Elect.

"The Man of Sin"

Perhaps we can now better understand what Paul meant when he said: **"For the mystery of iniquity doth already work: only he who now letteth [Gr. *restrains*] will let [*restrain*] until he be taken out of the way" (vs. 7).** With most of the apostles martyred, the apostle Paul and John were the only ones left to restrain the "mystery of iniquity" or apostasy that was now entering into the Church to change God's laws!

Let's review why this interpretation appears to be the most logical: 1) the "Mystery of Iniquity" was already in existence during Paul's day, and did not refer to something that would only occur at the end-time, 2) the Temple was in existence during Paul's time, and he thought these events would occur then, and were related to Daniel's prophecies describing the "Little Horn," 3) this prophecy is related to the book of Revelation describing the identical events as pertaining to the "False Prophet."

Clearly, the "Little Horn," "False Prophet," "Man of Sin," and "Antichrist" are all the same Being!

Most of the commentaries have assumed this scripture is referring to the individual known as the "Antichrist," and the "falling away" would be from religion in general. However, some have thought this verse is referring to yet another Judas [traitor] within the midst of God's true Church—that could cause the "falling away" of God's people? They believe it would not be possible for Antichrist to deceive God's own elect?

Furthermore, they believe this verse is referring to a "spiritual Temple" [the Church] and not a literal Temple in Jerusalem. They claim, because Paul referred to the Temple as, "The Temple of God," this could only refer to the Church, as God will never designate the *apostate* anti-Christian Church as "The Temple of God." It is true that the original Greek word for Temple can be interpreted in a literal or spiritual sense [we will cover this subject in more detail under "The Eight Temples of God" in vol. 3]. Therefore, the word "sitteth" could imply his occupying the place of power and majesty.

Chapter Seven

TYPES OF THE HOLY SPIRIT

The Tree of Life and Death

Were you aware that the *two trees* in the garden of Eden were *symbolic* of two different life styles? The *tree of life* is analogous to receiving *spiritual knowledge* to attain ETERNAL LIFE! This divine knowledge which can only come through *God's Holy Spirit*; teaches one how to be "giving" or "loving" to his fellowman.

Diametrically opposite this way of life was the second tree which contained *the knowledge of good and evil*. This tree represented a way of life that would give one *worldly wisdom* which would ultimately lead to ETERNAL DEATH. This way of life would teach one how to "acquire" or "get" from his fellowman. It would make one think having *physical* material possessions were the ultimate satisfaction in life!

Now here's an interesting thought. What if Adam had taken of *the tree of life* instead of *the tree of the knowledge of good and evil*? Would Adam have received eternal life immediately?

Well, stop and think for a moment. Adam, like all human beings was made of *temporary* physical elements that will someday perish. There is no lasting [eternal] life in these elements. But God has made a way in which each physical human being can attain eternal life through His Holy Spirit. A loving and just God offered Adam and

Eve the free gift of eternal life through His Holy Spirit (*symbolic* of the tree of life).

Had Adam and Eve accepted God's Holy Spirit—they would still have had to live out their normal life spans like all flesh and blood human beings. Converted humans do not receive eternal life instantaneously—it is a GROWTH PROCESS! There is no human being that is an exception to this rule!

God's Holy Spirit gives man *revealed spiritual knowledge* that ultimately leads to eternal life. Our first parents, like all human beings, needed God's Holy Spirit to impart *divine knowledge* to solve their earthly problems and increase their faith.

It is through God's Spirit that humans can contact their heavenly Father and learn how to get along with others. Adam and Eve were only created with materialistic knowledge (knowledge that teaches how to build and use material things). They lacked spiritual knowledge as do all humans, who are void of God's Spirit of LIFE!

There are really only two ways of life, each one of them symbolized by one of the two trees in the Garden of Eden. The tree "of knowledge of good and evil" might also be called "the Tree of Death." It *symbolized* the way of get—the way of greed, competition, strife, vanity, pride, jealousy, envy, arrogance, and every evil lust of the flesh and mind. It *symbolized* the way of Satan the devil. The taste of that forbidden fruit is still in our mouths—and the world around us has been following that way, and partaking of the fruit of that tree, ever since that ancient time! No wonder the world around us is in the grip of a mad passion, and in the final death throes and agonies of self-destruction and incipient doom.

But the other tree—what a marvelous tree it is! It *symbolizes* the way of "life." It is called the "Tree of Life." It leads to everything that is good, wonderful, marvelous, happy, peaceful, joyous, pleasant, enriching, delicious, and good! It *symbolizes* the "way of God"—the way of obedience to His Commandments, which show us how to love God and how to love our neighbor.

It could be called "the Tree of Love." For God is love! It is also "the tree of humility," as opposed to pride. It is the "Tree of Give" verses the other "tree of get." It is the tree of giving, loving, sharing, concern for others, helpfulness, serving, abasing self and honoring others, seeking the welfare of others, and not self.

It is also the "tree of self sacrifice," It is truly the tree of humility and happiness, because true happiness comes through humility. True happiness is wanting to give rather than get. It does

TYPES OF THE HOLY SPIRIT

not compare itself with others and become jealous, envious or rude. It loves to see others prosper, succeed, and get ahead. It is not vain, ambitious, or competitive. Not at all!

This tree is also "the Tree of Faith." It *symbolizes* the way of faith. It is the tree of spiritual Power. In reality, this tree *symbolizes* not only God's way of Life, and obedience to His Laws, but it is also a *symbol* of God's Holy Spirit which produces the fruits of love, joy, peace, patience, gentleness, goodness, kindness, faith, meekness and self control, in our lives (Gal. 5:22).

This is the tree which we should be eating of every day! If Adam and Eve had partaken of the tree in the Garden of Eden that represented God's Holy Spirit—the "tree of [eternal] life"—they would have received the spiritual mind of God, and ultimately eternal life, *if they had continued to obey God*.

Adam and Eve had to desire the Spirit of God and surrender themselves to God's will in order to receive His Holy Spirit of eternal life—exactly as all must do today to receive it. There has never been but this one way to salvation! But Adam and Eve chose not to receive the Holy Spirit and eternal life God's way!

Water—A Type of The Holy Spirit

The Holy Spirit is referred to as "living water" in many places in the Bible. The analogy being, as water "flows" so does the Holy Spirit flow through us from God. Here are some scriptures that enhance this concept:

Jer. 17:13	"Living water."
Ps. 36:9	"Fountain of Life."
Jn. 7:37	"...Jesus said, if any man thirst, let him come unto me and drink. He that believeth on me, as the scripture hath said, *out of his belly shall flow rivers of living water.*"
Judges 15:19	God actually gave His spirit to Samson through water.
Jude 12	False preachers are like demons, "...clouds they are *without* water..."

1 Cor. 12:13	You will die without physical water, and also spiritually without "living water" from God. The water in our bodies is *constantly moving*, just as the Holy Spirit. That is why the scripture says, "we must *stir up* this gift in us" (11 Tim. 1:6). See also (Rev. 21:6,; 22:1,17).
Jn. 4:1	God's Spirit should be stirred up day by day (Psalm 51:10), or like water, it will become stagnant. See also (Ps. 42:2).

The rock that Moses struck was also a *type* of Christ sending forth His Holy Spirit as the source of the river of life! Paul tells us that "...the Rock that followed Israel was Christ" (1 Cor. 10:4). But Moses lacked *faith* in God's Word to strike the rock only once! Unlike the Israelites of old, Christians must have a deep abiding faith in Christ—and God will send them His Holy Spirit as a free gift!

The river of God is a beautiful *type* of God's Holy Spirit and its waters flow throughout the Word of God! God's *river of life* flowed from the garden of Eden and was channeled to the entire earth via various rivers and streams. God's river found its way into the wilderness, as evidence of the rock that Moses struck. In Canaan, the waters of Shiloah flowed to irrigate the land of milk and honey. During the Millennium, the river of life will flow from under the sanctuary, and water the entire city of Jerusalem (Ezek. 47; Joel 3; Zech 14; Ps. 46:4; 65:9). These healing waters will go down into the desert, and go into the sea to heal the entire earth!

After the Millennium, when God the Father dwells with His children, a pristine river will flow out of the throne of God and of the lamb (Rev. 22:1). As during the Millennium, wherever this "water of life" flows, trees will bear healing fruit (Ezek. 47:12; Rev. 22:2).

The Holy Spirit— A Type of Cleansing Agent

There are all kinds of cleansing agents on the market today to make one's clothes cleaner than clean. God also has a cleansing agent from sin—His Holy spirit that will make us *whiter than white*!

TYPES OF THE HOLY SPIRIT

We have already shown that God uses physical water as an analogy to understanding what the Holy Spirit does. Now God uses the CLEANSING ACTION of water to describe how the Holy Spirit *cleanses us from sin*.

God told the ancient Israelites to do things of a *physical* nature so that we today can have a better understanding of *spiritual* matters (1 Cor. 10:6).

He told the Israelites to wash themselves up with water when ever they sinned (Heb. 9:6-14). The high priest could not enter the holy place without washing his clothes in water (Lev. 16:1-4). The priest had to wash his clothes and take a bath in water before sacrificing an animal (Num. 19:1-7). God gives more instructions for the cleansing of clothes by the people and priests in (Exodus 19:10-14 and Leviticus 8:6). But this was only a *schoolmaster* to bring them unto Jesus Christ who "cleanses us" now, or spiritually washes us up with the Holy Spirit (Gal. 3:24-25). David knew sin had to be cleansed. He wrote, **"Wash me thoroughly from iniquity and cleanse me from my sin" (Ps. 51:1-3,12,13).**

The apostle Paul shows how the Old Covenant ablutions [washings] were done away with by the cross. They could only be a sign—they could never really cleanse the mind itself (Heb. 9:9-10). God says in Jeremiah 2:22 RSV, **"Though you wash yourself with lye [a harsh cleansing agent] and use much soap [in water] the stain of your guilt is still before me."**

Christ now *cleanses* us *symbolically* by His blood (1 John 1:7-9) and with the washing of water by the Word (Eph. 5:26). This is the washing of regeneration and renewal of the Holy Spirit (Tit. 3:6).

Christians have their bodies washed with pure water, having a High Priest in Jesus who gives us the Holy Spirit that cleanses us of sin (Heb. 10:19-22).

There is an old expression that says, "You can lead a horse to water but you can't make him drink." Jesus Christ is and was that spiritual drink (1 Cor. 10:4). God says that His people have forsaken Him—the foundation of LIVING WATERS and hewn them out cisterns, broken cisterns, that can hold no water (Jer. 2:13).

Jesus said that He would give unto him that is athirst of the foundation of water of life freely (Rev. 21:6). All will be able to come to the well where the Holy Spirit dwells very soon! In these last days, God is going to pour out His Holy Spirit upon all flesh (Acts 2:17).

Wine—A Type of The Holy Spirit

In another *analogy*, the Holy Spirit is described as *wine* spiritually, Notice: **"Neither do men put wine into old bottles [bodies or old ways of life] else the bottles break and the wine runneth out, and the bottles [bodies] perish: but they put new wine [a new way of life] into new bottles [bodies with a new mind] and both [the Holy spirit] are preserved" (Matt. 9:17).** We will study this meaning more deeply under the parables.

When the Holy Spirit came on the day of Pentecost to start the New Testament Church, many mocked them, saying they were drunk with new wine. But Peter rose up and declared they were not drunk, but rather filled with God's Holy Spirit (Acts 2:13-17).

Oil—A Type of The Holy Spirit

The Holy spirit is also used *symbolically* as oil in the Bible. In the parable of the 10 Virgins of (Matthew 25), five of them didn't have enough oil [the Holy spirit] to make it to the wedding supper and hence into God's Kingdom! This parable will be discussed more fully also under the Parables.

The "Two Witnesses" depicted by two olive trees (Zech. 4:1-3), receive their *power* in the form of *oil* (Zech. 4:6).

The Holy Spirit—A Powerful Force

The Holy Spirit [Gr. *pneuma*] is *pictured* as a mighty *force* like the wind (Jn. 3:8). On the Day of Pentecost, He came like the sound of a rushing wind (Acts 2:2). He is *invisible*, yet you can see His effects. The Holy Spirit is like electricity that cannot be seen, but His effects can (such as lighting up a bulb). He is the dynamic *energy* that flows—like the energy flowing to a light bulb. God is the power source, we are the light bulb! Christians are called the "light of the world!" Like electricity, it can be controlled in amounts (11 Kings 2:9). Jesus had the full measure of the Holy Spirit (Jn. 3:4).

God's Holy spirit is described as the POWER that formed the earth in (Romans 15:19 and Jeremiah 32:17). It is God's Holy Spirit that gives us *power* or *ability* to do His work or to act (Acts 1:8).

TYPES OF THE HOLY SPIRIT

By God's breath [*symbolic* of the Holy Spirit] life came into Adam. God's spirit is compared to *wind* that imparts life into the resurrected Israelites (Ezek. 37:9,14).

The Dove—A Type of The Holy Spirit

In (Matthew 3:16) we read how the Holy Spirit descended like a dove. A dove is *symbolic* of *peace*. This is one of the fruits of the Holy Spirit (Gal. 5:22).

The Palm Tree—A Type of The Holy Spirit

During the Feast of Tabernacles, the Israelites would march through the streets of Jerusalem for seven days waving branches of the Palm tree and Citron, boughs of leafy trees and willows.

This *picturesque* event was known as "sucough" or portable tabernacles and is referred to in (Leviticus 23:40).

During this very special occasion, the people would sing *halleuhah* "praise ye the Eternal" and *hosannah* "save now."

There can be little doubt that these four types of trees were reminders of the wilderness trek, as the Palm pointed to the valleys and plains, the 'boughs of thick trees,' the bushes on the mountain heights, the 'willows of the brook,' the many brooks God gave them to drink from, and the 'citron' the many fruits of the "promised land."

These *four* types of trees would be waved toward the east with singing (Ps. 118:1-3,25), and *symbolically* stood for 4 geographical areas that needed RAIN!

The Citron [Citrus] was a *type* of the heart of man, the Palm, a *type* of the spine, the Myrtle, a *type* of the eye and the Willow, a *type* of the lips.

Like the parts of God's Church, these parts of the body were all united to serve God (1 Cor. 12).

On the eighth day of the Feast of Tabernacles, the people looked forward to *rain,* dressed in white robes and carrying Palms, singing "Hosannah, salvation to our God" (Rev. 7:9,10).

This very graphic custom was still performed during New Testament times, as the people marched down to the pool of Siloam with torches in their hands, singing praises and pouring water into the pool (Jn. 9:7-11).

Anciently, this ceremony was performed on the last Sabbath during the feast of Tabernacles, in which the Jews took a bowl of water from the pool of Siloam and *poured* it into a silver bowl and placed it on the altar in the Temple. This non-biblical custom was a petition to God for rain and a bountiful crop. The water *pictured* the "pouring out" of God's Holy Spirit and the healing during the Millennium (see 1 Sam. 7:5-6; Jn. 7:38).

From the events that occurred that day, in the time of Christ the Last Great Day of the Feast of Tabernacles fell on a weekly Sabbath during the time that Jesus was preaching and healed the blind man (Jn. 9:7).

This ancient ceremony became a charade instead of a parade as the self-righteous would wear broad their phylacteries [scriptures worn on their head and arms] to be seen of men (Matt. 23:5).

These pious Jews would literally sew fringes on the corners of their garments to remember to keep God's Law (Deut. 22:12).

This entire procession was a beautiful *type* of the wedding proposal or *betrothal* to Israel (Hosea 2:19). We will study the literal Hebrew custom of marriage, as it relates to the actual marriage of the Church to Christ in time sequence under the parables.

For seven days during the Feast, an offering was to be made by fire (Lev. 23:36), but on the eighth day of the Feast the Israelites looked forward to the latter rains, notice:

> **Also day by day, from the first day [of the Feast] unto the last day, he read the book of the law of God. And they kept the feast seven days; and on the eighth day was a solemn assembly, according unto the manner (Neh. 8:18).**

This eventful time *pictured* the spiritual rain [God's Holy Spirit] that will cover the earth during the Millennium!

Manna—A Type of The Holy Spirit

Jesus referred to Himself as our *heavenly manna* in (John 6:31-33), notice:

> **Our fathers did eat manna in the desert; as it is written, He gave them bread from heaven to eat. Then Jesus said unto them, Verily, verily, I say**

> unto you, Moses gave you not that bread from heaven: but my Father giveth you the true bread from heaven. For the bread of God is he which cometh down from heaven, and giveth life unto the world.

Jesus further explained: **"I am the bread of life: he that cometh to me shall never thirst" (vs. 35).** Our Savior becomes even more direct in verse 51:

> I am the living bread which came down from heaven: if any man eat of this bread, he shall live for ever: and the bread that I will give IS MY FLESH, which I give for the life of the world.

Recall it was *physical manna* that rained from heaven to sustain the physical nation of Israel, while journeying in the wilderness on their way to the "promised land."

Like the physical manna that kept the Israelites "alive" in the physical wilderness of this world, Christians must partake of God's Holy Spirit internally on a daily basis in order to be sustained spiritually for all eternity!

Christians, like the example of ancient Israel, should find their spiritual nourishment early in the morning [prayer] and then will receive the DEW [symbolic of God's Holy Spirit] (Ex. 16:8,12,13,21).

Israel was instructed by God not to leave any manna till the morning (Ex. 16:19). This was a *type* of the Holy Spirit in the sense that Christians need a daily supply—you can't store up God's Holy Spirit! God's Holy Spirit needs to be stirred up and renewed day by day (11 Cor. 4:16).

"The Laying On Of Hands"—A Type of The Holy Spirit

The "laying on of hands" is one of the fundamental doctrines taught in God's Word (Heb. 6:2). By definition, it is a physical method that God uses to show TRANSFER. This *transfer* can be in the form of special gifts, blessings, authority or even sin!

There are (5) basic categories that this transfer method of "laying on of hands" was used in the word of God:

1) **Substitution:** Under the Old Covenant, God told the congregation of Israel to "lay their hands" upon the person who cursed—then to stone him (Lev. 24:14). This ceremony depicted the transfer of sin. Whenever a priest, the entire congregation or a common Israelite sinned—a "Sin-- offering" was required. Whenever an Israelite was to make an offering for sin, he laid his hand on the head of the sin offering, *symbolically* designating the *transfer of sin* to the animal.

   The animal, of course, was *representative* of our Lord and Savior who took our sins upon Him. The animal was then killed, and its blood smeared upon the horns of the altar in the courtyard (Lev. 1:5).

   On the Day of Atonement, the high priest was to "lay his hands" upon the head of the live goat [*symbolic* of Christ], who bare our sins (Lev. 16:21). This goat was selected by lot of two goats that God designated to represent Christ and Satan. The goat, which God selected to represent Christ as the "Sin-offering" for the people, was killed (vs. 15). Thus, the sins of the people were borne by this goat, even as Christ, finally, once and for all bore our sins on the cross.

   Of course, the real perpetrator of all sin, is Satan the devil, represented by the other goat that was let free into the wilderness. This goat *symbolically* represented Satan's freedom to roam in the wilderness of this world until he is bound and chained upon Christ's return. As a matter of speculation, in final fulfillment of the Day of Atonement, Satan may have "hands laid upon him" as the ultimate fulfillment of the Day of Atonement in a *future* formal ceremony.

2) **Bestowal of Inheritance:** Jacob blessed Ephraim and Manasseh, and "laid hands" upon them (Gen. 48:10-16). This act showed parental bestowal of inheritance rights through *transfer*.

3) **Blessing of Children:** Jesus blessed the little children by placing His "hands upon them" (Mk. 10:16). Children of a believing mate can receive a special

blessing of protection, and even answered prayer (1 Cor. 7:14).

4) **Anointing and Healing:** Jesus Christ healed by the "laying on of hands" (Lk. 4:40; Mk. 6:4-5; Matt. 8:15). The apostle Paul healed by the "laying on of hands" (Acts 28:8). Jesus told His disciples to "lay hands upon the sick and they shall be made well" (Mk. 16:18). The apostles healed by anointing with oil (Mk. 6:13; Jas. 5:14). God brought special miracles by the hands of Paul (Acts 19:11). God brought faith, signs and iracles by the hands of the apostles (Acts 14:3).

5) **The Holy Spirit:** The Holy Spirit came after baptism when hands "layed upon them" (Acts 19:1-6; 8:14 18).
Paul councils us to: **"Neglect not the gift that is in thee, which was given thee by *the laying on of hands"* (1 Tim. 4:14; Acts 6:6).** Rather, stir up the gift that God gave you by the putting on of hands (11 Tim. 1:6). Paul was an example of receiving the Holy spirit by the "laying on of hands" (Acts 9:19-20).It must be pointed out that there is nothing spiritual, mystical or magical in the hands of the Minister. He is merely an instrument performing a *symbolic* ceremony, just as baptism and the anointing with oil. These are not ritualistic ceremonies—but rather authoritative expression of faith! The water does not take away sins in baptism, and there is nothing magical or sacred in the oil the Minister uses to anoint people. These are physical ceremonies that *symbolically* describe a spiritual meaning.

And it is a good thing the Minister does not have sole power to give God's Holy spirit—for he may be fooled by the insincerity of an individual—but not by God! A case in point is found in (Acts 8), where Philip mistakingly baptized Simon Magus. On the other hand, false Ministers cannot even perform this ceremony without God's authority. A case in point was the demon who refused to heed the Jewish exorcist (Acts 19:12-16). This account clearly shows as with all of God's ceremonies, that performing a ritual does not produce results without God's authority backing up that person!

Chapter Eight

TYPES OF BAPTISM

A Type of Death and Resurrection

The use of the word *baptizo* in Jewish usage first appears in the Mosaic laws of purification (Ex. 30:17-21; Lev. 11:25; 15:8; 17:15; Num. 19:17,18; 31:22,23) where it is evident to mean a mere "washing" or "cleaning." In the *Septuagint Version* of the Old Testament, translated into the Hellenistic idiom of the New Testament, the word *baptizo* is only used on three occasions: (11 Kings 5:14; Eccl. 34:35; Isa. 21:4), where the meaning also has reference to a "cleansing."

It's root word "baptize" is not an English word, but a Greek word meaning "immerse." It means to "plunge into", not "sprinkle." Water baptism [immersion] is a *type* of spiritual DEATH and RESURRECTION pertaining to the Christian.

John the Baptist baptized around Enon near Jerusalem, **"…because there was *much* water there" (Jn. 3:23).**

Jesus set the example for us and our elder Brother was put *down into* the water, for He went up OUT OF the water (Matt. 3:16). Philip baptized the Eunuch INTO the water (Acts 8:38-39).

Baptism is a BURIAL in a watery grave, and a raising from it (Col. 2:12). Neither sprinkling nor pouring is a burial, and one rises up out of neither. They do not picture the *symbolic* meaning of baptism!

Paul summed it up very succinctly in Romans 6:3-5:

> **Know ye not, that so many of us as were *baptized* into Jesus Christ, were baptized *into* His *death*? Therefore we are *buried* with Him by baptism into *death:* that like as Christ was *raised up* from the dead by the glory of the Father, even so we also should walk in newness of life. For if we have been planted together in the likeness of His death, we shall be also in the likeness of His *resurrection*.**

There is the beautiful *symbolism*—the real meaning of baptism! It portrays, in *symbol,* the death, burial, and resurrection of Christ!

Baptism also *pictures* the CRUCIFIXION of the old self (vs. 6): **"Knowing this, that our old man is crucified with him..."** This *portrays* the burial of our old sinning self, and coming up out of this watery grave, is *symbolic* of a changed person resurrected to a new spiritual life in Christ Jesus.

Going down into the water *envisions* the death of Christ, and the old self. Coming up out of the water, *pictures* Christ's *resurrection*, and a spiritually resurrected person walking henceforth "in newness of life."

Jesus said of His baptism: **"...Suffer [permit] it to be so now: for thus it becometh us *to fulfill all righteousness...*" (Matt. 3:15).**

Then, there had to be a law that He had to obey in order to fulfill all righteousness. Indeed, there was!

Remember, Jesus was going to be a priest [our High Priest] and all priests had to be baptized (Ex. 29:4). Moses performed the baptism ceremony of Aaron and his sons [the priests] and did all that the Lord commanded (Lev. 8:3,36).

God the Father did the *anointing* of Jesus Christ (Acts 4:27, 10:37-38). Christians, who are also going to become priests (Rev.1:6; 5:10), if possible, may desire to follow in their elder Brother's footsteps and become baptized by water immersion.

TYPES OF BAPTISM

Old Testament Types

The apostle Paul waxes eloquent in (1 Corinthians 11:1) as he challenges us to follow Christ's example: **"Be ye followers of me, even as I also am of Christ."** Certainly, Paul did follow the example of Jesus in regards to baptism when Ananias said to him: **"Get up, be *baptized* and wash your sins away..." (Acts 22:16, NIV).**

From this statement, it is apparent that the baptismal ceremony was important to the apostle Paul even after one has repented.

What then is the purpose of the baptismal ceremony?—the answer is found in the Old Testament.

Being a Pharisee, the apostle Paul was well versed in the Old Testament scriptures and understood the meaning of baptism as he stated in 1 Corinthians 10:1,2 RSV:

> **I want you to know, brethren, that our fathers were all under the cloud, and all passed through the sea, and *all were baptized into Moses* in the cloud and in the sea.**

This *symbolic* baptism of Israel represented their leaving corrupt Egypt [a type of sin] and emerging into the newly revealed truths of God.

This *pictured* the repentant sinners willingness to bury the old way of life, and be cleansed from old sin or past sin (unleavened bread).

In Noah's day, God cleansed the earth [baptized] of universal sin by a universal flood of waters (Gen. 7). Peter wrote of Noah's flood, also a *type* of New Testament baptism:

> **Eight souls were saved by water. The like *figure* where even baptism doth now save us... by the resurrection of Jesus Christ (1 Pet. 3:20-21).**

Both of these examples show that baptism is a *cleansing* or *purification* process.

The following examples are also *types* of New Testament baptism. Aaron, the first high priest of Israel was not allowed to enter the Holy of Holies [representative of God's throne] without first bathing his flesh in water (Lev. 16:1-4).

Lepers that had their leprosy disappear had to wash their clothes in water before they could return to society after being quarantined (Lev, 14:8). Both husband and wife had to bathe themselves after marital relations (Lev. 15:16-18). The high priest was to wash his clothing and take a bath after many an animal sacrifice (Num. 19:1-7).

Through His prophet Elisha, God's instructions to Naaman, the chief general of the Syrian army who had contracted leprosy, was: **"Go and wash in the river Jordan seven times."** This didn't make too much sense to this skeptical Gentile General and his reply was: **"Are not Abana and Pharpar, the rivers, of Damascus, better than all the waters of Israel? Could I not wash in them and be clean? So, he turned and went away in a rage" (11 Kings 5:12, RSV).** Later, Naamans' aides talked him into doing as God's prophet had said—and he was healed completely of his leprosy!

These Old Testament examples show us very plainly—that God used the physical act of bathing of the flesh, and clothing that touched the flesh, to rid the Israelites and consenting Gentiles of physical and mental diseases. This clearly shows that God wants all mankind to be physically, mentally and spiritually clean!

But these cleansing ceremonies with water in the Old Testament could not really wash sins away and were only a *forerunner* to the New Testament "spiritual cleansing" in Christ.

Jeremiah exemplifies this: **"Though you wash yourself with lye [a harsh cleansing agent] and use much soap [in water], the stain of your guilt is still before me" (Jer.. 2:22, RSV).**

Again, Paul relates the meaning of the Old Testament ceremonial washings in Hebrews 9:9:10 (RSV):

> **According to this arrangement, gifts and sacrifices are offered which cannot perfect the conscience of the worshipper, but deal only with food and drink and various ablutions [washings], regulations for the body imposed until the time of reformation (Christ's blood sacrifice on the cross).**

TYPES OF BAPTISM

The sacrifice of Jesus Christ did what all the offerings, sacrifices and ceremonial washings could not do.

The baptismal bridge between the Old and New Testaments was crossed by John the Baptist who baptized unto REPENTANCE. This paved the way for Christ's baptism of the Holy Spirit. John said of this event:

I baptize you with water for repentance, but he [Christ] who is coming after me is mightier than I...He will baptize you with the Holy Spirit and with fire (Matt. 3:11, RSV).

Once we have *repented* and been *baptized*—God stands by His promise to give us the *gift* of His Holy Spirit as stated by the apostle Peter in (Acts 2:38)!

3 Baptisms

Baptism as a doctrine is found in (Hebrew 6:1-2).

The apostle John described 3 different types of baptisms in Matthew 3:11, **"I indeed baptize you with *water unto repentance*: but he that comes after me shall baptize you with the *Holy Spirit* and with *fire*."** Exactly what is the meaning of these *three* baptisms?

1) **Baptism of Repentance:** This is what John the Baptist brought, as recorded in (Mk.1:4; Acts 19:1-6). John the Baptist preached the baptism of *repentance*. The apostle Peter proclaimed the same message in Acts 2:38, **"Repent and be baptized..."** This baptism was done by *water emersion*. As many New Testament examples affirm, total immersion is *symbolic* of a watery grave. Only a complete submerging could properly picture the death of the "old man" (Rom. 6:3-6). There is only one baptism (Eph. 4:4-5).

Actually, full immersion was practiced until the late 1200's A.D.. In the year 1155, the theologian Thomas Aquinas wrote: "Baptism may be given not only by immersion, but also by affusion of water, or sprinkling with it. But is not the safer way to baptize by immersion, because that is the most common custom?" (quoted by Wall, *His Baptism*, vol,11, pp. 391-393).

Further: "Thirteen hundred years was baptism generally and regularly an immersion by the person under the water, and only in extra-ordinary cases a sprinkling or pouring with water; the latter [sprinkling or pouring], moreover, was disputed—nay, even forbidden" (Brenner, *Catholic History* p. 306).

The word Baptize in the Greek is "Baptizo" meaning immerse. It means to [lunge into, or put into]. Jesus set us the example (1 Pet. 2:21) by being totally immersed! Notice in Matthew 3:16 that He: ***"came up out of the water."*** John Baptized at Eaan, near Jerusalem because there was *much* water there (Jn. 3:23). Philip baptized the Eunuch who *came up* out of the water (Acts 8:38-39). Jesus said to be baptized as He was (Matt. 20:22-23). Our Savior said He wanted to be baptized for it becomes us *to fulfill all righteousness* (Matt. 3:13-17).

In Jesus' name— Jesus commanded that His disciples baptize in the *name of the Father*, and the *Son*, and the *Holy Spirit* (Matt. 28:19-20). In (Acts 2:38), the apostle Peter proclaimed to be baptized in the name of Jesus Christ. Peter baptized in the name of Jesus (Acts 10:46-48). Philip also baptized in the name of Jesus Christ (Acts 8:5,12).

The Bible says that there is no other name under heaven by which we must be saved (Acts 4:12). We are baptized "into" the Father, Son and Holy Spirit. That is how we come into His Church. By *one spirit* are we baptized [put into] *one body* (Eph. 4:4). For by *one spirit* are we baptized into *one body* (1 Cor. 12:13).

The one who does the baptism, does it in place of Jesus, since He is no longer here physically, and does it in His name. That's why Jesus made and baptized more disciples than John [though He didn't baptize any Himself], (Jn. 3:22, 4:1).

The *three* that bear record in (1 John 5:7-12) are the *spirit*, *water* and the *blood*: and these three agree in one (even as the Father, Son, and Holy Spirit). These are three things that all repentant Christians must accept.

Jesus said: **"...he that believes the Gospel and is baptized shall be saved..." (Mk. 16:16).** Christians in the early Church showed their belief by being baptized (Acts 16:33).

2) **Baptism of the Holy Spirit**—Jesus announced that John baptized with water—but, before many days, the apostles and early Christians would be baptized with the Holy Spirit (Acts

TYPES OF BAPTISM

1:5). Jesus declared in John 3:5, **"Truly, truly, I say to you, unless one is born of water, and the spirit, he cannot enter the Kingdom of God."**

Jesus said He came to give this baptism (Lk. 12:50). Jesus asked His disciples if they could drink of the baptism that He was baptized with (Mk. 19:38). For by *one spirit* were we all baptized into *one body* (1 Cor. 12:13). Once we repent and are baptized with water, we will receive the gift of the Holy Spirit (Acts 2:38), or the Baptism of the Holy Spirit!

3) **Baptism by Fire**—John the Baptist spoke of his cousin Jesus Christ—He would baptize with the Holy spirit and with fire (Matt. 2:11). Jesus spoke of this *fiery baptism* in the parable of the tares as in relation to the wicked who will be *burned up* at the end of the age (Matt. 13:40). **"And death and hell were cast into the lake of fire. This is the second death" (Rev. 20:14)**, and the Baptism of fire! (see also Mal. 4:1,3; Matt. 13:40; 25:41; Rev. 20:13-15).

Circumcision—A Type of Baptism

To God, everything and everyone in the world is either a Jew or Gentile, circumcised or uncircumcised, clean or unclean. There are many physical analogies in the Word of God that help us to understand this vital truth.

Fruit was considered as "uncircumcised" for three years as we read in (Leviticus 19:23).

As a *sign* between God and Abraham's seed of the Old Covenant, every male child was to be circumcised the 8th day (Gen. 17:10-12).

Gentiles could also become a part of the covenant by being circumcised (Gen. 17:13). Circumcision was an initiation that made you a part of the covenant and its promises—and part of the promise to Abraham was that of Christ coming out of his seed to save the world. That is why Abraham is called **"...the Father of the circumcision" (Gal. 4:1-25).**

And if we are Christ's, then we are Abraham's, and heirs according to the promise. The promise of ETERNAL LIFE through Abraham's seed culminated in Jesus Christ and the New Testament!

THE FOOLISHNESS GOD

Circumcision in the New Testament was to have a greater meaning—that of the *heart* and to love God with all your heart and soul (Lev. 26:41; Deut. 10:16; 30:16; Ezek. 44:7; Jer. 9:25,26; 4:4).

God considered a Jew [or Christian] which is one *inwardly* and *circumcision is that of the heart* (Rom. 2:17-29; Gal. 5:1-12).

God speaks through the apostle Paul that circumcision is nothing; but the keeping of the Commandments [that's something] (1 Cor. 7:19; Col. 3:11). Circumcision, like baptism, is not needed for salvation (Acts 15); but like baptism, it is an *initiation* of a Christian under the New Testament. It is a *physical operation* that depicts a "spiritual operation" of the mind—A CHANGED HEART!

Christians are made circumcision through Christ's shed blood (Eph. 2:11-20). We are the circumcision that worships God in the spirit (Phil. 3:3).

No uncircumcised person could take the Passover in the Old Covenant (Ex. 12:48), and Christians should not partake of the New Testament sacriments unworthily (1 Cor. 11:24-29).

The uncircumcised [spiritually] will not enter the holy city during the Millennium! (Isa. 52:1).

The apostle to the Gentiles brings out this analogy of circumcision to conversion further in the book of Romans:

> **For circumcision verily profiteth, if thou keep the law: but if thou be a breaker of the law, thy circumcision [conversion] is made uncircumcision [or of none affect]. Therefore, if the uncircumcision keep the righteousness of the law, shall not his uncircumcision be counted for circumcision? And shall not uncircumcision which is by nature [nonbeliever] if it fulfill the law, judge thee, who by the letter and circumcision dost transgress the law? For he is not a Jew, which is one outwardly; neither is that circumcision, which is outward in the flesh: But *he is a Jew [Christians are spiritual Jews], which is one inwardly; and circumcision is that of the heart,* in the spirit, and not in the**

TYPES OF BAPTISM

letter; whose praise is not of men, but of God (Rom. 2:17-29).

God shows here, very lucidly, that eternal life can now be given to ALL—both Jew and Gentile alike (a Gentile is one who is not born a national Jew, or spiritually in God's eyes is a nonbeliever).

But there are certain conditions that must be met by all! You must accept Jesus as your personal Savior and try to overcome your human nature by repenting of sin, and if possible be baptized—to show God you want to change it! You can't overcome it without His Holy Spirit!

Through His apostle, God tells us we must all become spiritual Jews for salvation!

Purity and Purification

What did the tree in the garden of Eden represent? All of the *types* that God gave the nation of Israel (water, wine, blood, oil, baptism, circumcision)—PURITY and PURIFICATION!

The concept of "purity" was very deep within the religious social structure of the children of Israel, as witnessed by the over zealous attitude of the Pharisees (Mk. 7:3,4).

When the Eternal gave the ceremonial laws to Moses, they were for the following reasons: 1) the birth of a child [circumcision of males], and isolation of the mother for a varying periods of time (Lev. 12:1-5); 2) contact with a dead corpse (Num. 19:1-10); 3) diseases such as leprosy (Lev.13:8); and 4) uncleanness due to a running sore (Lev. 15).

Throughout the Old Testament, family "purity" was stressed concerning sexual relations (Lev. 20:1-21; Deut. 22:20,21).

Family "purity" continued to be highly emphasized in the New Testament (Matt. 5:27; 19:3-9; Mk. 10: 2-11; 1 Cor. 5:9-13; 6:18-20; 7:8).

Several New Testament Greek words bring out this "purity concept:"

KATHAROS: "free from impure admixture, without blemish, spotless, blameless" (Matt. 23:26; 27:59; Jn. 13:10; Heb. 10:22; Rev. 15:6; 19:8,21).

KATHARIZO: "to make clean, to cleanse from physical stains, dirt and utensils, to pronounce clean in a Levitical sense" (Matt. 23:25; Matt. 8:2; Acts 15:9; 2 Cor. 7:1; Heb. 9:14).

KATHARISMOS: "to make pure in a Levitical and moral sense from sin" (Mk. 1:44; Lk. 2:22; Jn. 2:6; Heb. 1:3; 2 Pet. 1:9).

HAGNOS: "pure from defilement, not contaminated [from the same root as *hagios*, holy], chaste" (Phil. 4:8; 1 Tim. 5:22; Jas. 3:17; 1 Jn. 3:3).

Purified by Blood

The Old Testament sacrifices used BLOOD to also *symbolize* the cleansing of sin as the apostle Paul wrote: **"And almost all things are by the law purged with blood; and without [the] shedding of blood is no remission [of sins]" (Heb. 9:22).**
The blood of Jesus Christ *purges* our conscience us of all sin (Heb. 1:3; 9:14); and *cleanses* us of all sin (1 Jn. 1:7).
The Hebrew word "toher" connotes CLEANSING and PURITY as determined from the following scriptures:

Psalm 12:6:	"The words of the LORD are *pure* words: as silver tried in a furnace of earth, *purified* seven times."
Psalm 19:8:	"The statutes of the LORD are right, rejoicing the heart: the commandment of the LORD is *pure,* enlightening the eyes."
Psalm 51:2:	"Wash me thoughly from mine iniquity, and *cleanse* me from my sin."
Psalm 52:5:	"Purge me with hyssop, and I shall be clean: *wash* me, and I shall be whiter than snow."
Psalm 51:10:	"Create in me a *clean* heart, O God; and renew a right spirit within me."

TYPES OF BAPTISM

Through the vehicles of water, fire and blood, the Eternal is going to PURIFY the mind of man and the earth—and pardon the iniquity of Israel! Notice the Eternal's merciful words to Israel:

> **I have seen thine adulteries, and thy neighings, the lewdness of thy whoredom, and thine abominations on the hills in the fields. Woe unto thee, O Jerusalem! wilt thou not be made clean? when shall it once be? (Jer. 13:27). And I will cleanse them from all their iniquity, whereby they have sinned against me; and I will pardon all their iniquities, whereby they have sinned, and whereby they have transgressed against me (Jer. 33:8). See also (Ezek. 36:25,33; 37:23; Isa. 4:3-4; Jer. 24:7; Micah. 7:18-19; Zech. 13:9).**

Biblically, the word *sanctify* means "to make holy," and is used in conjunction with *cleansing*, notice:

> **...that He might sanctify and cleanse it [Christ's Church] with the washing of water by the word, that He might present it to Himself a glorious church, not having spot or wrinkle or any such thing, but that it should be holy (Eph. 5:26-27).**

To be spiritually "clean" or "sanctified" [set apart, made holy] is to be "set apart" from filthiness!

All through the Word of God, the Eternal desires that His people be *sanctified* and cleased by the washing of His Word (Eph. 5:26); to be *uncorrupt* in works (Tit. 2:7); to *cleanse* ourselves from all filthiness of the flesh, perfecting *holiness* in the fear of God (11 Cor. 7:1); and to draw near to God by having our hearts *sprinkled* from an evil conscience, and our bodies *washed* with *pure* water (Heb. 10:22).

There was innocence and evil contained in the *symbolic* trees in the garden of Eden. Adam and Eve chose to eat of the forbidden fruit—and it's bitter taste has been in our mouths ever since!

Our first parents thought they could make a "spiritual cocktail" by mixing a little bit of evil with good. In essence, they thought they could mix a little bit of arsenic with apple juice and get a tropical drink!

Let us heed the many wrong examples of sin in the Bible and cease to do evil, and never forget our loving God's promise to those who do— that He will *wash* us, and make us *clean*! (Isa. 1:15).

Chapter Nine

TYPES OF THE TWO WITNESSES

And I will give power unto my two witnesses, and they shall prophecy a thousand two hundred and threescore days, clothed in sackcloth. These are the two olive trees, and the two candlesticks standing before the God of the earth. And if any man will hurt them, fire proceedeth out of their mouth, and devoureth their enemies: and if any man will hurt them, he must in this manner be killed (Rev. 11:3-5).

Although it is impossible to forecaste the exact identity of *who* will be the "Two Witnesses", there is a great deal we can learn about them from the *types*, such as *what* their message will be, *who* they will preach to, and *where* they will preach.

God's "Two Witnesses" will exist at the same time the "Beast" and "False Prophet" will be in power. They will be God's comtemporary Moses and Aaron withstanding Satan's idolatrous system.

They are *cameos* of Moses and Aaron who performed MIGHTY MIRACLES in the sight of Pharaoh through the power of the Almighty God.

Even as Moses and Aaron warned Pharaoh of the impending plagues if he would not let God's people go—so will these two servants of God. The apostle John writes of their supernatural powers in Revelation 11:6 :

> **These have *power* to shut heaven, that it rain not in the day of their prophecy: and have *power* over waters to turn them to blood, and to smite the earth will all *plagues*, as often as they will.**

"Two Olive Trees" and "Two Candlesticks"

But why are these "Two Witnesses" labeled as *"two olive trees"* and *"two candlesticks"* as well? What could these *symbols* possibly represent?

In (Revelation 1:12), the apostle John saw a vision in which he saw a *seven branched golden candlestick*, [a "minorah"] and in the middle of the seven candlesticks one like unto the Son of man. The explanation of the seven candlesticks are explained in (Revelation 1:20), as being *God's seven Churches* or era's. In other words, God's Church would exist throughout the ages, as Christ said His Church would never die (Matt. 16:18).

Of course, the Son of Man who sits [in authority] in the middle of the candlesticks is Jesus Christ, who is the invisible head of the Church (Eph. 5:23). Jesus is the invisible head of the True Church, even as Satan is the invisible head of the false church! There are also seven stars which are angels [Gr. *Messengers*] over the Churches (Rev. 1:20).

The "seven candlesticks" may possibly represent God's seven Church eras throughout history. If this is true, the wording seems to suggest that the last two eras exist during the tribulation period. Because the "Two Witnesses" are two candlesticks, the only logical conclusion we can draw is that they *symbolically* represent the last two Church era's!

Perhaps these messengers *symbolize the leaders of the last two eras*, as God has most likely chosen a person to represent each era based on his character. For example, the leader of the Philadelphia era would be a person who God finds little fault with (Rev. 3:10), whereas the leader of the Laodicean era will be a person who is *lukewarm* in character [until repentant] (Rev. 3:16). The Laodiceans will have to go through the *Tribulation* [fire] in order to qualify to be in God's Kingdom (Rev. 3:18).

TYPES OF TWO WITNESSES

Types of Zerubbabel and Joshua

And the angel that talked with me came again, and waked me, as a man that is wakened out of his sleep. And said unto me, What seest thou? And I said, I have looked, and behold a candlestick all of gold, with a bowl upon the top of it, and his seven lamps thereon, and seven pipes to the seven lamps, which are upon the top thereof. And two olive trees by it, one upon the right side of the bowl, and the other upon the left side thereof (Zech. 4:1-3).

Immediately we recognize that John's prophecy of the "Two Witnesses" is related to the prophecy concerning Zerubbabel and Joshua of the Old Testament as recorded in the book of Zechariah. Zerubbabel was the governor and prince of ancient Judah (B.C. 520) and Joshua was the high priest as we have already learned.

Zerubbabel led God's people out of captivity in Babylon to build God's house in Jerusalem. The very name Zerubbabel means "out of Babylon." Working along side Zerubbabel was Joshua the high priest of Judah.

As we have previously learned, the Bible uses oil [olive] as *symbolic* of God's Holy Spirit. In these last days, God is going to *anoint* His "Two Witnesses" with the power of His Holy Spirit to perform *mighty miracles* once again!

Likewise, a modern-day Zerubbabel will lead His people out of "spiritual Babylon." He will thunder God's warning, **"Come out of her, my people, that ye be not partakers of her sins, and that ye receive not of her plagues "** (Rev. 18:4).

This end-time Zerubbabel will help build God's "spiritual house" and his *counterpart* in the nation of Israel most likely will be instrumental in building a religious center in Jerusalem in the last days.

Just as Joshua and Zerubbabel began a "new work", **not by might** [Heb. *hayel*, i.e., sheer force of labour], **nor by power** [Heb. *koah*, i.e., ability], **but by my Spirit** [Heb. *ruah*], so will the Two Witnesses!

This will be a "new work" in Jerusalem performed by God's Holy Spirit working in and through them. It will be a unifying Spirit, the same Spirit that worked in many of the prophets of old that will bring about the glorious completion of God's work!

This unifying and completing end-time work is also symbolic of the capstone mentioned in (Zech. 13:2), which completes and unifies the physical and spiritual Temple.

In (chapters 3,4 and 6 of Zechariah) we find additional information concerning the "Two Witnesses." Jesus Christ, the head of the Church is represented as a candlestick of all gold with a bowl upon it (Zech. 4:2)—and his seven lamps thereon and seven pipes to the seven lamps. These seven lamps represent God's seven Church eras, even as the seven candlesticks did in (Revelation 1:20).

The seven pipes leading to the lamps, represent the connection to Jesus Christ by which His Holy Spirit [in the form of oil] can flow to His Church (Zech. 4:12). It is by this medium that the "Two Witnesses" will receive their power (Zech. 4:6). These "Two Witnesses" will have power to shut heaven that it rain not, and turn water into blood and to smite the earth with all plagues. They will have *power* and *authority* to kill anyone who tries to overcome them (Rev. 11:6 7). They are the Lord's anointed Ones that stand by the Lord of the whole earth (Zech. 4:1; Rev. 11:4).

The Last Two Eras

These "Two Witnesses" will be very instrumental in building God's "spiritual Temple." Joshua and Zerubbabel built God's physical Temple after the Jews were released from their captivity in Babylon in 536 B.C. God uses them *symbolically* to show what the "Two Witnesses" will also do in these last days.

Although the historical context of the book of Haggai and Ezra is to rebuild the "physical Temple", the book of Zechariah is primarily directed towards building God's "spiritual Temple."

During the time of the rebuilding of the Temple—Haggai, Zechariah and Malachi were God's living prophets. But it wasn't untill 400 years after Malachi, that Israel had another prophet through the preaching of John the Baptist.

During this interval of time, the Temple was not filled with God's shekinah glory! God's Holy Spirit was *among* them, but

TYPES OF TWO WITNESSES

not *in* them! God's glory only returned *symbolically* to the Temple when Jesus Christ entered with the LIGHT of truth!

Speaking to the *spiritual* Zerubbabel, God says he will help lay the foundation of His house and finish it (Zech. 4:9). Concerning God's "spiritual Temple," Jesus Christ is the ultimate fulfillment of laying the foundation. Other apostles throughout the ages have helped Jesus Christ build the spiritual Temple, including the apostle Paul (1 Cor. 3:11). Because the "Two Witnesses" may represent two Church eras, it seems evident that they will *symbolize* the Philadelphia and Laodicean eras—as these will be the last two eras in time sequence prior to Christ's return. However, they will not be the only eras in existence! We will study more about the eras of the Church under "Symbolism in Revelation" in volume 4.

Zerubbabel appears to represent the Philadelphia era as it will have little strength (Rev. 3:8; Zech. 4:6). Joshua who has "filthy garments" [symbolic of sin] needs to repent and go through the Tribulation (Zech. 3:2-4). Notice, God's inspired wording: **"...is not this a brand plucked out of the fire?" (3:2).** This appears to correspond to the Laodicean character. Notice the words "the true and faithful *witness"* in (Revelation 3:14) to the leader of the Laodicean Church.

Once this individual repents as well as those representative of this era [his fellows—Zech. 3:8], they will qualify to become *judges* in God's Kingdom (Zech. 3:7). This also corresponds with the Laodiceans as they will sit with Christ in His throne (Rev. 3:21). This is *symbolic language* for their responsibility, meaning they will be doing what Christ does. Jesus will be a *judge* over the nations (Acts 10:42; 1 Pet. 4:5; Jn. 5:22,27).

Jesus indicated in (Luke 7:41-50) the relationship of one who had many sins also had much love, because they also knew how much they needed forgiveness. Certainly, this type of individual would be more qualified as a judge, since they have first hand experience in repentance and mercy. God chastens every son He loves, and He loves repentant Laodiceans (Rev. 3:19).

Zechariah 3:8 speaks of these "fellows" as "men wondered at" [Heb. "men of wonder" margin]. These "men of wonder" or repentant Laodiceans will reign with Christ, the BRANCH (Zech. 3:8) who is building God's "spiritual Temple" (6:12).

It is also fitting that the Philadelphia era will have the responsibility of being the *educators* in God's Kingdom—

because they are represented spiritually as *pillars* that hold up God's Temple (Rev. 3:12). A physical pillar is a structural support.

Because prophecy is often *dual* to the nation of Israel and the Church, there most likely will be a physical *counterpart* in the nation of Israel to spiritual Joshua and Zerubbabel. These converted Israelites may be instrumental in building God's physical Temple in the last days (Zech. 6:11-13,15). This Temple would be in Jerusalem, the holy city (Rev. 11:1-3). No doubt this would cause a great deal of confusion since the "False Prophet" is also associated with God's Temple (11 Thess. 2:4).

Joshua's "Filthy Garments"

Joshua's "filthy garments" (Zech. 3:3) *symbolized* the sins of Israel as well as his own. Notice Isaiah's parallel wording to the national sins of Israel:

> **...behold, thou art wroth, for we have sinned: in those is continuance, and we shall be saved. But we are all as an unclean thing, and all our righteousness are as** *filthy rags*... **(Isa. 64:5-6).**

The changing of Joshua's garments characterizes the RESTORATION, and moral cleansing of the nation of Israel! Under Zerubbabel, 4,289 priests returned to restore the Temple service. Previously, the priesthood had become corrupted and the offerings polluted (Mal. 2:5-9). Thus God "cleaned up" the nation of Israel and Judah at this time, and made them ceremonially clean to rebuild the Temple!

This moral cleansing of the physical nation of Israel may also *parallel* the spiritual cleansing of the last church era under spiritual Joshua. After Zerubbabel died, the priesthood became corrupt, and the people turned away from God. Realize, God does things in DUAL stages. Zerubbabel and Joshua worked side by side building the *material Temple* of stone, wood and other materials, and are *forerunners* or *types* of God's end-time *spiritual Temple*!

Could it be that two close associates building the Church in the last days would parallel the lives of Zerubbabel and Joshua. Remember, the problem with the Laodicean's is in their attitude producing lukewarm works! God commands them to repent and be zealous [Gr. *zeo*], meaning "to boil." These "works" would have to begin *prior* to the Tribulation, as it is these "lukewarm works" that has caused them to be sent into the Tribulation! Therefore, we may conclude that the Laodicean era will exist at the same time, and may even be affiliated with the Philadelphia era.

Zechariah 3 and 4 detail the characteristics of Joshua, and may very well be a *type* of spiritual Joshua. Here we find that Joshua was God's chosen leader and then Satan found his weakness, and overpowered him (Zech. 3:1). After Joshua repented, he was given a new mitre [a symbol of government] and new garments (Zech. 3:5). Clearly, Joshua had a problem following God's government that had been previously layed down and enforced by Zerubbabel.

Those who are "his fellows" have a similar problem, and will also have to go through the great Tribulation to "open their eyes" (Zech. 3:8). In other words, they were not walking in God's ways! (Zech. 3:7).

Just as God has always had a *duality* between the physical and the spiritual—there may also be a *duality* between Spiritual Joshua and Zerubbabel of the Church and their *counterpart* in the physical nation of Israel. Two Witnesses may be instrumental in building a physical Temple in Jerusalem in the last days as did the literal Joshua and Zerubbabel (Zech. 6:11-13, 15).

Lest there be any doubt that a remnant of Israelites will form a part of the Laodicean Church and be "plucked out of the fire" let's read Amos 4:11: **"...ye [Israel] were as a firebrand plucked out of the burning: yet have ye not returned unto me, saith the LORD."**

During "Jacob's trouble" in the last days, when the nation of Israel is held in captivity in the Great Tribulation—a remnant of Israel will repent as the Eternal pours out His Holy Spirit! When Jesus Christ returns to the earth, He will lead them out of captivity, and back to their land! We will study more of the intricate details of this scenario under God's Holy Days in volume 3.

Now here is something interesting concerning the changing of Israel's filthy garments!

On the Day of Atonement, the high priest entered the Most Holy Place in the Temple, not in his ordinary golden garments, but in a *white linen* dress with matching girdle. Although his mitre was the same shape, it was of a different material than he ordinarily wore.

Thus, on this most sacred and solemn day, the high priest appeared, not as the *Bridegroom* of our Lord, but *symbolically* as the *Bride!* White linen is the *symbol* of righteousness (Rev. 3:4,5; 4:4; 7:9,13; 15:6; 19:8,14).

The removal of Joshua's "filthy garments" and the clothing of him with a change of righteous clothing was *emblematic* of the perfect purity that will eventually happen to Israel and the Church—Christ's "spotless Bride"!

John The Baptist
A Type of the Prophet Elijah

Malachi the prophet, who lived about the time of Zechariah the prophet, declared:

> **Remember ye the law of Moses my servant, which I commanded unto him in Horeb for all Israel, with the statutes and judgments. Behold, I will send you Elijah the prophet before the coming of the great and dreadful day of the Lord: and he shall turn the heart of the fathers to the children, and the heart of the children to their fathers, lest I come and smite the earth with a curse (Mal. 4:4-6).**

Elijah, of course, was the greatest prophet of God in ancient times. In his days, as in our modern times, the people had strayed far from the knowledge of God. King Ahab, the wickedest king who ever lived, sat on the throne of Israel, and Jezebel, his wicked and treacherous wife, ruled with him. The truth of God had been buried under a mountain of superstition inspired by the "Babylonian Mysteries." Israel had fallen into paganism, and Baal worship was rife. In fact, the prophets of Baal outnumbered the servants of God 450 to one!

Says *Unger's Bible Dictionary*, "Ahab had taken for wife Jezebel, a Canaanite woman, daughter of Eth baal. Of a weak and yielding character, he allowed Jezebel to establish the Phoenician worship on a grand scale—priests and prophets of

TYPES OF TWO WITNESSES

Baal were appointed in crowds—the prophets of Jehovah were persecuted and slain, or only escaped by being hid in caves. *It seemed as if the last remnants of true religion were about to perish"* (art; *Elijah*, p. 302).

In the face of stiff persecution and the threat of violent death at the hands of Jezebel's police, Elijah, under inspiration of God, proclaimed with dynamic power:

> **As the Lord God of Israel liveth, before whom I stand, whose constant servant I am, there shall not be dew nor rain these years, but according to my word.**

He had the same power as the "Two Witnesses" described in (Revelation 11)!

For three years and six months [a time, times, and half a time!] there was no rain (Jas. 5:17). The full horrors of famine, caused by crop failure, descended on Samaria and the northern Ten-Tribed Kingdom.

Then Elijah returned from hiding out, and confronted Ahab and Jezebel once more. Before Ahab, he challenged the prophets of Baal to the supreme test, that the controversy as to who really represented the true God, and who was the true God, would be resolved once and for all time!

Unger's Bible Dictionary relates:

> **There are few more sublime stories in history than this. On the one hand the servant of Jehovah, attended by his one servant, with his wild, shaggy hair, his scanty garb, and sheepskin cloak, but with calm dignity of demeanor and the minutest regularity of procedure. On the other hand, the prophets of baal and Ashtaroth—doubtless in all the splendor of their vestments (11 Kings 10:22), with the wild din of their 'vain repetitions' and the maddened fury of their disappointed hopes—and the silent people surrounding all; these form a picture which brightens into fresh distinctness every time we consider it.**

> The Baalites are allowed to make trial first. All day long these false prophets cried to Baal, they leaped upon the altar, and mingled their blood with that of the sacrifice—but all is in vain, for at the time of the evening sacrifice the altar was still cold and the bullock lay stark theron- 'there was neither voice, nor any to answer, nor any that regarded.'
>
> Then Elijah repaired the broken altar of Jehovah, and having laid thereon his bullock and drenched both altar and sacrifice with water until the trench about it was filled, he prayed, 'Lord God of Abraham, Isaac, and of Israel, let it be known this day that thou art God in Israel, and that I am thy servant, and that I have done all these things at thy word.' The answer was all that could be desired, for 'the fire of the Lord fell, and consumed the burnt sacrifice, and the wood, and the stones, and the dust, and licked up the water that was in the trench.' The people acknowledged the presence of God, exclaiming with one voice, 'The Lord, he is God; the Lord he is God' (*Unger*, p. 303). See (1 Kings 18:38).

Elijah also had power to kill his enemies as will the "Two Witnesses" (Rev. 11:5). However, Elijah was not perfect. His faith weakened at times. He had "like passions" as we do (Jas. 5:17). Even after this mighty miracle, after which the prophets of Baal were all slain, Jezebel sent him a threatening letter and he fled for his life! In the wilderness, he sat down under a juniper tree, discouraged, depressed, and despondent.

John the Baptist was a voice crying out in the *physical* wilderness of the Jordan River, preparing the way for Jesus' First Coming. This Coming was to a *material* Temple and to a *physical* nation (Judah). This *physical* Coming was but a *prototype*, or forerunner to Jesus' second Coming, in which one in the "spirit and power" of John and Elijah will prepare the way for Jesus' second Coming.

TYPES OF TWO WITNESSES

Spiritual Elijah will cry out amidst today's *spiritual wilderness* of sin and religious confusion, announcing Christ's Second Coming to His *spiritual* Temple (the Church). This time Jesus will be coming in a *glorified* spiritual body, not a *physical* body!

The Elijah to come in these last days, before the second coming of Christ, will be a prophet in the "spirit and power" of Elijah—not Elijah himself. John the Baptist fulfilled this role before Jesus' first coming. Zacharias, the father of John the Baptist, was told by an angel that his son would:

> **...be great in the sight of the Lord, and shall drink neither wine nor strong drink; and he shall be filled with the Holy Spirit, even from his mother's womb. And many of *the children of Israel* shall he turn to the Lord their God. And he shall go before him [the Messiah] *in the spirit and power of Elias [Elijah]*, to turn the hearts of the fathers to the children, and the disobedient to the wisdom of the just; to make ready a people prepared for the Lord (Lk. 1:15-17).**

Who will fulfill this role in these last days?

Who will turn the hearts of the nation of Israel to their Father in heaven? This end-time messenger will turn the hearts of them of Judah in Jerusalem as did Elijah and John the Baptist (Mal. 3:4-6). He will convert 144,000 hearts of the nation of Israel back to God! Once again, this prophecy is *dual* to the nation of Israel.

Notice a little more about the precise role John the Baptist, the "Elijah" of his day, was to fulfill as his father Zecharias, inspired by God's Holy Spirit announced:

> **And thou, child shalt be called the prophet of the Highest; for thou shalt go before the face of the Lord to prepare his ways; to give knowledge of salvation unto his people by the remission of their sins, through the tender mercy of our God; whereby the day-spring from on high hath visited us, to give light to**

them that sit in darkness and in the shadow of death, to guide our feet into the way of peace (Lk. 1:76-79).

When the Pharisees asked him, John himself said he was not Elijah (Jn. 1:21). His answer was, **"I am the voice of one crying in the wilderness, Make straight the way of the Lord, as said the prophet Isaiah" (vs. 23).**

But Jesus plainly said of John, **"And if ye will receive it, this is Elias [Elijah], which was for to come" (Matt. 11:7-14).** Later, the disciples had forgotten Jesus' words, so they asked Him again:

> **And his disciples asked him, saying, 'Why then say the scribes that Elias must first come' And Jesus answered and said unto them, Elias truly shall first come,** *and restore all things.* **But I say unto you, That Elias is come already, and they knew him not, but have done unto him whatsoever they listed. Likewise shall also the Son of man suffer of them. Then the disciples understood that he spake unto them of John the Baptist (Matt. 17:10-13).**

Clothed in Sackcloth

Although the substance of their preaching is not revealed by scripture, the message of the "Two Witnesses" is suggested by the clothing of these end-time messengers:

> **And I will give power unto my two witnesses, and they shall prophesy a thousand two hundred and threescore days, clothed in sackcloth (Rev. 11:3).**

Thayer defines this sackcloth [Gr. Sakkos] as follows:

> *a coarse cloth, a dark coarse stuff made especially of the hair of animals*: a garment of the like material, and clinging to the person like a sack, which was wont to be worn by

> mourners, penitents, suppliants...and also by those, who, like the Hebrew prophets, led an austere life (*A Greek-English Lexicon of the New Testament*, p, 566).

Here are more startling facts between the *dual* lives of Elijah and John the Baptist. Both were crude men dressed in sheepskin (11 Kings 1:8; Heb. 11:37) and camels's hair (Matt. 3:4). Interestingly, Joshua, another *type* of the "Two Witnesses" had unusual [filthy] garments (Zech. 3:3).

Both men were audacious and rebuked kings. Elijah rebuked king Ahab of Israel, while John the Baptist reprimanded king Herod. Both were preachers of righteousness and acquired the animosity of a queen, whose king tried to kill them. Jezebel and Herod's wife are *types* of the false church while Ahab and Herod are *types* of the "False Prophet."

Elijah was well known to the nations around him. One thing more is worth speculating upon. When Elijah's work on earth was over, he passed his mantle to Elisha. Once spiritual Elijah completes his work on the earth, one has to wonder if there will be an Elisha work afterwards?

Someone, on the earth in these last days will fulfill this tremendous prophecy. He will restore the true worship of God, and turn the hearts of the fathers to their children, and "***restore all things***" preparing a people to meet God, proclaiming the good news of the coming Kingdom of God to the nations of the world!

Both Elijah and John the Baptist were prophets sent to the house of Israel in a time of apostasy, to call the nation to REPENTANCE! With the ministry of the "Two Witnesses," we see once again the sign of their message in their very special clothing—hair cloth, which was a SIGN of national mourning and repentance!

It may therefore be concluded, from their distinctive dress, that the "Two Witnesses" are announcing the same message as did John—that of *repentance* because the Messiah is coming!

Not Moses and Elijah

According to the literalist theory, the "Two Witnesses" will be Moses and Elijah. They base their claims on several scriptural references.

Because it is predicted in (Malachi 3:1-3; 4:5-6) that Elijah would come before the second coming of Christ, and since he did not appear to experience physical death (2 Kings 2:9-11), literalists assume that Elijah will be one of the "Two Witnesses."

It is true that there are many similarities between the life of Elijah and the "Two Witnesses", including power to withhold the rain for 3 1/2 years (1 Kings 17:1; Rev. 11:3,6), and power to kill his enemies (Rev. 11:5).

Literalists also identify Moses as one of God's end-time messengers because Moses appeared with Elijah in the transfiguration (Matt. 17:3), and he performed similar miraculous feats such as turning water into blood (Ex. 7:19-20; Rev. 11:6).

Now the theory continues. Moses' body was preserved by God so that he would be restored (Deut. 34:5-6; Jude 9) as one of the Witnesses [representing the Law], with Elijah [representing the Prophets], in witnessing and proclaiming the coming of the Messiah!

However, there are several fallacies with this theory. The *transfiguration* was a *vision* of the Kingdom of God, and not a resurrection of Moses since Christ is the *firstfruit* of the resurrection (1 Cor. 15:20,23). The answer to this perplexing scripture is found in (Matthew 17:9), where Jesus told them, **"Tell the VISION to no man."** A vision is not a material reality, but a supernatural picture observed by the eyes.

The Witnesses have mortal bodies and are subject to death. Elijah and Moses on the Mount of transfiguration evidently did not have mortal bodies, for they "appeared in glory." It is hardly likely that they would be given mortal bodies again.

Ezekiel's Message—A Type for The End Time

God used the prophets, naming them Isaiah, Ezekiel, Hosea and Joel, to warn Israel about punishments He would bring upon them for their constant rebellion against His laws. These prophets were to use their voices like trumpets to blare their warnings to God's people.

Notice, for example, God's instruction to Isaiah:

> **Cry aloud, spare not, lift up thy voice like a trumpet, and shew my people their**

transgression, and the house of Jacob their sins (Isa. 58:1). See also (Hosea 5:8 and Joel 2:1).

Portions of the prophets' warnings were fulfilled in *type*, by ancient Israel's captivity. Yet many of these prophecies are *dual*, having both ancient and modern fulfillments. Such is the case with the message of the prophet Ezekiel.

God set Ezekiel as a watchman to Israel. Ezekiel, through his message, *symbolically* blew a trumpet of warning to God's people (Ezek. 33:1-7).

Ezekiel's warning, however, did not reach the house of Israel, because they had already gone into captivity! Ezekiel's visions of Israel's impending destruction were given "...in the fifth day of the month, which was the fifth year of king Jehoiachin's captivity" (Ezek. 1:2). Jehoiachin went into captivity in 597 B.C. or about 125 years after the removal, to Assyria, of the last of the northern tribes, which occurred from 721-718 B.C.

If Ezekiel's message did not reach ancient Israel—for whom was it intended?

God's warning through Ezekiel was intended for the modern descendants of ancient Israel—very possibly the peoples of Israel, the United States, Britain and in general, northwestern Europe today!

Levitical Types

Over the years, there have been many different interpretations as to the identity of these two exalted individuals known biblically as the "Two Witnesses." Theologians have speculated these two end-time miracle workers to be everyone from the resurrected Moses and Elijah, to angelic beings! Although it would be preposterous to give actual names of the "Two Witnesses", their nationality and origin can be safely speculated upon, based on our previous knowledge of the *types* and scripture!

Note this first of all!

Whoever these "Two Witnesses" of God will be, they definitely will be human! Scripture is emphatic on this point because they are *killed* in the holy city (Rev. 11:7,8).

Because a Levitical system is yet to emerge in Jerusalem with a sacrificial system and possible Temple [this will be covered in more detail in volume 3]—it is my personal belief that these two end-time servants of God will be of Israelite origin. This understanding is also based upon our knowledge of past *types* of the "Two Witnesses." As already mentioned, there may be a *duality* between the "Two Witnesses" in Jerusalem representing the physical nation of Israel and the spiritual Church.

Also, as already shown, Moses, Aaron, Joshua, and Zerubbabel, Elijah and John the Baptist were all *types* of the "Two Witnesses." The first *type* of the "Two Witnesses" were Moses and Aaron—who turned water into blood and caused a devastating drought (Ex. 7:17). The "Two Witnesses" will perform similar feats (Rev. 11:6).

Realize this important truth—both Moses and his brother Aaron were Levites!

Next, we come to Elijah who brought fire down from heaven (1 Kings 18:38) and prophesied a 3 1/2 year drought (1 Kings 17:1; Jas. 5:17). Again, these are identical powers the "Two Witnesses" will receive (Rev. 11:5,6).

Although the Bible does not give Elijah's nationality, other than he was a Tishbite of Gilead—he is believed to be a Levite. For him to erect an altar and make a sacrifice without being a Levite (1 Kings 18:31-38)—would have been an abomination to the Eternal! Also, because our Savior said that John the Baptist was a *type* of Elijah (Matt. 17:12,13)—and John was a Levite (Lk. 1:5,13).

In these last days—a third *type* of Elijah is yet to come, **"Behold, I will send you Elijah the prophet before the coming of the great and dreadful day of the Lord" (Mal. 4:5).**

What is this coming Elijah to do? Let Christ give us the answer: **"...Elijah truly shall come first, and *restore all things*" (Matt. 17:11).** This was also prophesied by Peter in Acts 3:20-21:

> **And he shall send Jesus Christ, which before was preached unto you: whom the heaven must receive until the times of *restitution* [restoring] of all things...**

TYPES OF TWO WITNESSES

But what things are the coming Elijah to *restore* before Christ returns? He will begin to *restore* the Kingdom to Israel! The apostles were well aware that this would someday occur as they inquired of Christ: **"...Lord, wilt thou at this time *restore* again the kingdom to Israel?" (Acts 1:6).**

Now we come to the final *type* of the "Two Witnesses" to learn *what* will be *restored* by the coming Elijah!

The account of Joshua and Zerubbabel *parallels* what the "Two Witnesses" will do to a tee! They, like the "Two Witnesses" were God's "two olive trees" that stood before God on earth.

Now what did Joshua and Zerubbabel do? They *restored* the Aaronic *priesthood* and *sacrificial system* in a *rebuilt Temple!* Because they *symbolically* stood on each side of the seven branched candlestick in the holy place of the Temple (Zech. 4:2,3)—they must be Levite priests! Scripture tells us that Joshua was a high priest (Zech. 3:8). No Gentile or other Israelite tribe was permitted to enter the Holy Place in the Temple where the seven branched candlestick was located (Ex. 30:27).

Let's notice further similarities between Joshua and Zerubbabel, and the "Two Witnesses."

Both are called "two olive trees" and "two candlesticks" or "two anointed ones" that stand by the Lord of the whole earth (Zech. 4:2,3,14; Rev. 11:4).

Both have something to do with measuring a Temple in Jerusalem! Notice the resemblance in wording:

> **Therefore, thus saith the LORD, I am returned to Jerusalem with mercies:** *my house* **shall be built in it, saith the LORD of hosts, and a line shall be stretched forth upon Jerusalem...I lifted up mine eyes again, and looked, and behold a man with a** *measuring line* **in his hand (Zech. 1:16; 2:1).**

Zerubbabel is then seen with a *plummet* in his hand [a carpenter's tool for making walls perpendicular] to *measure* and complete God's house [Temple] (Zech. 4:9,10). This has spiritual reference to measuring the "straightness" or the level of deviation the Church has strayed from God's truth! Now notice the similar wording of (Revelation 11) in reference to the "Two Witnesses":

> **And there was given me [John]** *a reed like unto a rod*: **and the angel stood, saying, Rise, and** *measure the temple of God*, **and the** *altar*, **and them that worship therein. But the** *court* **[court of the Gentiles] leave out, and** *measure it not; for it is given unto the Gentiles: and the holy city shall they tread under foot forty and two months (Rev. 11:1,2).**

Undoubtedly there are spiritual implications of this Temple to God's Church—however, to "spiritualize" the entire context as applying to a "spiritual Temple" is a gross error!
Consider!

As noted previously, Joshua and Zerubbabel were *types* of the "Two Witnesses" and built a *literal* Temple! Gentiles will *literally* tread down God's holy city of Jerusalem for forty two months [3 1/2 years] (Lk. 21:24). If this Temple is "spiritual"—why connect the "court of the Gentiles" to it which is *literal*, and will be *literally* trodden under foot by Gentile armies? The "court of the Gentiles" can only be interpreted in a literal sense—for what is it's spiritual implication?

After viewing the *types* of the "Two Witnesses"—we can only come to one possible conclusion. They will be of Israelite origin, and be instrumental in building a house for the Lord in Jerusalem. Most likely one of them will be of priestly origin as was Aaron, Joshua, Elijah and John the Baptist.

Jerusalem is to be the focus of attention in these last days. It is where the "Two anointed" servants of God will perform mighty miracles that will convert thousands in Israel! This will be similar to what John the Baptist did and Peter on the Day of Pentecost (Acts 2:41: 21:20).

So great will be the conversion of Israel that 144,000 Israelites (12,000 from each tribe) will be protected from the seven last plagues of God (Rev. 7:1-8). Unbelievable miracles are about to occur in Jerusalem, and in fact may parallel what happened during the first century. Notice Jesus' prophetic words:

TYPES OF TWO WITNESSES

> **But ye shall receive power, after that the Holy Spirit is come upon you: and ye shall be witnesses unto me both in Jerusalem, and in all Judaea, and in Samaria, and unto the uttermost part of the earth (Acts 1:8).**

This will be the time that all things will be *restored* in Jerusalem including a Temple, Levitical priesthood and sacrificial system. This will occur in Palestine as a result of the conversion of thousands of Jews to a *type* of Jewish Christianity that was experienced during the first Century!

Chapter Ten

TYPES OF SIN

Babylon, Egypt and Sodom—Types of Satan's System

Three sister cities are mentioned in the Bible more than any others that spiritually represent *types* of sin. This is confirmed in the eighth verse of Revelation eleven: **"And their dead bodies [the 'Two Witnesses'] shall lie in the street of the great city [Jerusalem], which *spiritually* is called Sodom and Egypt, where also our Lord was crucified."**

These ancient cities were *figures* of those who would turn from the truth and live in open REBELLION of God's laws! Babylon is mentioned in the 17th and 18th chapters of Revelation in reference to a religious system that has deceived the entire world!

It seems apparent that ancient Babylon was the city where Satan started his *counterfeit religious system* under Nimrod as we have already read. This pagan counterfeit system was carried on through the *Babylon Mysteries* during the days of King Nebuchadnezzar. They have spread to *all* nations, and God's Word lashes out against this false worship very vehemently in (Revelation 17).

Babylon means "confusion"! That's why God confused the tongues of those in Babylon when they made the tower of Babel under Nimrod's direction. God made their tongues "babel" in different languages so they would repent of their evil ways! But this did not stop Satan's influence. Abraham was called out of

Babylon or "confusion" into a new world of *enlightenment*. Christians are to follow his faithful example!

King Nebuchadnezzar's Babylonian monarchy was the grandest kingdom of its time. It was described *symbolically* by a head of gold in a dream the King had, as interpreted by Daniel in the second chapter of his book.

Nebuchadnezzar's Dream

King Nebuchadnezzar of Babylon had a most unusual dream in which he saw an image, mighty and with exceeding brightness stand before him. It had a frightening appearance in which the head of this image was of fine gold, it's breast and arms were of silver, it's belly and thighs of bronze, it's legs of iron and it's feet were partly of iron and partly of clay.

The King then saw a stone, made by a *supernatural source* hit the image in it's feet of iron and clay, and broke them in pieces. Further, the iron, the clay, the bronze, the silver and the gold were all broken in pieces and blown away by the wind. Finally, the stone that struck the image became a great mountain and filled the earth.

Daniel interpreted the image to mean *four* successive world ruling empires that would arise throughout history—the fourth one existing at the end of man's age. Any history student knows that the Persian Empire, under Cyrus, conquered the Babylonian Empire [head of gold] in 538 B.C. Therefore, *symbolically* the Persian Empire represented the breast and arms of silver. It is also common knowledge that Alexander's Grecian Empire conquered the Persians in 330 B.C. (the belly and thighs of bronze). Finally, the Grecian Empire was swallowed up by the Roman Empire in 31 B.C. represented by the legs of iron and feet partly of iron and clay.

The *symbolic stone* made without hands that *smashes* the Roman Empire is Jesus Christ and His coming Kingdom. The interpretation of the STONE is given in many places in the Bible. **"Jesus of Nazareth...is *the stone* which was set at nought of you builders, which is become HEAD of the corner" (Acts 4:10-11; Eph. 2:19 22; 1 Pet. 2:4 8; 1 Cor. 10:4; Dan. 7:13-14).**

Each of these FOUR world ruling Empires became more degenerate in morals than the one it had conquered, yet stronger

TYPES OF SIN

militarily. Just as each metal was more precious than it's successor, yet softer in hardness. Gold is more valuable than silver, silver is more precious than bronze, and bronze is more esteemed than iron. Yet iron is harder and stronger than bronze, bronze is more enduring than silver, and silver is harder than gold.

It would be the Roman Empire, the fourth kingdom that would be stronger in military strength, yet *morally inferior* to the previous kingdoms, that would be smashed by the coming Kingdom of Jesus Christ. The two legs of this image that looked like a man, represented the two divisions of the Roman Empire, namely Constantinople in the East and Rome in the West.

THE FOOLISHNESS GOD

**NEBUCHADNEZZAR'S DREAM
DANIEL 2**

Head of gold
CHALDEAN EMPIRE
609 - 538 B.C.
DANIEL 2:38

Breasts & arms of silver
MEDO PERSIA EMPIRE
538 - 330 B.C.
DANIEL 2:32, 39

Belly & thighs of brass
GREECE
330 - 31 B.C.
DANIEL 2:32, 39

Legs of iron
ROMAN EMPIRE
1 B.C. - 476 A.D.
DANIEL 2:40

Stone cut out without hands
JESUS
DANIEL 2:45

Toes, part iron, part clay
ROMAN EMPIRE
yet future
DANIEL 2:41

TYPES OF SIN

The Synagogue of Satan

In the days of Christ, Simon the Sorcerer would revive the centuries old "Babylon Mystery Religion" as we have already read. Now read Revelation 2:9: **"I know the blasphemy of them which say they are Jews, and are not, but are THE SYNAGOGUE OF SATAN."**

Notice, this is a *synagogue of* Satan! A synagogue is merely the Hebrew word for church. Then Jesus is not speaking of a race, but of a church that belongs to the devil!

So here was a church made up of Gentiles, claiming salvation, claiming to be Jews inwardly, masquerading as a "Christian" church, yet the very tool of Satan himself!

Many religious commentators believe this synagogue of Satan is the great apostate church which developed after 70 A.D. and ultimately became recognized as the State Religion of the Roman Empire.

In (Revelation 2:13-14), Christ, speaking to the Church of Pergamos, says, **"I know thy works, even where Satan's seat is...thou hast there, them that hold *the doctrine of Balaam.*"** Balaam led the children of Israel away from their God and Jesus relates that this synagogue of Satan has led His Church away from him because of their false doctrine (Num. 25:1-3, 31:16).

The False Church (Babylon The Great)

Many prophetic writers have commented that the New Testament contains many warnings of "false doctrines" inspired by Satan and promoted by a false church. It is a part of the world, actually ruling in its politics over many nations, and united with the "Holy Roman Empire." It will be brought to a complete focus in (Revelation 17).

This church is pictured with pomp, ritual and display, decked in purple, scarlet and gold—while God's colors are blends of reds, lemon yellows, rich browns, emerald greens and bright sea blues (Rev. 2:13 14). It sits on 7 hills (Rev. 17:9) and rules over many peoples, nations, and tongues (Rev. 17:15).

She is pictured as a universal deceiver...the whole world spiritually drunk from her. Notice also that this woman is labeled as one who commits *fornication*, not adultery (vs. 2)—which means it is a church not married to Christ!

THE FOOLISHNESS GOD

The Bible labels this fallen woman [church] as a WHORE! (Rev. 17:1). Continuing in verse 5 we read of this harlot woman:

> **And upon her forehead was a name written, MYSTERY, BABYLON THE GREAT, THE MOTHER OF HARLOTS AND ABOMINATIONS OF THE EARTH.**

Revelation 17 & 18 describe this "fallen woman" as losing her throne over the kingdoms of the earth!

Thoughout the ages commentators have made a Babylonian connection with the church of Rome? Why it is called Babylon the great, and not Persia or Greece the great? This false church is described as "the daughter of Babylon" in (Isaiah 47:1-5).

In his *Lectures on the Revelation,* pp. 287-95; H.A. Ironside explains the development of the same system:

> **The woman is a religious system, who dominates the civil power, at least for a time. The name upon her forehead should easily enable us to identify her. But in order to do that we will do well to go back to our Old Testament, and see what is there revealed concerning literal Babylon, for the one will surely throw light upon the other...**
>
> **...we learn that the founder of Bab-el, or Babylon, was Nimrod, of whose unholy achievements we read in the 10th chapter of Genesis. He was the arch-apostate of the patriarchal age...he persuaded his associates and followers to join together in "building a city and a tower which should reach unto heaven."...**
>
> **Ancient lore now comes to our assistance and tells us that the wife of Nimrod-bar-Cush was the infamous Semiramis the First. She is reputed to have been the foundress of the Babylonian mysteries and the first high-priestess of idolatry. Thus, Babylon became**

the fountainhead of idolatry, and the mother of every heathen and pagan system in the world. The mystery religion that was there originally spread in various forms throughout the whole earth...and is with us today...

Building on the primeval promise of the woman's Seed who was to come, Semiramis bore a son whom she declared was miraculously conceived! And when she presented him to the people, he was hailed as the promised deliverer. This was Tammuz, whose worship Ezekiel protested against in the days of the captivity. Thus was introduced the mystery of the mother and the child, a form of idolatry that is older than any other known to man. The rites of this worship were secret. Only the initiated were permitted to know its mysteries. It was Satan's effort to delude mankind with an imitation so like the truth of God that they would not know the true Seed of the woman when He came in the fullness of time...

From Babylon this mystery-religion spread to all the surrounding nations...Everywhere the symbols were the same, and everywhere the cult of the mother and the child became the popular system; their worship was celebrated with the most disgusting and immoral practices. The image of the queen of heaven with the babe in her arms was seen everywhere, though the names might differ as languages differed. It became the mystery-religion of Phoenicia, and by the Phoenicians was carried to the ends of the earth.

Astoreth and Tammuz, the mother and child of these hardy adventurers, became Isis and Horus in Egypt, Aphrodite and Eros in Greece, Venus and Cupid in Italy, and bore many other names in more distant places. Within 1000 years Babylonianism had become the religion of the world, which had rejected the Divine revelation.

Linked with this central mystery were countless lesser mysteries...Among these were the doctrines of purgatorial purification after death, salvation by countless sacraments such as priestly absolution, sprinkling with holy water, the offering of round cakes to the queen of heaven as mentioned in the book of Jeremiah, dedication of virgins to the gods, which was literally sanctified prostitution, weeping for Tammuz for a period of 40 days, prior to the great festival of Istar, who was said to have received her son back from the dead; for it was taught that Tammuz was slain by a wild boar and afterwards brought back to life. To him the egg was sacred, as depicting the mystery of his resurrection, even as the evergreen was his chosen symbol and was set up in honor of his birth at the winter solstice...The sign of the cross was sacred to Tammuz, as symbolizing the life-giving principle and the first letter of his name. It is represented upon vast numbers of the most ancient altars and temples, and did not, as many have supposed, originate with Christianity.

The chief priests wore mitres shaped like the head of a fish, in honor of Dagon, the fish-god, the Lord of life—another form of the Tammuz mystery, as developed among Israel's enemies, the Philistines. The chief priest when established in Rome took the title Pontifex Maximus, and this was imprinted on his mitre. When Julius Caesar [who, like all young Romans of good family, was an initiate] had become the head of State, he was elected

TYPES OF SIN

> Pontifex Maximum, and this title was held henceforth by all the Roman emperors down to Constantine the Great, who was, at one and the same time, head of the church and high priest of the heathen!
>
> The title was afterwards conferred upon the bishops of Rome, and is borne by the pope today, who is thus declared to be, not the successor of the fisherman-apostle Peter, but the direct successor of the high priest of the Babylonian mysteries, and the servant of the fish-god Dagon, for whom he wears, like his idolatrous predecessors, the fisherman's ring.
>
> During the early centuries of the church's history, the mystery of iniquity had wrought with such astounding effect, and Babylonian practices and teachings had been so largely absorbed by that which bore the name of the church of Christ, that the truth of the Holy Scriptures on many points had been wholly obscured, while idolatrous practices had been foisted upon the people as Christian sacraments, and heathen philosophies took the place of gospel instruction...

Today's Babylon

C. I. Scofield fills in more of the details as to modern-day Babylon's identity in his renowned *Scofield, Reference Bible*, pp. 1346-47:

> Two "Babylons" are to be distinguished in the Revelation: ecclesiastical Babylon, which is apostate Christendom, headed up under the Papacy; and political Babylon, which is the Beast's confederated empire, the last form of Gentileworld-dominion.Ecclesiastical Babylon is "the great whore" (Rev. 17:1), and is destroyed by political Babylon (Rev. 17:15-18),

> that the beast may be the alone object of worship (2 Thess. 2:3, 4; Rev. 13:15). The power of political Babylon is destroyed by the return of the Lord in glory...The notion of a literal Babylon to be rebuilt on the site of ancient Babylon is in conflict with Isaiah 13:19-22. But the language of Rev. 18 (e.g. vs. 10, 16, 18) seems beyond all question to identify "Babylon," the "city" of luxury and traffic, with Babylon the ecclesiastical centre, viz. Rome. The very kings who hated ecclesiastical Babylon deplore the destruction of commercial Babylon.

The sins of Babylon had spread to other nations including Egypt. Egypt is also described as a *type* of sin in the Bible. It was here that the Israelites were held in *bondage* to the cruel taskmasters of Egypt. This is a *type* of the spiritual captivity Christians are in—until they can escape by the miraculous power of God!

The Pharaoh of Egypt is a subsequent form of Satan holding God's *chosen* people in his power.

Sodom and her sister Gommorha were two of the most sin filled cities of their day. Sodom was a haven for illicit sex—hence the term "sodomy." Sin was so prevalent there, they actually flaunted it (Isa. 3:9).

The Bible describes Christ's Church and the false church as *typified* by Jerusalem the Bride, and it's *counterpart* in Babylon, the Harlot.

An enormous metropolis, "Babylon the great" stands for the corrupt system that seduces the whole world. The book of Revelation contrasts this city, so full of wickedness, with the *purity* and *perfection* of the "New Jerusalem." This glorious spiritual city, the New Jerusalem, also stands for the future ruling headquarters of God's perfect sovereignty.

Earthly Babylon is a physical *counterpart* of spiritual Babylon which is a spiritual city, similar to our "Jerusalem Above." She is a prison house of demonic spirits, and we are told that she is the source of every abomination in the earth, and the mother of the harlots [false religions] in the earth (Rev. 17:5).

This spiritual city of demons has ruled the whole earth through witchcraft and other methods of the occult!

The story of Babylon is a sobering one. The old city beneath the Mesopotamian plain has come to represent human society as it develops apart from God. It has been both the pinnacle of man's achievements, and a millstone arournd his neck.

When the angel of the Lord lifts that millstone and *symbolically* casts Babylon the great into the depths of the sea, a great weight will have been lifted off human civilization!

"The Image of The Beast"

Renowned author Henry Halley says in his *Halley's Bible Handbook:*

> This description of Babylon the Great Harlot, seated on the Seven-Headed Ten-Horned Beast, while it may have ultimate reference to a situation yet to appear, exactly fits Papal Rome. Nothing else in World History does fit. The desire for Worldly Power began to manifest itself in the Church, on a broad scale, in the 4th century, when the Roman Empire ceased its persecutions, and made Christianity its State Religion. The spirit of Imperial Rome passed into the Church. The Church gradually developed itself into the pattern of the Empire it had conquered.
>
> Rome fell. But Rome came to life again, as a World-Power, in the Name of the Church. The Popes of Rome were the heirs and successors of the Caesars of Rome. The Vatican is where the Palace of the Caesars was. The Popes have claimed all the authority the Caesars claimed, and more. The Papal Palace, throughout the centuries, has been among the most luxurious in all the world. Popes have lived in Pomp and Splendor unsurpassed by earthly kings. In no place on earth is there more ostentatious pageantry and show of magnificence than at the coronation of a Pope. The City of Rome, first Pagan, then Papal, has been the Dominating

Power of the World for Two Thousand Years, 200 B.C. to A.D. 1800.

Full of names of Blasphemy (17:3). Popes claim to hold on earth the place of God, to have Supreme Authority over the Human Conscience, to Forgive Sin, to Grant Indulgences, and that Obedience to Them is necessary to Salvation. How could anything be more Blasphemous? "Scarlet" (17:3,4) color of the Beast and the Harlot, and also of the Dragon (12:3), is the Color of the Papacy. The Papal Throne is Scarlet. It is borne by twelve men clad in Scarlet. The Cardinals' hats and robes are Scarlet. Originally the Devil's color (12:3), it has now become the Color of Atheistic Communism: they are commonly spoken of as Reds, Red Army, Red Territory, the Red Square in Moscow, the Devil again marshalling his hosts from without. "Filthiness of her Fornication" (17:6). The Horrors of the Inquisition, ordered and maintained by the Popes, over a period of 500 years, in which unnumbered millions were Tortured and Burned, constitute the MOST BRUTAL, BEASTLY and DEVILISH PICTURE in all history. It is not pleasant to write these things. It is inconceivable that any Ecclesiastical Organization, in its mania for Power, could have distorted and desecrated and corrupted, for its own exaltation, the beautiful and holy religion of Jesus, as the Papacy has done. But facts are facts. And History is History. And, most amazing of all, it seems exactly prefigured in Revelation. No wonder John's vision made him sick at heart (10:10). P. 731-732, article, *An Apostate Church on the Throne of a World-Empire.*

TYPES OF SIN

A Type of "The Lake of Fire"

The terrible destruction of Sodom and Gomorrah by "fire" is a *graphic illustration* of the end-time "fire" which will literally consume and annihilate the wicked!

Here is what Jude wrote concerning this infamous event:

> **Even as Sodom and Gomorrah, and the cities about them in like manner, giving themselves over to fornication, and going after strange flesh, are set forth** *for an example,* **suffering the vengeance of** *eternal fire***! (Jude 7).**

Jude says the annihilation of these twin sin cities is an example for us! Their fate depicts the fate of all the incorrigibles at the end of this hell-bent age!

Exactly what happened to these sin cities is recorded in God's Word in Genesis 19:24-28:

> **Then the Lord rained upon Sodom and Gomorrah brimstone and fire [a type of the "lake of fire"] from the Lord out of heaven; and he overthrew those cities, and all the plain, and all the inhabitants of the cities, and all that which grew upon the ground....and lo, the smoke of the country went up as** *the smoke* **of a great furnace.**

Now notice the *parallel* end-time account concerning the fate of Babylon the Great in Revelation 18:8-10:

> **Therefore, shall her plagues come in one day, death, and mourning, and famine; and she shall be utterly** *burned with fire:* **for strong is the LORD God who judgeth her. And the kings of the earth, who have committed fornication and lived deliciously with her, shall bewail her, and lament for her, when they shall see** *the smoke of her burning,* **Standing afar off for the fear of her torment, saying, Alas, alas**

that great city Babylon, that mighty city! for in one hour is thy judgment come.

Adam and Eve's Nakedness—A Type of Sin!

God sacrificed an animal to make the clothes for Adam and Eve after they sinned to *cover* their nakedness (Gen. 3:21). This event has spiritual implication to the sacrifice of Jesus Christ who *clothes* Christians from their sins or from their spiritual nakedness (Rev. 3:17). The moment Adam ate of the forbidden fruit, "Jesus was slain from the foundation of the world" (Rev. 13:8).

May God help us to make our election sure, and not trample upon the sacrifice of His faithful Son—lest we be cast into the "lake of fire" as despicable chaff!

Satan's Fate Described

The fate of Satan, in *type*, is vividly described in (Ezekiel 28). The first ten verses of this chapter describe the fate of the prince of Tyre, the proud human ruler of the commercial capital of the ancient world, a city overflowing with wealth and commercial success, the envy of nations.

Let's read several translations of this evil despot's fate which is *typical* of our adversary, Satan the devil! Here is what the *Living Bible* says:

> **Son of dust, weep for the king of Tyre. Tell him, the Lord God says: You were the perfection of wisdom and beauty. You were in Eden, the garden of God; your clothing was bejeweled with every precious stone—ruby, topaz, diamond, chrysolite, onyx, jasper, sapphire, carbuncle, and emerald—all in beautiful settings of finest gold. They were given to you on the day you were created. I appointed you to be the anointed GUARDIAN CHERUB. You had access to the holy mountain of God. You walked among the stones of fire.**

TYPES OF SIN

> You were perfect in all you did from the day you were created until that time when wrong was found in you. Your great wealth filled you with internal turmoil and you sinned. Therefore, I cast you out of the mountain of God like a common sinner. I destroyed you, O overshadowing cherub, from the midst of the stones of fire. Your heart was filled with pride because of all your beauty; you corrupted your wisdom for the sake of your splendor.
>
> Therefore, I have cast you down to the ground and exposed you helpless before the curious gaze of kings. You defiled your holiness with lust for gain; therefore, I brought forth fire from your own actions and let it burn you to ashes upon the earth in the sight of all those watching you. All who know you are appalled at your fate; you are an example of horror, you are destroyed forever (verses 12-19).

Notice! This anointed "guardian Cherub"—obviously Lucifer, the devil—according to several translations of the Bible in modern English—will be consumed with fire from his own actions which will burn him to ashes upon the earth in the sight of all the nations. He will be an example of horror—the ultimate example of the fate of the wicked. All who have known him will be appalled at his final fate. God says he will be "DESTROYED FOREVER." Moffatt translates this verse that God will make him "set fire to himself" with flames that will "CONSUME" him.

Now let's notice the authorized *King James Version*. In (Ezekiel 28), speaking of the king of Tyre, which blends into the *antitype* of satan the devil, God says:

> Thou hast defiled thy sanctuaries by the multitude of thine iniquities, by the iniquity of thy traffick; therefore, will I bring forth a fire [remember the "lake of fire"] from the midst of thee, it shall DEVOUR THEE, and I will

bring thee to ashes upon the earth in the sight of all them that behold thee (Ezek. 28:18).

How could God do this if Satan is a spirit being and therefore "cannot die"? Perhaps we have overlooked the simple explanation.

Could God not change Satan's spirit into flesh or physical matter, and then destroy him? Even Christ, very God, the Logos, "became flesh" and subsequently died on the stake. God died! If God Himself could die, surely, he could likewise terminate the devil.

Does this verse only refer to the king of Tyre, or could it also be referring to Satan's fate in the lake of fire? Only time will tell!

Summary of Dualities

Through the understanding of the dualities or *types* in God's Word, is His beautiful plan of salvation revealed! By these basic types, God's general outline for His awesome plan is understood.

That is, there is a great God family in heaven, and an insidious *adversary* called the devil and Satan, who is trying to prevent human beings from becoming members of that eternal ruling family!

There is also a Church that God works through to help those He is calling into that family. The instrument of the Church provides potential members of the God family with spiritual knowledge! Upon repentance, God will send these devoted Saints His Holy Spirit which enables them to keep His royal Law of Love!

Satan also has a church and ministers that he works through to DECEIVE, subvert and confuse individuals as to their transcendental purpose.

There are really only two ways of life an individual may choose to live within the parameters of planet earth—the way of God or the way of Satan! Those who refuse to live God's way will be destroyed, while the righteous will shine forth as the sun in glory in the family of God forever! Christ and His spotless Bride will stand TRIUMPHANT over the serpent who was permitted to bruise the heel of the woman's seed at first.

Throughout the remainder of this series, God will restate, emphasize and magnify His MASTER PLAN through the

TYPES OF SIN

various agencies of Names, Numbers, Offerings, Parables, Holy days; etc. Each agency will be a stepping stone through progressive revelation until the sum total of God's magnificent plan is revealed!

Chapter Eleven

GOD'S GOVERN-MENTAL PLAN OF NUMBERS

Have you ever felt that the world's problems are so prodigious that there's absolutely nothing you can do about them?

You sort of feel so small—like a flea on a dog's tail which is part of the dog, who is part of the house, which is part of the neighborhood, which is part of the city, which is part of the state, which is part of the nation, which is part of the earth, which is part of the galaxy, which is part of the universe, which is part of...?

You'd like to solve the worlds problems of crime, unemployment, famine, racial prejudice, water and air pollution, disease, war, drugs, over-population, inflation, government corruption; etc. But you begin to realize you are powerless, and simply throw your arms up in frustration, and say to yourself, "what's the use, nobody seems to care anyway." Maybe you've considered demonstrating against these evils by marching"?

Perhaps you have thought of joining a small militaristic radical organization that is planning to overthrow the government? Then you could surely bring about your ideas and really help the poor and those being treated unjustly by government—right!

Wrong! Soon you realize that many have already tried that route and it didn't get them anywhere.

This book deals with the world and the problems in it—and HOW those problems WILL be solved! Christians can have an active part in a world ruling government that WILL solve these problems. Only it won't come about by man, rather in spite of him!

The government of God is soon coming to planet earth to replace Satan's diabolical *counterfeit* religious and governmental system! Followers of Christ can have a vital role, and play an ACTIVE part in it!

Restoring The Government Of God

Precisely how is God's government going to function? What kind of government is it going to be—Communistic, Democratic, Theocratic or Dictatorship?

The answer to these bewildering questions can only be understood by certain *numerical values*. Numbers are very significant in the understanding of the government of God. But in order to understand the relationship of specific numbers mentioned in the Bible, we must first understand God's *governmental* structure.

Back now to a brief synopsis of God's first government on earth. Apparently, Lucifer, and one third of the angels were placed upon planet earth to further God's plan for man.

Realizing also that man, like the angels, would ultimately rebel against His authority—God designed a full-proof system through Jesus Christ to bring man salvation. When man followed in the footsteps of those sinning angels, God said in effect:

> **Because man has rejected my government I will cut off all mankind, except for a select few till my Son [the second Adam] should come and supplant Satan. Then I will RESTORE my government over the earth and universe through Him and man!**

Let me clarify a point of confusion here. Even though God realized the angels had the potential to sin—man was not an after-thought!

It was always God's intention to create man—His highest creation. The angels were created to help God carry out His government throughout the universe through man! In essence, they were created to be man's servants! (Heb. 1:14).

God Starts His "Fail-Safe" Government

Immediately, God started the machinery in motion for His master plan. Prior to the flood, only Enoch is recorded as "walking with God." Noah and his family were spared the destruction of the flood so God could pave the way to REDEEM mankind and again restore His government on earth. The rest of humanity perished in the flood, only to be resurrected at a later time.

Several generations after the flood, God the Father called Abraham to carry out His purpose. It was to Abraham that God gave the promise of Salvation through his seed—which finally culminated in Jesus Christ, the savior of the world!

Moses was chosen of God four hundred and thirty years later—to bring Abraham's descendants out of the bondage to the Egyptians and into the promised land. God would use these physical Israelites to begin *restoring* His Government on earth. The Eternal made a covenant with these Israelites to be His model nation on earth—and to show what the government of God would be like.

God, in the personage of Jesus Christ, dwelt among these Israelites in a "cloud" and guided and directed them. He fought their battles and provided food for them. But eventually the Israelites rebelled against the Father's Spokesman and desired a human king over them that they could see—like the heathen nations about them. The Eternal then appointed Saul to reign over them, who eventually was replaced by David because of REBELLION against the government of God!

The history of Israel's many kings is recorded, as well as their eventual captivity because of refusal to be God's model nation. God's Holy Spirit was simply not given to the nation of Israel as a whole, but rather only to the prophets. It was only when Jesus Christ came to *restore* God's government that the Holy Spirit could be given in general (Jn. 7:37-39).

Jesus was Born to Rule

Jesus was born to be a king (Jn. 18:37) and to take over the throne of David in Israel and thereby RESTORE the government of God on earth (Lk. 1:31-33).

Jesus was born to be the Savior of the world and to share the government of God with Christians.

Adam had failed to supplant the former archangel Lucifer on God's throne on the earth—but Jesus [the second Adam] came to replace Lucifer, fulfilling God's master plan as outlined from the very beginning.

The prophetic message Jesus brought [the Gospel] was that the Kingdom of God was now going to be imminently established on the earth. Now the government of God would be *restored* and administered by God's chosen servants.

A Pyramid Government

When God instructed His servant Moses to institute His model government upon the earth, He inspired Moses to set up a PYRAMID form of government through his father-in-law. We read of this in the eighteenth chapter of Exodus:

> **(Vs. 13) And it came to pass on the morrow, that Moses sat to judge the people: and the people stood by Moses from the morning unto the evening. (Vs. 17) And Moses' father-in-law said unto him, the thing that thou doest is not good. Thou wilt surely wear away, both thou, and this people that is with thee: for thou art not able to perform it thyself alone.**

Moses' father-in-law perceived Moses was taking on too much responsibility himself, and therefore the people were not benefiting. Moses' father-in-law suggested he appoint able men over smaller matters, and to bring the more urgent and important matters to him personally. Notice:

> **So, Moses hearkened to the voice of his father-in-law, and did all that he had said. And Moses chose able men out of all Israel, and made**

> them heads over the people, rulers of *hundreds,* rulers of *fifties,* and rulers of *tens.* And they judged the people at all seasons: the hard causes they brought unto Moses, but every small matter they judged themselves. (Ex. 18:24-26).

This structure of human government that Moses was inspired to institute, was PYRAMIDAL with Moses at the top, then rulers of l0's, 50's, l00's and l000's.

Through this system, God as it's divine invisible head spoke with Moses via a cloud and Israel was guided (Ex. 24:15-18). God instructed Moses to build a Tabernacle in the 25th chapter of Exodus through which the Eternal led the entire congregation:

> Then a cloud covered the tent of the congregation and the glory of the Lord filled the tabernacle. And Moses was not able to enter into the tent of the congregation, because the cloud abode thereon, and the glory [Heb. *shekinah*] of the Lord filled the tabernacle. And when the cloud was taken up from over the tabernacle, the children of Israel went onward in all their journeys: But if the cloud were not taken up, then they journeyed not till the day that it was taken up... (vss. 34-37).

After the death of Moses—Joshua, the son of Nun was chosen by God to be the *mediator* between God and His chosen people (Joshua 1:1). When Joshua died, the Eternal raised up judges to lead Israel (Judges 2:8,16). The most righteous judge was Samuel (1 Sam. 4:1).

Now when Samuel was old and ready to die, he was going to appoint his sons to be judges over Israel (1 Sam. 8:1). But this displeased the congregation of Israel and, instead, they wanted a physical king to rule over them. Let's read this account:

> But the thing displeased Samuel, when they said, give us a king to judge us. And Samuel prayed unto the Lord. And the Lord said unto Samuel, Hearken unto the voice of the people

in all that they say unto thee, for they have not rejected thee, but *they have rejected me,* that I should not reign over them (1 Sam. 8:6-7).

Here, God thunders through His servant Moses: "**...they have rejected me...**" Israel rejected the GOVERNMENT OF GOD! Israel desired to look upon a physical king like all the heathen nations around them. This was the end of God's ordained government on earth—and the beginning of man's self imposed rule!

Based upon this sad commentary—it was *never* God's intention to have the form of government we have today! This has been mankind's own choosing!

The Eternal is now preparing, through Christians, individuals who will RESTORE His government to the earth, However, in this interim, they have certain obligations to meet as they wait patiently for Christ's return.

Christianity and Politics

Because Christians are a part of God's government—exactly what is a Christian's responsibility to the governments of this world? Should he participate in its politics and elections? Let us look into the pages of our Bible for the answer!

Dan. 2:20-21	The first point to realize is that God Himself sets up the basest of men in government and removes them at His will. No amount of ballot casting can sway God's mind if He desires a particular individual in office! Several Presidents have in fact been elected into office who did not get the popular vote. See also (Dan. 4:17-25).
Acts 17:26	God sets up the boundaries of nations—not men!
Jn. 19:10-11	All government power comes from God almighty as Jesus told Pilate.

GOD'S PLAN OF NUMBERS

11 Cor. 4:4	Satan is the god of this world and God allows him to have his people in office until he is dethroned by Jesus Christ.
Matt. 4:8	Satan offered his government to Jesus Christ.
Lk. 4:4	
Jn. 18:35	Jesus said His Kingdom was not of this world.
Jn. 17:9-16	Christians are not of this world [age or society] even as Christ was not!
11 Cor. 6:17	Paul admonished Christians: "Wherefore come out from among them [the world's ways] and be ye separate..."
Rom. 12:2	"And be not conformed to this world..."
1 Jn. 2:15	"Love not the world, neither the things in the world. If any man love the world, the love of the Father is not in him."
Gal. 1:4	Christ gave himself to deliver us from this present evil world.
1 Pet. 1:4	A Christian's citizenship is now reserved in heaven.
Eph. 2:19	Christians are merely ambassadors for Christ representing God's Kingdom to this world. See also (Phil. 3:20; 11 Cor. 5:20).

A Christian's Responsibility

Rom. 13:1-7	"Let every soul be subject unto the higher powers. For there is no power but of God: The powers that be are ordained of God, whosoever therefore resisteth the power, resisteth the ordinance of God: and they that resist shall receive for themselves damnation. For rulers are not a terror to

THE FOOLISHNESS GOD

good works, but of the evil. (vs. 7) Render therefore to all their dues: tribute to whom tribute is due: custom to custom ..."

Matt. 22:21   Jesus said: "...Render therefore unto Caesar the things which are Caesars, and unto God the things that are Gods."

1 Pet. 2:13-14   "Submit yourselves to every ordinance of man for the Lord's sake: whether it be to the King as supreme, or unto governors, as unto them that are sent by him for the punishment of evildoers, as for the praise of them that do well."

Tit. 3:1   "Put them in mind to be subject to principalities and powers, to obey magistrates, to be ready to every good work."

Eccl. 10:20   "Curse not the king, no not in thy thought.."

Acts 23:5   "...Thou shalt not speak evil of the ruler of thy people"

1 Tim. 2:1-2   "I exhort therefore, that first of all, supplications, prayers, intercessions, and giving of thanks, be made for all men; For kings, and for all that are in authority; that we [Christians] may lead a quiet and peaceable life in all godliness and honesty."

Matt. 5:34-36   Christians should not swear when under oath, but rather affirm. See also (Jas. 5:12).

Acts 5:29   "...We ought to obey God rather than men." This is in reference to when man's law contradicts God's higher spiritual law.

Why Man's Government Will Fail

GOD'S PLAN OF NUMBERS

The Bible is the study and commentary of two kinds of government, 1) Man's and 2) God's. The Bible shows us clearly that man is incapable of governing himself collectively, and without the intervention and return of Jesus Christ to the earth to set up God's government—would eventually end up in worldwide cosmoside.

Contrariwise, Christians can *now* accept the rule of God in their lives, and govern themselves by the laws of God!

The following points convincingly portray the reasons as to *why* the prodigious problems facing mankind today—will NEVER be solved by man:

1) **Accusations:** Satan is called the *accuser* of the brethren in the Bible (Rev. 12:9). He appeals to government leaders to accuse each other rather than to help each other. This is clearly demonstrated by the vicious "character assassination" attacks made by opposing candidates and parties. Witness the Carter-Reagan, Bush-Dakakis and Trump-Clinton debates (accusations). The apostle Paul says that "debates" are a work of the flesh (Rom. 1:29) which bring forth contention [backbiting, envy, wrath; etc.] (11 Cor. 12:20).

2) **Human Nature:** Human nature is anti-law as Paul writes in Romans 8:7: **"Because the carnal mind is enmity against God: for it is not subject to the law of God, neither indeed can be."** That is precisely why Jesus said of the last days: **"...iniquity [lawlessness] shall abound..." (Matt. 24:12).** Until people want to be governed by God's Holy Spirit, no human government will work!

3) **Competition:** Jesus made this prophetic statement: **"...every kingdom divided against itself is brought to desolation; and every city or house divided against itself shall not stand" (Matt. 12:25).** Because of the competitive "party" strife of human nature —man's government will always be divided against itself! Each party literally "sandbags" the other. God's government of "love" will not seek its own benefit (1 Cor. 13:5).

4) **Lust For Power:** James wrote concerning the nature of war: **"From whence come wars and fightings among you?**

Come they not hence, even of your *lusts* that war in your members" (Jas. 4:1).** Until human nature is conquered by God's Holy Spirit there will always be war and killing. Peter explains that human nature must give heed to divine nature in order that corruption through lust be conquered (11 Pet. 1:4). Mankind was corrupt in the days of Noah (Gen. 6:12) and will be until the return of Jesus Christ (11Tim.3)! The Bible says they are all corrupters! (Jer. 6:28). When was the last time you saw an "honest politician"?

5) **Demonic Influence:** That demons sit at the throttle behind the throttle of human counterparts in world government is made clear by the apostle Paul in Ephesians 6:12: **"For we wrestle not against flesh and blood, but against principalities, against powers, against THE RULERS OF DARKNESS of this world, against spiritual wickedness [wicked spirits] in high places."**

The tenth chapter of Daniel reveals that Satan's demons controlled the kingdom of Persia (vs. 13) and Greece (vs. 20). Certainly, no human being could withstand a spirit being for 21 days, only to have the archangel Michael intervene. Only when the Kingdom of God is set up with Jesus Christ at it's helm—will government really work! Then, there won't be a two party system between Jesus and Satan!

6) **Bribes:** God's Word emphatically forbids the taking of bribes, and for good reason, notice: **"And thou shalt take no gift [bribe]: for the gift blindeth the wise, and perverteth the words of the righteous" (Ex. 23:8).** "He that is greedy of gain troubleth his own house: but he that hateth gifts [bribes] shall live" (Prov. 15:27). **"A wicked man taketh a gift [bribe] out of the bosom to pervert the ways of judgment" (Prov. 17:23). (See also Prov. 29:4).**

Certainly, we are all familiar with the many scandalous cases of bribery in Washington including Abscam and the following scripture is quite applicable: **"Thy princes [leaders] are rebellious, and companions of thieves: every one loveth gifts [bribes] and followeth after rewards..." (Isa. 1:23).** Only when God pours out His Holy Spirit upon all flesh and human nature is completely reoriented, will bribery cease and government really work!

7) **Unrighteous Judgment:** The apostle Paul spells out loud and clear the evil minds rebellious individuals have in the first chapter of Romans: (Vs. 25): **"Who changed the truth of God into a lie..." (Vs. 26): "For this cause God gave them up unto vile affections..." (Vs. 28): "And even as they did not like to retain God in their knowledge, God gave them over to a reprobate mind, to do those things which are convenient; being filled with ALL UNRIGHTEOUSNESS..."**

God gives sinful rebels a reprobate mind (margin—a mind void of proper judgment). Look at some of the stupid and perverted judgments that have been made in our courts today.

Men have been let go who have raped women because their rights were supposedly violated when the arresting officer failed to read their rights in proper sequence. There are thousands of such heinous judgments in our land today, and will only be changed with a change of heart!

8) **Born Liars:** King David wrote these pungent words about today's society in Psalm 58:3: **"The wicked are estranged from the womb: they go astray as soon as they be born, *speaking lies*." "Thou lovest evil more than good; and *lying* rather than to speak righteousness" (Ps.52:3).** Because of distrust in government, a system of checks and balances had to be devised. This has cost the people billions of dollars! Each year more groups and departments are created to check each other. Democracy breeds bureaucracy and the cost of this madness has grown into the billions!

Man's heart is truly **"deceitful above all things" (Jer. 17:9),** and until changed by God's Holy Spirit will always speak lies and never achieve an honest government for the people!

9) **Disloyalty:** The foundation of man's government is built around disloyalty through political analysis of reporters. Bad news is good news to them—while the Bible says, **"...love covers sins" (Prov. 19:11).** Only when man receives a new heart to forgive and understand, will government be capable of working!

His Number is 666

There has been a great deal of speculation as to the meaning of the number 666. The movie "The Omen" showed the number 666 inscribed on the head of a demon possessed individual.

Some have thought that eventually all of mankind would have a separate computer number and the one whose number was 666 would be the "False Prophet." Even the crown of the Pope is said to contain letters which numerically add up to 666 in Latin.

If the letters of a man, organization or government are to add up to the numerical value of 666, which language are we to use?

One very original concept is to use the English language, correlating the alphabet to intervals of 6, since 6 is the number designated to represent man or the government of man in the Bible. This way, A becomes 6, B becomes 12, C becomes 18; etc. And interestingly enough, Kissinger adds up to 666.

The Apostle John told us to COUNT the number and he wrote in the GREEK language, so why would anyone think of counting in the English language? Furthermore, the Old Testament was written in the Hebrew language and the New Testament in the Greek. If we are to count in any particular language, surely it would be one of these.

The Hebrew, Greek and Roman languages all use letters to substitute for numbers. Roman numerals equal I=1, V=5, X=10; etc. and the Greek A=1, E=5, I=10; etc.

We have already identified the Roman Empire to be most likely the "Beast". The Roman Empire was founded and named after ROMULUS, its first king. John said to count the number of a MAN that represents the ROMAN EMPIRE and all it's inhabitants. Romulus is written LATEINOS in the Greek language meaning "Latin man" or "Latium," after the city the Romans adopted as their heritage.

Strange as it may seem [or is it DESIGN], Romulus adds up to 666 in BOTH Hebrew and Greek languages.

It is also very ironic, that there has NEVER been two words that have ever been translated into two languages whose numerical value adds up to 666.

Clearly, the number 666 IDENTIFIES the ROMAN EMPIRE!

**The Crucifixion and
the 318 Circumcised of Abraham**

That the *crucifixion* was revealed by God through the circumcision of the three hundred and eighteen men of Abraham's house is most remarkable!

God made a covenant with Abraham when he was one hundred years old (Gen. 17:1-2). Abraham was to circumcise his household as a condition of this covenant as told in verse 10:

> **This is my covenant which ye shall keep, between me and you and thy seed after thee; Every man child among you shall be circumcised.**

Abraham was faithful in what God had commanded as recorded in verse 23:2:

> **And Abraham took Ishmael his son, and all that were born in his house, and all that were bought with his money, every male among men of Abraham's house; and circumcised the flesh of their foreskin in the selfsame day, as God had said unto him.**

How many males were in Abraham's household is revealed in Genesis 14:14:

> **And when Abraham heard that his brother was taken captive, he armed his trained servants, born in his own house, *three hundred and eighteen*...**

It follows that Abraham circumcised all three hundred and eighteen males of his household as God commanded. Now, what is the significance of the number 318? The writer of the book of *Barnabas* writes thusly:

> **Wherefore he has circumcised our ears that we should hear his word, and believe. But as for that circumcision in which the Jews trust, it is abolished. For the circumcision of which God spake, was not of the flesh; But they have**

transgressed his commands, because the evil one hath deceived them. For thus God bespeaks them; 'Thus saith the Lord your God [Here I find the new law] Sow not among thorns; but circumcise yourselves to the Lord your God.'

And what doth he mean by this saying? Hearken unto your Lord. And again he saith, 'Circumcise the hardness of your heart, and harden not your neck.' And again, 'Behold, saith the Lord, all the nations are uncircumcised, (they have not lost their foreskin): but this people is uncircumcised in heart.' But you will say the Jews were circumcised for a sign. And so are all the Syrians and Arabians, and all the idolatrous priests: but are they therefore of the covenant of Israel? And even the Egyptians themselves are circumcised. Understand therefore, children, these things more fully, that Abraham, who was the first that brought in circumcision, looking forward in the spirit to Jesus, circumcised, having received the mystery of three letters. For the Scripture says that *Abraham circumcised three hundred and eighteen men of his house.* But what therefore was the mystery that was made known unto him?

Mark, first the eighteen, and next the three hundred. For the numeral letters of ten and eight are I H. And these denote Jesus.
And because the cross was that by which we were to find grace: Therefore, he adds, three hundred; the note of which is T (the figure of his cross). Wherefore by two letters he signified Jesus, and by the third his cross. He who has put the engrafted gift of his doctrine within us, knows that I never taught to any one

GOD'S PLAN OF NUMBERS

a more certain truth; but I trust that ye are worthy of it.

"As the Hebrew alphabet has no numbers they are represented by full words or by the individual letters themselves standing for numbers; letters 1-9 represent the numerals, letters 10-18 the tens, and letters 19-22 cover the first four hundreds. It has gone unnoticed that Abraham's chief servant, Eliezer, and described as his sole heir in Genesis 15:2, has a Hebrew name that adds up to 318 = 200 ר+ 7 ז+ 70 א+ 10 י+ 30 ל+ 1 ע.

"In the early church, in the late first and second centuries, some writers made use of 318 (made up of 300+10+8, rather than as in Eliezer's name) to signify Jesus on the cross. In Greek, which can also use the numerical=alphabetical system as it too is without numerals, *Tau*=300 and is equivalent to the Hebrew letter, *Tau*, both of which represent a cross in the shape of a capital 'T', which is closer to the shape of a crucifixion cross than a modern crucifix. The 18 comes from *Eta* plus *Iota*, which stood in the Greek alphabet order where ח *cheth* and י *yodh* stand in the Hebrew, thus they stood for 8 and 10 respectively, making the 18. Now, *IH*, in Greek is *Iota-Eta*, the first two letters of Jesus' name ΙΣΟΥΣ, *iêsous*, just as God's name, *YHVH*, could be represented by its shorter version *YH* (*Yah*). So the Epistle of Barnabas, written between 70-135 A.D. says:

"For [the Scripture] saith, 'And Abraham circumcised ten, and eight, and three hundred men of his household.' What, then, was the knowledge given to him in this? Learn the eighteen first, and then the Writing later in the 3rd century, Clement of Alexandria in his *Stromata*, 'Miscellanies', on 'The Mystical Meanings In The Proportions Of Numbers, Geometrical Ratios, And Music' says:

"As then in astronomy we have Abraham as an instance, so also in arithmetic we have the same Abraham. For, hearing that Lot was taken captive, and having numbered his own servants, born in his house, 318, he defeats a very great number of the enemy. They say, then, that the character representing 300 is, as to shape, the type of the Lord's sign, and that the *Iota* and the *Eta* indicate the Savior's name; that it was indicated, accordingly, that Abraham's domestics were in salvation, who having fled to the Sign and the Name became lords of the captives, and of the very many unbelieving nations that followed them. (Clement, *Stromata*, Book 6, Chapter 11)

"So Christian numerological interpretation is just as fanciful as some Jewish numerical word plays. Certainly, we can give full marks for ingenuity and there is no harm done in the meaning given. Nonetheless, it is more probably in a book like Genesis of history not prophecy that historical accuracy rather than symbolism is intended and what is being portrayed is Abraham's wealth and status in being able to raise 318 fighting men." (StudlyLight.org).

Chapter Twelve

GOD'S PLAN REVEALED BY NAMES

Many may gloss over the enumerable uninteresting names of people mentioned in the Bible—yet the keen observer will recognize these names to be *highly significant* in the understanding of God's MASTER PLAN.

The names that God gave certain men, described *specific nations* that would eventually come out of their seed to fulfill future prophecies.

The ancient Israelites named their children after natural or personal qualities desired, in following the example of God Almighty. Oftentimes people were named after their particular occupation such as tent maker or horse trader.

Sometimes names were changed by God as in the case of Abram, Saul and Jacob once they had fulfilled a certain personal quality.

Solomon, the wisest man that ever lived once wrote: **"A good name is rather to be chosen than great riches" (Prov. 22:1).** And, **"A good name is better than precious ointment" (Eccl. 7:1).**

Let us now understand some of the more interesting Biblical names and their "complex meanings" to better understand God's fantastic earthly play. For a complete listing of all of the men's names in the Bible; the reader is encouraged to read *ALL the Men of the Bible*, by Herbert Lockyer, published by Zondervan.

Adam—"Red Mud" Or Taken Out of The Red Earth

Adam, the "first man", was God's masterpiece in human perfection as He molded him out of the *red earth*. Physically, he was healthy and masculine. Mentally, he was perfect in that he had "free choice" or volition. Adam was as perfect a human specimen, as Christ, the second Adam, was a perfect spiritual creation (l Cor. 15:45). Adam is a *type* of Christ. (See Types of Christ).

Eve—Life Giver

Truly Eve was a *life giver* in that she gave life to all the races through birth. Eve is a *type* of the Church—"the Mother of us all" being the husband of Adam, even as Christ, the second Adam, is the husband of the Church. (See Types of the Church).

Cain— Acquisition, Fabrication or Possessed

Cain was the firstborn son of Adam and Eve and represented the wicked nature that man was to *acquire* through Satan's influence as he slew his brother Abel. Truly he was *fabricated* in Satan's image (1 John 3:12) and *possessed* with a satanic nature. (See Types of Satan).

Abel—Meadow, Vanity or Vapor

Abel, the second son of Adam and Eve was slain by his brother Cain denoting the abruptness of his life as a *vapor*. His death is associated with that of Jesus Christ in that both had their blood shed (Heb. 12:24). (See Types of Christ).

Seth—Compensation, Appointed or Substituted

Seth was the third son of Adam and Eve and represents Abel's *substitute,* [the 2nd Abel] Notice: **"And Adam knew his wife** again; and she bore a son, and called his name Seth: For God she said, hath appointed me another seed instead of Abel, whom Cain slew" (Gen. 4:25).**

Enos—Man in His Frailty

The son of Seth. Men began to call upon the name of the Lord after his birth (Gen. 4:26). Enos lived 905 years (Gen. 5:19).

Enoch—Dedicated, Teacher, Initiated

Enoch was the firstborn son of Cain and began to *walk with God* when his son Methuselah was born (Gen. 5:24). Enoch represents the life of a repentant sinner—born a child of bad seed, yet overcoming and becoming a child of grace. Enoch represents a *type* of the Church. (See The Days of Noah, Vol. 4). His life was *dedicated* to God and he was a teacher of prophecy (Jude 14).

Methuselah—It Shall be Sent

Methuselah is the son of Enoch and grandfather of Noah. He lived 969 years, the longest period of time recorded in the Bible. His name implies *"It shall be sent"*—the flood, in which his death was the sign. See (The Days of Noah, vol. 4). Methuselah, like his father Enoch, is also a *type* of the Church.

Noah—Rest

Noah lived when the earth was universally corrupt and the human race did every imagination of *wickedness* of his heart (Gen. 6:5). But despite all this corruptness of mankind, Noah remained *faithful* to God and was a just man (Gen. 6:9; Heb. 11:7; 11 Pet. 2:5).

When the flood came, Noah and his family were saved as the ark *rested* upon Mount Ararat. The earth was finally at *rest* from all of man's rebelliousness as well.

Noah and his family represent those who will have to go through the Great Tribulation of which the flood is a *type*. Like Noah, many will be saved; but only after the wicked will once again perish. Then will God's *rest* of His glorious millennial reign begin with Jesus Christ ruling over the nations. (See The Days of Noah vol. 4).

Abraham—The Father of a Multitude

Abraham's original name was Abram, meaning "father or height" and was changed to Abraham by God after he proved to be faithful to Him. God changed Abraham's name after He made a covenant with him that a *multitude of nations would spring from his seed* (Gen. 17:5). Abraham represents the new spiritual seed of faith and is therefore called "the father of the faithful" (Gen. 4:16). He is a *type* of God the Father offering up his only son Isaac (Heb. 11,17). (See Types of Christ).

Nimrod—Mighty Hunter, Strong He that Rules

Nimrod was a "mighty hunter" before the Lord in that he was a tyrant (Gen. 10:9). He defied God by building the tower of Babel. Other names of Nimrod are:

Pluto to the Greeks.
Baal to the Phoenicians meaning "my lord."
Osirus to the Egyptians.
Merodach or Marduk to the Babylonians.
Tammuz to the Semites.
Nimrod of the Bible or Baal (Judges 2:13).
Ninus king of the Assyrians.
Saturn to the Romans meaning "hiding one."
Othothis the 2nd king of Egypt or Osirus husband and son of Isis (Semiramis).

Semiramis—Goddess of Love and War

Her name is spelled Ashtoreth, Astarte, Ishtar [in Babylonia]; etc. Other names of Semiramis are:

Astarte to the Babylonians or Aphodite.
Hept to the Egyptians or "the veiled one".
Isis to the Egyptians or the mother of Osirus.
Isis, Hept, Ishtor, Semiramis to the Assyrians.

Ashtoreth of the Bible and Israel.
Venus to the Romans.
Ceres to the Greeks.
Diana to the Ephesians.
Shengmoo to the Chinese.
Hertha to the Germans.
Disa to the Scandanavians.
Virgo to the Druids.
Indrani or Isi in India.
Cybele in Asia.
Nana to the Semerians.
Baalti in deified form to the Latins meaning "mea Domina."
Madonna to the Italians.
Mylitta meaning "the mediatrix" or mediator between heaven and earth. She was "Queen of heaven" (Jer. 7:18-20; 44:17). She was prayed to and became a substitute in Mary (see *Outline of History*, by H.G. Wells, pg. 544).

Tammuz

The false god Tammuz is mentioned in the book of Ezekiel (Ezek. 8:14). Ezekiel describes a vision he had, saying the Lord "brought me to the entrance of the north gate of the house of the LORD, and I saw women sitting there, mourning the god Tammuz." God calls the idolatrous practice of weeping for Tammuz a "detestable" thing, made even worse in that it was happening at the temple in Jerusalem.

Gilgamesh references Tammuz in Tablet VI of the *Epic of Gilgamesh* as one of Ishtar's past lovers, who was turned into an *allalu* bird with a broken wing. Dumuzid was associated with fertility and vegetation and the hot, dry summers of Mesopotamia were believed to be caused by Dumuzid's yearly death. During the month in midsummer bearing his name, people all across Mesopotamia would engage in public, ritual mourning for him.

During the late twentieth century, scholars widely thought that, during the Sumerian Akitu festival, kings may have established their legitimacy by taking on the role of Dumuzid and engaging in ritualized sexual intercourse with the high priestess of Inanna as part of a sacred marriage ceremony. This notion is now generally rejected by scholars as a misinterpretation of Sumerian literary texts. The cult of Dumuzid was later spread to the Levant and to Greece, where he became known under the West Semitic name Adonis.

The cult of Ishtar and Tammuz continued to thrive until the eleventh century AD and survived in parts of Mesopotamia as late as the eighteenth century (article Dumuzid, *Wikepedia*).

Other names of Tammuz are:

Kenkenes
Kenken
Othothis
Horus to the Egyptians
Tammuz in Mesopotamia
Gilgamesh to the Babylonians
Saturn or Jupiter or Fortuna in Rome
Bacchus or "god of wine" in Rome
Hercules
Myrthia
Chrishna
Iswara in India
Deoius in Asia

Isaac—He Laugheth, or Laughing One

The firstborn of Abraham and Sarah. Born by *promise* of God when Abraham was one hundred years old and Sarah about ninety (Gen. 17:19, 21; 21:3-12; 22:2-9). This event did indeed make Sarah and Abraham *laugh* (Gen. 21:6). Isaac is a *type* of Christ in that he consented to become a sacrifice for God (Gen. 22:12; 26:5; Heb. 11:17). His wife Rebekah is a *type* of the Church. (See Isaac and Rebekah under Types of Christ and the Church).

Ishmael—God Heareth

Ishmael was Abraham's son by his Egyptian handmaid Hagar. It was not God's will that Ishmael be the inheritor of the promises to Isaac, nontheless *God did hear* the cry of his mother and said: **"I will make him a great nation" (Gen. 21:18).** The great nation to eventually come out of Ishmael according to most Bible scholars is the modern-day Arab nations. That is why there is so much contention over Israel, the promised land. Both Jew [descendants from Isaac's seed] and Arab contend Israel is rightfully their land based on the birthright promise of their father Abraham. In Isaac and Ishmael are an allegory of the two covenants as recorded in (Gal.4:22-30) by the apostle Paul. Christians, as Isaac, are the children of promise; not born after the flesh [fleshly desires] as was Ishmael.

Moses—Drawn Forth, Taken out of The Water

Certainly, everyone is familiar with how Moses was *drawn out of the water* by the Pharaoh's daughter when the Pharaoh of Egypt resolved to kill every male baby of the Israelites. Moses was raised by Pharaoh's daughter and schooled in royalty. Unbeknown to Moses, God had allowed all of this grooming so Moses could lead his people out of Egyptian bondage, and be God's historian, legislator and leader. (See Types of Christ).

Joshua—Deliver

Moses called Joshua Oshea (Num. 13:16). His name went from deliver to delivered or "god saved." He became delivered or selected by God somewhere in time as God was judging him. (See Types of Christ).

Aaron—Mountain of Strength or Enlightened. "Very High"

Aaron was the elder brother of Moses and chosen to be his *mountain of strength* in speaking. It seems Moses may have had a speech impediment as he was slow in tongue (Ex. 3:10; 4:11,12) and therefore God used Aaron to be the spokesman for Moses.

Aaron was the second son of Levi; the third son of Jacob. Aaron became the first high priest of Israel and his sons carried out the priestly functions as described in the book of Leviticus. In Aaron we have a *type* of Christ—our High Priest and Spokesman for God, and His sons—the Church carrying out priestly functions of the ministry.

Jacob—Supplanter

Jacob was the second son of Isaac and Rebekah and twin brother to Esau. It was through Jacob's deceitful nature that he *supplanted* the birthright promise from his brother Esau. Jacob deceived his blind father Isaac by covering his body with hairy kid skins to appear as Esau.

Israel—Ruling or Striving with God, Champion of God, Prevailer, Overcomer

God "wrestled" with Jacob one night and brought him to a point of total submission (Gen. 32:25; Hos. 12:4). By thus yielding his life to God's purpose; Jacob achieved victory and God changed his name to Israel, which means **"He strives with God [and prevails]" (Gen. 32:28; 35:10).**

It was through Jacob's or Israel's 12 sons [known as the children of Israel] that God was to fulfill His redemptive purpose for mankind. God was also going to fulfill His covenant with Jacob's grandfather Abraham; that his seed would be the inheritors of physical blessings of land mass, including Palestine.

Esau—Hairy

Esau was Jacob's twin brother and was very *hairy* from birth (Gen. 25:25). Being the firstborn of Isaac [though only minutes before Jacob] he was entitled to the birthright promise. But for a bowl of pottage, Esau sold his birthright promise to his younger brother Jacob.

This story relates a spiritual lesson to Christians as we read in Hebrews 12:16-17: **"Lest there be any fornicator, or profane person, as Esau, who for one morsel of meat sold his birthright. For ye know how that afterward, when he would have inherited the blessing, he was rejected: for he found no place of repentance, though he sought it carefully with tears."**

Esau was a cunning hunter and man of the field (Gen. 25:27), which implies he was "worldly" spiritually. The lesson for Christians to learn from Esau's example, is that we can lose our "spiritual birthright" [God's Kingdom] if we refuse to repent with sincerity. Tears are not enough—action speaks louder than words or tears! Esau became the progenitor of the modern nation of Turkey as Esau is Edom (Gen 36:1).

Judah—Praise of The Lord

Judah was Jacob and Leah's fourth son. The nickname of the tribal family of Judah became known as "Jews" (Gen. 29:35; Num. 26:19-21; 1 Chron. 2:3-6). When Judah was conceived, his mother said: **"...now will I *praise the Lord*: therefore, she called his name Judah; and left bearing" (Gen. 29:35).** The *lion* became the national *symbol* of this tribe (Num. 2:3-4) and our Lord sprang out of Judah.

Jesus—Jehovah is Salvation

To Abraham and his seed were the *Birthright* and *Sceptre* promises made. The Birthright promise was a promise of physical prosperity through *race* for Abraham's descendants. The Sceptre promise was that of *grace* coming through Abraham's *seed* culminating in the Messiah. Matthew traces the genealogy of Jesus Christ the Savior of the world to the son of David being a son of Abraham (Matt. 1:1).

The promise that the Messiah would be born of the "seed of a woman" (Gen. 3:15) and without sin (Heb. 4:15) fully qualified Jesus to be the Savior of the world.

Jesus called Himself "The Son of Man" as a title in refering to one of His important attributes. He had divested Himself of His glory to be born a human, suffer and be sacrificed for the sins of humanity. Using the title "Son of Man" emphasized the vital role played by His humanness. There are approximately 365 names and titles given to the personage of Jesus Christ which describe His power and *authority* such as:

CHRIST_____	"The anointed one."
LORD_____	"His sovereign majesty."
SHILOH_____	"One who pacifies" in reference to peacemaker.
EMMANUEL_____	"God with us."
WONDERFUL_____	"Wonderful in all His works."
COUNSELOR_____	"Perfect wisdom and knowledge."

PRINCE OF PEACE	"His kingdom of peace and righteousness."
THE WORD	"The Spokesman of God."
MELCHISEDEC	"King of RIGHTEOUSNESS" or JUSTICE.
"SON OF MAN"	Jesus, in His human form, epitomizing His humanness.

Lucifer—Light Bringer or Shinning One

Lucifer was a super-archangel—God's epitome of angelic perfection of beauty and wisdom till iniquity [sin] was found in him (Ezek. 28:13-17). He was God's *bringer of truth* [light] until he decided to usurp God's throne, as indicated from his Hebrew name *hellel* ("brightness" or "morning star of the dawn"). After his rebellion, God changed his name to Satan, meaning *adversary* or *enemy* (Rev. 12:9).

Baal—Possessor or Controller, Lord

The pagan deity sun-god. Nimrod claimed to be the priest of Baal and spread this idolatrous heathen practice.

Balaam—Consumer of The People

Balaam means "Consumer or devourer of the people." He had the power to *curse* or to *bless* the people. The association between "Balaam" and the "Nicolaitanes" is given in (Revelation 2:13-15) in Jesus' rebuke of the Pergamos era. Here we find that the false doctrines of Balaam were creeping into the true Church!

Nicolaitane means "conqueror of the people," and both names connote the bringing of people to sin—that would bring about the wrath of God! Nimrod was also a "conqueror of the people." (See Simon Magus under Types of Satan).

Magus—Magician

Simon Magus was a sorcerer magician who bewitched the people of Samaria and was the new priest of Baal worship during the time of Christ (Acts 8:9).

Iscariot—Man of Murder

The disciple who betrayed our Lord with a kiss and then proceeded to hang himself in an act of repentance. He became possessed by Satan himself and was called "the son of perdition," the same title given to the end-time "man of sin". (See Types of Christ and Satan).

Shem—Renown or Name

Firstborn of Noah's three sons who escaped the flood (Gen. 5:32). Shem's name infers "a distinguished person." It was through Shem's seed that our Lord would come. Shem was a *forerunner* of Christ whose greater "name of renown" will make every knee bow (Lk. 3:36). Noah said, in offering praise to God: "Blessed be the Lord of Shem" (Gen. 9:26). The Caucasian races are said to have come from the seed of Shem.

Ham—Black, Colored, Dark, Hot, Swarthy

Ham was the youngest son of Noah and father of Cush whose son was the infamous Nimrod. He is said to be the father of races such as the Egyptian, African, Babylonian, Philistine and Canaanite. A curse was placed upon him by his father when he committed a perverted act when Noah got drunk with wine (Gen. 9:24-26). The curse was that the nations to come out of his seed would be servants to his brother Shem.

Japheth—Let Him Enlarge

The second son of Noah is said to be the father of the yellow races who spread over the north and west regions of the earth (Gen. 9:27). The Medians, Greeks, Romans, and Gauls of old and the Russians, Indians, Chinese, Japanese of the present. The modern nations are identified under Gog in (Ezek. 38,39). Many have been vagabonds dwelling in tents as his father Noah prophesied (Gen. 9:27).

David—Beloved

David was the youngest of eight sons of Jesse. He was Israel's second and greatest king. David's life is most interesting and an example to Christians for overcoming the trials set before them. He is a man after God's own heart because he repented of his heinous sins. David is a man of tremendous faith slaying the giant Goliath when only a boy. He was a courageous warrior, skillful musician and talented poet. He is a *type* of Christ. No wonder David was *beloved* of God!

Job—Hated, One Ever Turning to God

Job was an Old Testament patriarch who lived in the land of Uz—he was the original "Wizard of Uz." His character was perfect and flawless except for the sin of "self-righteousness." Job was a model in faith, patience, prayer, and overcoming trials of injustice. Though accused wrongly by his friends, God allowed him to suffer only to show His justice. Job's life is a *type* of Christ [a righteous man] suffering injustice for God's purpose, and an inspiration for all Christians who likewise suffer persecution.

Peter—A Rock of Stone

A fisherman chosen by our Lord to be one of His leading disciples. Peter became the leading spokesman of the apostles as Jesus appointed him steward with authority when He stated: **"And I say unto thee, that thou art Peter, and upon this *rock*, I will build my church; and the gates of hell shall not prevail against it"** (Matt. 16:18). Peter became the chief apostle to the Jews.

Paul—Little

Originally his name was Saul; but he was also called Paul (Acts 13:9). Paul was a tentmaker by trade (Acts 18:3). A Pharisee, and the son of a Pharisee (Acts 23:6). Paul had been a persecutor of Christians before his conversion when God be-*littled* him (Acts 8:1-4). He became the apostle to the Gentiles and author of fourteen of the twenty seven books of the New Testament. Paul was unsurpassed as a great missionary, orator, educator, evangelist and writer of New Testament times.

Lazarus—God Hath Helped

There are two accounts in the Bible in which the name Lazarus is used—both denote *God's helping hand.* The parable of Lazarus and the rich man shows how God will help those who have been treated unjustly in this life (Lk. 16:19-31). The other account is when Jesus raised Lazarus, the brother of Mary and Martha from the dead (Jn. 11; 12:1-17).

Antipas—Anti-Father.

Antipas was the early Christian martyr of Pergamos in Asia Minor where Satan's seat was located (Rev. 2:12-13). Some believe his name is *symbolic* for his refusal to go along with the dictates of the church of Rome—hence ANTI-PAPA or ANTI-POPE!

Chapter Thirteen

GOD'S NATURE AND CHARACTER REVEALED BY HIS NAMES

Every name or title of God as mentioned in the Bible reveals some attribute of the Divine CHARACTER OF GOD. In studying God's Word, we learn new facts about God's nature and CHARACTER with each new name by which He *reveals* Himself!

There are many Hebrew names used to describe God's very character, and for a complete listing (see *Bullingers Concordance*). However, we shall now give some of God's many names that are used more than others—and show how they relate to His divine attributes.

The two personal names of God in the Hebrew Scriptures are Elohim and Jehovah (or, more correctly, Yehweh). The former calls attention to the FULLNESS of divine power. The latter means "He who is" and thus declares the divine self-existence of God.

These terms are varied or combined with others to bring out or emphasize certain attributes of the Godhead. Such variations or combinations being rendered in our English version, "God Almighty," "The Living God," "The Most High," "The Lord," "The God of Hosts." The English word "God" is identical with the Anglo-Saxon word for "good," and therefore it is believed that the name God refers to *divine goodness*.

ELOHIM

ELOHIM is the only name God uses to describe His nature in the first chapter of the book of Genesis. This divine title is used 2,700 times in the Bible. It's first occurrence connects it with creation, and gives it its essential meaning of THE CREATOR!

The word *Elohim* is a uni-plural noun. It is a word like "church" or "family." Elohim denotes MORE than one member of the Godhead! It also means "the Mighty Ones."

Here then is another truth concerning the title Elohim. It establishes the COVENANT-RELATIONSHIP with His people! This relationship was first established with the 2nd member of the Godhead, "the Word" as we read in John 1:1-3:

In the beginning was the Word, and the Word was with God...all things were made by Him... For by him were all things created ...all things were created by Him and for him. And He is before all things and by Him all things consist (Col. 1:16-17).

God or "Elohim" in covenant with the personage who later became His faithful Son, also establishes His covenant-relationship with all those who are created to be HEIRS of SALVATION (Heb. 1:14).

From the following scriptures, it should be made evident "Elohim", refers to and implies one who stands in a COVENANT-RELATIONSHIP with our great heavenly Father.

Gen. 6:13-18   "And *Elohim* said unto Noah, the end of all flesh is come before me,... but with thee will I establish my *covenant*."

NAMES OF GOD

Gen. 9:9,17	"And I, behold I, establish my *covenant* with you, and with your seed, and with every living creature that is with you. And this is the token of the *covenant* which I make between me and you. I do set my bow [rainbow] in the cloud, and I will remember my *covenant*, which is between me and you and every living creature of all flesh that is upon the earth."
Gen. 17:1-8	Elohim established His covenant with Abraham, Isaac and Jacob as He said:
Gen. 26:24	"I am the Almighty God: walk before me and be thou perfect; and I will establish my *covenant* between me and thee, and thy seed after thee in all generations, to be a God to thee, and to thy seed, and I will be their *ELOHIM*." See also (Gen. 28:13,14).
Psalm 111:5	David believed and trusted God to "...be mindful of His covenant."
1 Kings 8:23	God is "Elohim" that is the "one who keepeth covenant."
Gal. 3:17	But "the *covenant* which was confirmed before of God in [or to] Christ, the law which was four hundred years after cannot disannul, that it should make the promise of none effect."

JEHOVAH

"YHWH"—The Hebrew letters written as "LORD" in the *King James* version meaning "The Eternal" or "Ever Living One." This Hebrew word, often translated "Jehovah" in some of the revised versions, showing God's everlasting office in a COVENANT-RELATION to those whom He has created.

Jehovah is indicated in the *Authorized Version* by small capital letters, "LORD", and by "God" when it occurs in combination with Adonai, in which case "Lord GOD" means Adonai Jehovah. The Jehovah titles, found in the Hebrew canon are:

1. JEHOVAH-JIREH—Jehovah will see, or provide (Gen. 22:14).

2. JEHOVAH—ROPHEKA—Jehovah that healeth thee (Ex.15:26).

3. JEHOVAH-NISSI—Jehovah my banner (Ex. 17:15).

4. JEHOVAH-MEKADDISHKEM—Jehovah that doth sanctify you (Ex. 31:13; Lev. 20:8; 22:32; Ezek. 20:12).

5. JEHOVAH-ZEBAOTH—Jehovah of hosts (1 Sam. 1:13 and frequently).

6. JEHOVAH—SHALOM—Jehovah sends peace (Judges 6:24).

7. JEHOVAVAH-ZIDKENU—Jehovah our righteousness (Jer. 23:6; 33:16).

8. JEHOVAH-SHAMMAH—Jehovah is there (Ezek. 48:35).

9. JEHOVAH-ELYON—Jehovah most high (Ps. 7:17; 47:2; 97:9).

10. JEHOVAH-ROI—Jehovah my Shepherd (Ps. 23:1).

Just as God established His covenant-relationship with His people through the name "Elohim"—now He *reveals* Himself as the God who "loves righteousness and hates sin," to maintain that relationship! Therefore, He must judge EVIL till it is swallowed up in victorious LIFE! This name epitomizes JUDGMENT!

NAMES OF GOD

Although Noah and Enoch walked with "Elohim" (Gen. 5:22)—Noah found GRACE in the eyes of "Jehovah" (Gen. 6:8,9).

Sometimes the names "Elohim" and "Jehova" are used interchangeably in the Bible as the following scriptures demonstrate:

Gen. 6:5 — "*Jehovah* saw the wickedness of man, that it was great upon the earth...and *Jehovah* said, I will destroy man whom I have created."

Gen. 6:12-18 — "And *Elohim* saw the earth, and behold it was corrupt, for all flesh had corrupted his way. And *Elohim* said, I will destroy them with the earth: for with thee will I establish my covenant."

However, whenever "Elohim" is used to indicate a "judgment," it appears when "judgment" will renew or restore the covenant relationship. It was "Elohim" that destroyed the earth and told Noah to gather "two of every living thing into the ark"—to continue the race or covenant relationship!

But the testimony of God's JUDGMENT through His name "Jehovah" remains adamant. Notice the following scriptures that show the correlation of "Jehovah" to "Judgment".

Psalm 11:7 — "Upon the wicked, *Jehovah* shall rain snares, *fire and brimstone*, and an horrible tempest: this shall be the portion of their cup. For the righteous *Jehovah* loveth righteousness, His countenance doth behold the upright."

Judges 10:7 — "...the *anger* of *Jehovah* was kindled against His people, and *Jehovah* sold them into the hands of their enemies."

It was because of Israel's continued REBELLION that "Jehovah" sold His people into slavery—"**...and His soul was grieved for the misery of Israel" (Judges 10:16).** Jehovah was grieved **"Forty years long with this generation in the wilderness" (Psalm 95:10).**

Once Israel REPENTS in the future—"Jehovah" will boast:

This is the covenant that I will make after those days, I will put my law into their mind, and will write it in their hearts, and I will be to them a God, and they shall be to me a people (Heb. 8:1-12).

JAH is Jehovah in a special sense and relationship—Jehovah as having become our Salvation (Exodus 15:2), He who is, and was, and is to come. It occurs 49 times in the Bible (see Psalm 68:4, 18).

EL is essentially the Almighty-Elohim in all His strength and power. It is rendered "God" as Elohim is, but EL is God the Omnipotent. Elohim is God the Creator putting His omnipotence into operation. El is the God who knows all (Gen. 14:18-22) and sees all (Gen. 16:13) and that performs all things for His people (Ps. 57:2). "El" appears no less than 225 times in the *Authorized Version* of the Old Testament.

ELOAH is Elohim, who is to be worshipped. Eloah is God in connection with His will rather than His power. The first occurrence associates this name with worship (Deuteronomy 32:15-17). Hence it is the title used whenever the contrast is with false gods or idols. Eloah is essentially "the living God" in contrast to inanimate idols.

EL SHADDAI

In every instance El Shaddai is translated "Almighty". It is God (EL), not as the source of strength, but of grace; not as Creator, but as the *Giver*. Shaddai is the ALL-bountiful. This title does not refer to God's creative power but to His power to supply all the needs of His people. It first occurs in (Genesis 17:1) where God shows Abraham, that He who called him out to walk alone before Him could supply all his needs.

"Elohim" described God as one who is in a covenant-relationship with His people. "Jehovah" depicts the virtue of "loving correction" of God toward His rebellious creation after "Judgment."

In these two names we find God's *love* and *judgment* of His people. After God chastises or corrects His children out of love—He ultimately extends MERCY to them. Here we find God's *dual* nature of love and correction. This nature holds true of the sacrifices as well. They could be a *sweet-Savour* AFTER they were a sin-offering. This is not a contradictory nature—but rather a complimentary one.

Love entails reward through correction or chastisement. "Sin-offerings" were necessary before they could be a "sweet-Savour" to God's nostrils. REPENTANCE or CORRECTION had to come before MERCY. And the same God can be a God of love or chastisement—as revealed by His many names!

"EL SHADDAI" reveals God's nature of "might" or "power"—THE ALMIGHTY! But the "almighty" what?

The prefix "EL" primarily has the connotation of physical "might" or "power" as used in (Nehemiah 5:5), **"Some of our daughters are brought into bondage, neither is it in our *power* (EL) to redeem them."** And in Proverbs 3:27: **"...withhold not good from them to whom it is due, when it is in the power (EL) of thine hand to do it..."** "Shaddai" describes the *power* or *might* of God as ALL-BOUNTIFUL! "Shaddai" comes from the Hebrew root word "SHAD" which means "the breast" (see Gen. 49:25).

This name of God expresses His almightiness of "the breast" as a loving, self-sacrificing and GIVING mother! Jesus is pictured as THE ALMIGHTY (Rev. 1:8), **"...clothed with a garment down to the foot, and girt about the *paps* with a golden *girdle*" (Rev. 1:13).** Even as the "breasts" of a woman feeds and nourishes a child to grow in strength—Jesus is envisioned in a woman's dress having "breasts" to *feed* His Church!

The name "EL Shaddai" is used several times in the Old Testament in conjunction with being "fruitful" and "multiplying." It was "EL Shaddai" that told Abraham:

> **...this is my covenant which ye shall keep. Ye shall circumcise your flesh, and I will make thee exceeding *fruitful*, and nations and kings shall come out of thee (Gen. 17:6).**

ELYON first occurs in (Genesis 14:18). ELYON with El is rendered "the most high (God)." It is El and Elohim, not as the powerful Creator, but as "the possessor of heaven and earth." It is Elyon as possessor of the Earth who divides the nations "their inheritance." In (Psalm 83:18) He is "over all the earth." This title occurs 36 times. ELYON is the Dispenser of God's blessings in the earth!

But this name, more than any other title of God—establishes Gods blessings to repentant Gentiles. It *symbolizes* God's COVENANT-RELATIONSHIP WITH GENTILES, more than the Church! This is made evident by several scriptures which we shall now take a closer look.

When Abraham was victorious over the heathen cities who took his nephew Lot with their spoil, **"Melchisedec, king of Salem brought forth bread and wine; and he was priest of THE MOST HIGH GOD" (Gen. 14:18).**

Through Melchisedec, Abraham received revelation of God's title, "The Most High God." Notice the words: **"I have lifted up my hand unto the Lord, the most High God, possessor of heaven and earth" (Gen. 14:22).**

The seventh chapter of the book of Hebrews explains the Melchisedec priesthood in more detail. Here we find that Abraham paid tithes to Melchisedec who is a *prototype* of Christ's priesthood (Heb. 6:20).

But why would Abraham pay tithes to Melchisedec? And why would this king of Salem be a priest of "the Most High God"?

Concerning the Melchisedec priesthood, the writer of Hebrews, **"has many things to say, and hard to be uttered"**—things that are **"strong Meat"** and hard to digest (Heb. 5:10-14).

The thought of "stronger meat" continues in the sixth and seventh chapters of Hebrews. In chapter six verse one, the author refers to the *milk* of the word as basic doctrines of "repentance from dead works", "faith towards God", "baptisms", "the laying on of hands", "the resurrection of the dead" and "eternal judgement".

These being "the milk of the word" contain the characteristics of God through His names! Surely "Elohim" is contained in covenant-relations through the virtue of "faith toward God", while "Jehovah" is characteristic of "repentance from dead works." "El Shaddai", characteristic of "pouring forth blessings" entails the doctrines of "baptisms", "laying on of hands" "resurrection" and "eternal judgement."

But these are all *basic principles* or truths that should not be a stumbling block to go on toward PERFECTION (Heb. 6:1).

Now WHAT GREATER TRUTH can we learn from the Melshisedec priesthood than these fundamental doctrines? And why is "EL ELYON" or "Most High God" connected with Melchisedec's priesthood?

Melchisedec was "king of salem" or "king of righteousness" and King of peace (Heb. 7:2). In this *dual* title we have the first two Hebrew names of God as already defined. "Elohim" in covenant-relationship is *synonymous* of "peace" while "Jehovah" with "righteousness." Melchisedec represents the amalgamation of God's *dual nature* into one! This title also describes God's plan to save the entire world, including Gentiles!

Now we get down to the deep "mysteries" of God which are *revealed* by His many names. Abraham and his seed represent the ELECT of God spiritually—who are to receive the covenant promises. They in turn being a kind of **"first fruits" (Jas. 1:18)**, will bless those who were not God's people.

Do you see the parallel to the event of Abraham and Melchisedec? Abraham representing the "elect" of God and inheritors of the promises—blesses a king whose title describes the character and plan of God for the UNCIRCUMCISED.

Paul elaborates upon God's plan for the Gentile world in the eleventh chapter of the book of Romans. There he expounds upon this "mystery" of God:

> **For I would not, brethren, that ye should be ignorant of this MYSTERY, lest ye should be wise in your own conceits; that blindness in part is happened to Israel,** *until the fullness of the Gentiles be come in.*

Paul explains this process in analogy to the grafting in of the branches of a tree. Gentiles will be grafted into God's family by THE MOST HIGH GOD even though they were not of the original promise!

This is the "meat" and the "mystery" behind the *dual* meaning of Melchisedec's name. It explains God's nature of "righteousness" by ultimately bringing "peace" to the Gentiles!

The New Testament priesthood of Jesus Christ is to emulate that of Melchisedec (Heb. 5:6; 6:20; 7:3). Why? Because the priesthood was now being changed from Levi by commandment, to that of Judah after the order of Melchisedec (Heb. 7:11-15).

Under the Old Covenant, Aaron and his sons [the Levites] were commanded by God to administer the services at the Temple. God paid them for their services from the people. But under the New Testament—Jesus Christ starts a new priesthood with a new tribe! Because our Lord was a descendant of the tribe of Judah—the Levitical priesthood now is ABOLISHED in Christ's ministry and those He desires to serve with Him!

Now Gentiles are invited to be priests in God's service, even as Melchisedec is king of the Most High God over all, including Gentiles!

The apostle to the Gentiles brings out this marvelous truth very poignantly to the hypocritical Jews:

> **Is he the God of the Jews only? Is he not also of the Gentiles? Yes, of the Gentiles also...whom God hath set forth to be a propitiation through faith in his blood, to declare his RIGHTEOUSNESS for the remission of sins that are past, through the forbearance of God (Rom. 3:29,25).**

Peter, who was the chief apostle to the Jews—had to learn this bitter lesson from the Gentile Cornelius centuries later. What Abraham learned from Melchisedec—Peter learned from Cornelius—that is, **"...call no man common or unclean" (Acts 10:28). "For there is no difference between the Jew and the Greek: for the same Lord over all is rich unto all that call upon him" (Rom. 10:12).**

Realize there are only three references to the title "Most High God" in the first five books of the Bible—and all three speak of THE GENTILE WORLD and God's relationship to it.

The first place the title "Most High God" is used in scripture is in reference to the Melchisedec priesthood. The second place is Balaam's prophecy concerning the judgment of Gentile

Nations such as "Sheth", "Amalek" and "Asshur" (Num. 23:7; 24:16). The third reference is in the "song of Moses"—"**...when THE MOST HIGH divided the nations their inheritance, when He separated the sons of Adam, He set the bounds of the peoples according to the number of children of Israel**" **(Duet. 32:8).**

Perhaps the most vivid example of the *implication* of the title "Most High God" and its relationship to the Gentile world—is the humbling experience of the Babylonian king Nebuchadnezzar—who was the first Gentile power depicted by a great beastly image representing the Gentile powers that would rule the earth till Christ's return (Dan. 2). But this nefarious king was made to eat grass like a wild animal till he learned "**...that *the Most High* ruleth in the kingdom of men, and giveth it to whomsoever He will...**" **(Dan. 4:30-34; 5:18-22).**

Melchisedec's priesthood was without a system of animal sacrifices—he only offered "bread and wine"—like Jesus Christ our PERFECT HIGH PRIEST! The lesson to be learned:

> **THE MOST HIGH dwelleth not in temples made with hands (Acts 8:48). Neither is He worshipped as though He needed anything, seeing He giveth to all life, and breath, and things (Acts 17:25, 26). Nay, rather God says...Love your enemies, and do good, and lend, hoping for nothing again: and your reward shall be great, and ye shall be the children of the Highest [MOST HIGH] for He is kind unto the unthankful and to the evil (Lk. 6:35).**

What a profound revelation of the Word of God! What a delight we have in our MOST HIGH GOD and His most benevolent plan for ALL mankind!

ADONAI

ADON is one of three titles [ADON, ADONAI, ADONIM] all generally rendered "Lord." Each has its own special usage and

THE FOOLISHNESS GOD

association. They all denote *headship* in various aspects. They have to do with God as "overlord."

ADON is the Lord as Ruler in the earth. ADONAI is the Lord in His relationship to the earth; and as carrying out His purposes of blessing in the earth. ADONIM is the plural of ADON. Adonim carries with it all that Adon does, but in a greater and higher degree; and more especially as owner and proprietor—as Adon may rule others who do not belong to him. Hence without the article it is often used of men. But Adonim is the Lord who rules His own.

God told Moses, the Hebrew patriarch, that He had appeared to Abraham, Isaac and Jacob by the name of "God Almighty" [Elohim]—but not by His name Jehovah or Yahweh (Exodus 6:3). In revealing His name to Moses, He stated: **"I AM THAT I AM" (EX.3:14).** God is the eternal, Self-existing One. He was, and is, and ever more shall be, the **"I AM."**

"Elohim" revealed God's unchanging love for His people in a covenant relationship. "Jehovah" established God's "righteousness" in maintaining that relationship, by rooting out sin. "EL Shaddi" reveals God's nature as "a giver or pourer" out of Himself for others. "EL Elyon" *symbolizes* the Most High over His creation that includes the Gentile world. Adonai reveals God as "lord" or "mother" or "husband."

Adonai expresses the relationship of a MASTER to his *slave* or *servant* or a HUSBAND to his *wife*. These relationships define certain inalienable rights of lordship and the individual.

Through the name "Adonai" or "Lord"—the relationship of husband to wife, or God to His ELECT is expressed! Here, the CHURCH realizes that as a "wife"—her *body* is not her own! That through the marriage relationship—she is "no more twain" but "joined to the Lord" as one "flesh" or "one spirit" (Matt. 19:5,6; 1 Cor. 6:17-19).

God's stringent love for His Church as husband is expressed through the prophets, notice: **"Thy Maker is thy husband" (Isa. 54:5). "I am married to you saith the Lord" (Jer. 3:14).**

Let's now read Ezekiel's account of *Adonai's* deep intimate relationship to His Bride:

> **Thus saith the Lord [Adonai] God... I made thee to multiply: thy breasts are fashioned. and thine hair is grown. Now when I passed by**

thee, and looked upon thee, behold, thy time was the time of *love*, and I spread my *skirt* over thee, and covered thy nakedness; I have caused thee to multiply as the bud of the field, and thou hast increased and waxen great, and thou art come to excellent ornaments: thy breasts are fashioned, and thine hair is grown, whereas thou wast naked and bare.

Now I passed by thee, and looked upon thee, behold, thy was the time of love; and I spread my skirt over thee, and covered thy nakedness: yea, I sware unto thee, and entered into a covenant with thee, saith the Lord God, and thou becamest mine. Then washed I thee with water; yea, I thoroughly washed away thy blood from thee, and I anointed thee with oil. I clothed thee also with broidered work, and shod thee with badger's skin, and I girded thee about with fine linen, and I covered thee with silk.

I decked thee also with ornaments, and I put bracelets upon thy hands, and a chain on thy neck. And I put a jewel on thy forehead, and earrings in thine ears, and a beautiful crown upon thine head. Thus wast thou decked with gold and silver; and thy raiment was of fine linen; and silk, and broidered work; thou didst eat fine flour, and honey. and oil: and thou wast exceeding beautiful, and thou didst prosper into a kingdom. And thy renown went forth among the heathen for thy beauty: for it was perfect through my comeliness, which I had put upon thee, saith the Lord [Adonai] God (Exek. 16:7-14).

Through His prophet Jeremiah, [Adonai] God speaks of His Bride: "**... as the bridegroom rejoiceth over the bride, so shall thy God rejoice over thee" (Isa. 62:5).** [Adonai] God finds deep joy in the intimate relationship He has with His wife. But joy to

THE FOOLISHNESS GOD

the husband can only come when his Bride is FAITHFUL and loyal regardless of how beautiful she looks!

If we fail in our relationship as a wife—we sever the relationship and BLESSINGS of [Adonai] God. This is apparent from the words God spoke through His prophet Ezekiel concerning *disobedient* Israel:

> **But thou didst trust in thine own beauty, and playedst the harlot because of thy renown, and pouredst out thy fornications on every one passed by; his it was. And of thy garments thou didst take, and deckedst thy high places with divers colours, and playedst the harlot thereupon: the like things shall not come, neither shall it be so.**
>
> **Thou hast also taken thy fair jewels of my gold and of my silver, which I had given thee, and madest to thy self images of men, and didst commit whoredom with them. And tookest thy broidered garments, and coveredst them: and thou hast set mine oil and incense before them.**
>
> **My meat also which I gave thee, fine flour, and oil, and honey, wherewith I fed thee, thou hast even set it before them for a sweet savour: and thus it was, saith the Lord God. Moreoever thou hast taken thy sons and thy daughters, whom thou hast borne unto me, and these hast thou sacrificed unto them to be devoured. Is this of thy whoredomes a small matter. That thou hast slain my children, and delivered them to cause them to pass through the fire for them...?**
>
> **Wherefore, O harlot, hear the word of the Lord: Thus, saith the Lord God; Because thy filthiness was poured out, and thy nakedness discovered through thy whoredoms with thy**

NAMES OF GOD

lovers, and with all the idols of thy abominations, and by the blood of thy children, which thou didst give unto them.

Behold, therefore I will gather all thy lovers, with whom thou hast taken pleasure, and all them that thou hast loved, with all them that thou hast hated; I will even gather them round about against thee, and will discover thy nakedness unto them, that they may see all thy nakedness.

And I will judge thee, as women that break wedlock and shed blood are judged; and I will give thee blood in fury and jealousy. And I will also give thee into their hand, and they shall throw down thine eminent place, and shall break down thy high places; they shall strip thee also of thy clothes, and shall take thy fair jewels, and leave thee naked and bare.

They shall also bring up a company against thee, and they shall stone thee with stones, and thrust thee through with their swords. And they shall burn thine houses with fire, and execute judgment upon thee in the sight of many women: and I will cause thee to cease from playing the harlot, and thou also shall find no hire any more (Ezek. 16:15-41).

EL OLAM

EL OLAM is translated from the original Hebrew in the *Authorized Version* as "Everlasting God" and literally means "God of the ages."

The title of "EL OLAM" first appears in scripture when the patriarch Abraham first encountered God and his name was *changed* to Abram. Here is the first clue as to what *significance* this title bears. It personifies CHANGE through revelation or by dispensation of an age.

THE FOOLISHNESS GOD

Whenever a "mystery" or "secret" is revealed—"EL OLAM" is rendered. It's name bears the connotation of "concealing" or "hiding" something for an indefinite period of time—hence it is often translated as "for ever" meaning "age lasting."

Such connotation is found in Exodus 21:6: **"...and he shall serve him *forever*" [olam]. And "...they shall be your bondmen *forever*" [olam] (Lev. 25:46).**

Wherever the word "olam" appears as *forever*, it's simply an expression of "time"—and has nothing to do with *eternity*!

The word "olam" refers to a specific period of time, rather than eternity—it is used to describe the Aaronic priesthood (Ex. 40:15); the Passover (Ex. 12:14,17); the Meat-offering (Lev. 6:18); and Tabernacle service of Levites with all the Old Testament washings and ordinances that have been done away (1 Cor. 3:7).

"Forever", in these verses simply means a "condition or period of time." However, when the time [or age] of these entities were fulfilled—they were abolished!

By placing an "EL" in front of "olam" in referring to God, we describe God as the "God of Ages" or "dispensations" to fulfill His *masterful plan* while God's purpose for mankind remains adamant! He reveals Himself in varying degrees through different means during different ages! This is God's kindergarten method of teaching His *crowning creation* what His purpose is for them!

Through the dispensation of the Mosaic law and ceremonial offerings of the Aaronic priesthood—the revelation came in the "flesh". Now it can be understood in the "spirit"!

The name "EL OLAM" teaches us that God is REVEALING His master plan through an APPOINTED ORDER. Through varied steps—God as "EL OLAM" is teaching us that the Old Testament examples were **"...shadows of good things to come" (Col. 2:17; Heb. 10:1).**

There was a time limit on the Noatian world, the Mosaic law, the Levitical Priesthood, and the Old Covenant. These were all "shadows" of better promises to come (Heb. 8:6-8). God, [EL OLAM]:

...hath in these last days spoken unto us by His Son whom He hath appointed heir of all things,

> by whom also He made the worlds [margin-ages] (Heb. 1:2).

Paul speaks of the glory of Jesus as: **"Unto him be glory in the church by Christ Jesus throughout all *ages* world without end" (Eph.3:21).** Paul continues his praise of Jesus in Ephesians 1:21:

> **Far above all principality, and power and might, and dominion, and every name that is named, not only in this world [margin-*age*], but also in that which is to come.**

Again, we read in Hebrews 9:26:

> **For then must he often have suffered since the foundation of the world: but now once in the end of the world [margin-*consummation* of the ages] hath he appeared to put away sin by the sacrifice of himself.**

Paul speaks of "EL Olam's" teaching methods of the Old Testament:

> **Now all these things happened unto them for ensample [examples]: and they are written for our admonition, upon whom the ends of the world [*margin-ages*] are come (1 Cor. 10:11).**

Finally, Paul speaks of "the ages to come" in which God "EL Olam" might show the exceeding riches of his grace in his kindness toward us through Jesus Christ (Eph. 2:7).

Clearly, the ages or DISPENSATIONS of grace outlining God's redemptive plan are revealed by these scriptures as every man will be granted grace in his own order, Christ the "first fruit"; then "they that are Christs'" (1 Cor. 15:22-28).

Those who have been *cleansed* by the flood, *purified* by the Tribulation and made *righteous* by the spirit—those who were "unclean" by nature, held in bondage to sin—will all be granted their rightful inheritance through God's mercy!

Then will the "mysteries" of God's redemptive plan be revealed to all! Then will be made manifest; the "revelation of the mystery, which has been kept secret from the agetimes, according to the commandment of the Everlasting or Age-working God" (Rom. 16:25-26).

Like the Jew who has been "blinded" in this dispensation, "EL Olam" will reveal deep SECRETS of His plan that have been *hidden* from past ages!

JEHOVAH SABAOTH

JEHOVAH SABAOTH rendered LORD OF HOSTS in our *authorized* version—pertains to God's ELECT being delivered from adversity by His HOLY ANGELS!

Like the righteous men of old—the names "Elohim" and "Jehovah", that is, "God in covenant, yet righteous", may be understood by the young Christian. As we grow in more knowledge of God's way of life, we shall know Him as the "Almighty", who helps us produce fruit in our lives.

Understanding that the Gentiles can NOW be partakers of His masterful plan—we shall know Him as the "Most High" God, who has a priesthood that encompasses more than just the "Elect." Abraham and Moses only understood the "God of Ages" after they went through sore trial! Abraham only understood this name when his handmaid Hagar was cast out of his camp. Moses understood this name only after he was told he would not lead Israel into the promised land—but would die before God's "elect" would inherit Canaan.

And so it is with us! Christians do not fully understand the name "LORD OF HOSTS" while we are in bondage to sin [as Israel was in Egypt], or while we are still in spiritual wilderness. We do not fully comprehend this title while we spiritually cross the Jordan into the promised land (*symbolic* of our accepting Christ through baptism). Nay, it is only when we begin to realize our human frailties—and we are POWERLESS without heavenly deliverance! In short, when we are placed between a rock and a hard place, or in situations beyond our physical ability to overcome—God's "heavenly hosts" stand ready to help!

The following scriptures show very vividly the intent of God's name—"Lord of Hosts." How in every case it is associated with

NAMES OF GOD

SUPERNATURAL DELIVERANCE by God via His Holy Angels!

1 Sam. 17:45	"Then said David to the Philistine, thou comest to me with a sword, and with a spear, and with a shield: but I come to thee in the name of the *Lord of Hosts*, the God of the armies of Israel, whom thou hast defied."
Isa. 9:13,19	"For the people turneth not unto him that smiteth them, neither do they seek the *Lord of Hosts*."
Isa. 10:12, 24-27	"Therefore thus saith the *Lord God of hosts*, O my people that dwellest in Zion, be not afraid of the Assyrian: he shall smite thee with a rod, and shall lift up his staff against thee, after the manner of Egypt. For yet a very little while, and the indignation shall cease, and mine anger in their destruction. And *the Lord of hosts* shall stir up a scourge for him according to the slaughter of Midian at the rock Orebi: and as his rod was upon the sea, so shall he lift it up after the manner of Egypt. And it shall come to pass in that day, that his burden shall be taken away from off thy shoulder, and his yoke from off thy neck, and the yoke shall be destroyed because of thy anointing."
Haggai 2:4, 6-9,23	"Yet now be strong, O Zerubbabel, saith the Lord; and be strong, O Joshua, son of Josedech, the high priest; and be strong, all ye people of the land, saith the Lord, and work; for I am with you, saith the *Lord of*

hosts." "For thus saith the *Lord of hosts.* Yet once, it is a little while, and I will shake the heavens, and the earth, and the sea, and the dry land. And I will shake all nations, and the desire of all nations shall come; and I will fill this house with glory, saith the *Lord of hosts.* The silver is mine, and the gold is mine, saith the *Lord of hosts.* The glory of this latter house shall be greater than of the former, saith the *Lord of hosts*; and in this place will I give peace, saith the *Lord of hosts.*"

Mal. 3:16,17

"Then they that feared the Lord spake often one to another: and the Lord hearkened, and heard it, and a book of remembrance was written before him for them that feared the Lord, and that thought upon His name. And they shall be mine, saith the *Lord of hosts,* in that day when I make up my jewels; and I will spare them, as a man spareth his own son that serveth him."

Gen. 19:1,16,17

"And there came two angels to Sodom at even; and Lot sat in the gate of Sodom: and Lot seeing them rose up to meet them; and he bowed himself with his face toward the ground." "And while he lingered, the men laid hold upon his hand, and upon the hand of his wife, and upon the hand of his two daughters; the Lord being merciful unto him: and they brought him forth, and set him without the city.
And it came to pass, when they had brought them forth abroad, that he said, Escape for thy life; look not

NAMES OF GOD

	behind them neither stay thou in all the plain; escape to the mountain, lest thou be consumed."
Gen. 16:7-11	"And the angel of the Lord found her by a fountain of water in the wilderness, by the fountain in the way to Shur. And he said, Hagar, Sarai's maid, whence camest thou? and whither wilt thou go? And she said, I flee from the face of my mistress Sarai? And the angel of the Lord said unto her, Return to thy mistress, and submit thyself under her hands. And the angel of the Lord said unto her, I will multiply thy seed exceedingly, that it shall not be numbered for multitude, And the angel of the Lord said unto her, Behold, thou art with child, and shalt bear a son, and shalt call his name Ishmael; because the Lord hath heard thy affliction."
Gen. 32:1-2	"And Jacob went on his way, and the angels of God met him. And when Jacob saw them, he said, This is God's host: and he called the name of that place Mahanaim."
Dan. 10:13	Michael the archangel, came to help Daniel.
Dan. 12:1	Michael will help God's people in the last days.
Rev. 12:7	Michael and his angels will cast the devil and his angels out of heaven in the last days.

Dan. 8:16	The archangel Gabriel appeared unto Daniel to give him understanding in prophecy. See also (Dan. 9:21).
Matt. 1:20	"But while he thought on these things, behold, the angel of the Lord appeared unto him in a dream, saying, Joseph, thou son of David, fear not to take unto thee Mary thy wife: for that which is conceived in her is of the Holy Spirit." The "angel" of the Lord also appeared to Zechariah (Luke 1:13,19); Mary (Luke 1:26,30); and the shepherds (Luke 2:9-13).
Matt. 2:13,19	Ministering angels helped Mary and Joseph escape into the haven of Egypt as Satan through Herod tried to kill the baby Jesus.
Matt. 4:11	Angels administered food to Christ after fasting forty days in preparation of Satan's temptation.
Lk. 22:43	Christ was strengthened by an angel in the garden.
Matt. 28:2,6	Angels were placed at the entrance stone to Christs' tomb. They rolled away the great stone and declared His resurrection to His disciples.
Matt. 26:53	Legions of angels were at Christ's disposal: "Thinkest thou that I cannot now pray to my Father, and He shall presently give me more than twelve legions of angels."
Jn. 1:51	"Verily, verily, henceforward ye shall see heaven open, and the angels

NAMES OF GOD

	of God ascending and descending upon the Son of Man."
Acts 12:6-11	The apostle Peter was delivered from Herod, in prison by the angel of the Lord.
Acts 8:26	Philip was given directions from an angel in the dessert.
Acts 27:23	The angel of God stood by Paul in the treacherous storm guiding the ship.
Rev. 1:1	An angel was sent to John on Patmos to verify the visions of Revelation.
Rev. 7:1-3	Angels will be very instrumental in carrying out God's plan in the last days. Cross references (Rev. 8:6-12; 9:14-15; 14:6; 15:1,7; 16:5; 19:17,18; 21:9).
Heb. 1:14	"Are they not all ministering spirits [angels] sent forth to minister for them who shall be heirs of salvation?"
Heb. 12:18,23	"Ye are not come unto the mount that may be touched, and to the sound of a trumpet, and to the voice of words...But ye are come unto Mount Sion, to THE CITY OF THE LIVING GOD, the heavenly Jerusalem, and to an innumerable company of ANGELS, to the general assembly and church of the first born, which are written in heaven, and to God, the Judge of all, and to *the spirits of just men* made perfect."

THE FOOLISHNESS GOD

The title "LORD OF HOSTS" bears record of God's desire to help His servants through thick and thin. Our hope, trust and faith is in heavenly Jerusalem—in which we are fellow citizens with an enumerable host of angels who stand ready to administer to us in perilous times. As the Psalmist states: **"The angel of the Lord encampeth round about them that fear him, and delivereth them" (Psalm 34:7).**

Summary

Every name or title of God reveals His nature and MASTER PLAN for the human race! God's name ELOHIM establishes the *covenant-relationship* with His true people. Once that covenant-relationship has been established—God chastises His people out of love when they break that covenant with Him. The title JEHOVAH denotes this *loving correction* from the God who "loves righteousness and hates sin."

Once God's children repent after being corrected, EL SHADDAI stands to bless His people with *fruitfulness*. God will feed, guide, protect, and lead His children in every good work, once their attention has been gained—followed by repentance!

Not only does God invite Israelites into His covenant-relationship, but ELYON invites *Gentiles* to become heirs of salvation also! ADONAI expresses God's relationship as master or husband of his people in a *marital relationship*! Each role is clearly defined and husband and wife must carry out their respective responsibilities to make God's plan work!

The title EL OLAM personifies *change* of God's plan through revelation or by dispensation of an age. JEHOVAH SABAOTH bears record of God's desire to *help* His servants in time of need. Many times administering angels are there to help us "supernaturally" without our realizing their invisible service.

Positively, each name or title of our great God opens new vistas of truth in comprehending His glorious universal plan for mankind!

Chapter Fourteen

GOD'S PLAN REVEALED BY THE SEVEN STAGES OF SONSHIP

Through the lives of *seven* men in the book of Genesis, *seven* distinct PHASES of salvation are revealed in which man must pass in order to become godlike! The number "seven" you will recall personifies "spiritual perfection."

These men are Adam, Abel, Noah, Abraham, Isaac, Jacob and Joseph. Each individual's life is an *abstract* of a *stage* every Christian will eventually experience personally, on his journey to Gods Kingdom. The stages of Christian development leading to *maturity* that these men represent are Human Nature, Repentance, Faith, Regeneration, Sonship, Service and finally Rulership!

Carnal Adam

In Adam we see a *prefigure* of our "

old man" or HUMAN NATURE. Christ is described as "the second Adam" because His nature was *divine* and totally opposite that of Adam (1 Cor. 15:45).

Giving heed to the temptations of the devil—then palming the blame on someone else is "human nature" in its most deceitful form. Every human being has this insidious nature in us and must contend with it daily. However, this nature is not inherited from our first parents as some believe. This will be explained in detail in a volume 4.

As a result of the first man and woman's sin—they were thrust out of Paradise, and contact with their Creator terminated at this point. This was *symbolically* demonstrated by the Cherubim securing the entrance door back into Eden! This *symbolically* cut off man's access to God's heavenly throne untill Christ came 4,000 years later.

Each of us, until converted, are like our first parents in that we have no contact with God. Our HUMAN NATURE had led us astray and down the path to sin and REBELLION just like Adam and Eve. But there is a way back to our heavenly home. This is the straight and narrow path of *repentance* leading to conversion. This straight and narrow path will allow us to spiritually pass by the sword of the Cherubim, and re-enter Paradise or God's heavenly throne!

There is yet another aspect of Adam's life which fulfills a phase of a Christian dispensationally. This is in the marriage of his wife—a *type* of Christ and His Church as already mentioned! While Adam slept, his wife was fashioned out of one of his ribs. She became "bone of his bone" and "flesh of his flesh."

The apostle Paul wrote concerning this *spiritual mystery*:

> **For no man ever hated his own flesh, but nourisheth and cherisheth it, even as the Lord of the Church: For we are members of his body,** *of his flesh, and of his bones.* **For this cause shall a man leave his father and mother, and shall be joined unto his wife, and they two shall be one flesh. This is a great mystery: but I speak concerning Christ and the Church (Eph. 5:29-32).**

The *mystery* of God building His Church out of the man [the second Adam] was revealed in Genesis 2:22. **"And the rib, which the Lord God had taken from the man, made [margin, Heb. *builded he into*] a woman, and brought her unto the man."**

So Christ, the second Adam is BUILDING a *woman* [Church] for Himself,, notice,

> **All the building fitly framed together groweth unto a holy temple in the Lord; in whom ye also are *builded together* for a habitation of God through the Spirit (Eph. 2:21-22).**

Just as Eve was made to be a *help-meet [mate]* for Adam, so likewise is the Church to become a "spotless bride" for Christ (Eph. 5:27).

Finally, like Adam and Eve who were given power and dominion over all the beasts of the earth—the *glorified* Bride of Christ will ultimately RULE the earth with her husband as "ALL things" are put under His feet! (Rev. 20:6; Heb. 2:8).

Cain And Abel—Two Ways of Life

Adam's sons Cain and Abel are also *prototypes* of this war with "human nature" within our flesh. The apostle Paul wrote more explicitly concerning this hostile nature:

> **For I know that in me [that is, in my flesh], dwelleth no good thing: for to will is present with me; but how to perform that which is good I find not. For the good that I would I do not: but the evil which I would not, that I do (Rom.7:18-19).**

Paul is confirming here that there is a law in our flesh [human nature]—that pulls us down to degradation and sin, which is contrary to what the "spiritual mind" tells us is right and good.

Paul continues to enlighten us as to this war in our mind:

> **For I delight in the law of God after the inward man [the converted spiritual mind]: But I see another law in my members [human nature] warring against the law of my mind, and bringing me into captivity to the law of sin which is in my members (verses 22,23).**

This is the plight of man and the *sequence* of conversion! First, mankind has the natural, unconverted, CARNAL MIND that is "enmity" or against God's law (Rom. 8:7). This mind is represented by the lives of Adam and his son Cain *symbolically*.

Afterwards comes the INWARD MAN or conversion through God's Holy Spirit:

> **That the righteousness of the law might be fulfilled in us, who walk not after the flesh, but after the Spirit. For they that are after the flesh do mind the things of the flesh; but they that are after the Spirit the things of the Spirit. For to be carnally minded is death; but to be spiritually minded is life and peace (Rom. 8:4-6).**

This is the *second Adam* or Christ-like nature that righteous Abel is the *archetype* who came *after* the carnal man: **"Howbeit that was not first which is spiritual, but that which is natural [carnal]; and afterward that which is spiritual" (1 Cor. 15:46).**

The *attitudes* of these two brothers represent the TWO NATURES of man. One is the life of the flesh, the other the Spirit. Just as Cain the firstborn struggled with his brother Abel—so is the inward spiritual man *wrestling* with the outer carnal man.

Cain thought nothing of being out of Paradise—Abel's eyes were always on the entrance gate. Abel was desirous to please his God and offered *a choice lamb* of his flock. Cain's offering of vegetables from the ground was an abomination to God.

Blood was offered by Abel [understanding that *blood* was required for sin], while Cain's mind was unaware of this atoning sacrifice! Burnt-offerings, requiring blood were to satisfy God (Lev. 27:13,14), whereas Meat-offerings of the ground were man's allotted portion (Gen. 1:29). Abel understood the need for repentance!

Here in *emblem,* is depicted two seeds or "two ways of life". The way of *acquiring* for oneself and the way of *love* and GIVING to others. These two seeds will exist all through the Bible side by side. They are *pictured* as the "Sheep and the Goats" or "Wheat and the Tares" by Jesus. They are also "two Churches" in this world. One is God's true Church, the other is *Satan's counterfeit system!*

Abel's seed continues in Seth, who walked with God and is the second Abel *spiritually*. His name means *replaced* and his seed culminates in righteous Noah.

Cain's very name means "a possession" and implies a sensuous life of worldly possessions. Notice, the striking words of Eve after Cain's birth: **"...I have gotten a man from the Lord"** (Eve thought Cain was the Messiah).

Cain's way of life *pictures* the "get" way of life. Contrariwise, Abel's name "a vapour" depicts his passing from a temporary physical life into a higher plane like a *vapour*.

These are the two ways of life—one carnal and one spiritual! According to *Clarks Commentary,* Cain and Abel may have been twins. This pictures the *dual natures* within all of us. To overcome the way of get—Christians must start "giving" ourself to our God, our family, the Church and to the world at large!

Righteous Noah

Noah's life is a *model* of the embryo Christian who is called out of the world of sin to be taken into a world of peace and *rest*.

The Bible says of righteous Noah, **"...Noah was a *just* man and *perfect* in his generations and Noah walked with God" (Gen. 6:9).** He was a preacher of righteousness, warning a corrupt world:

> **And God looked upon the earth, and, behold, it was *corrupt,* for all flesh had corrupted his way upon the earth (Gen.6:12). But,...Noah being warned of God of things not seen as yet, moved with fear, prepared an ark to the saving of his house, by the which he *condemned the***

world, and became *heir* of the *righteous* which is by faith (Heb. 11:7).

Because of Noah's *righteousness*, "**...the Lord said unto Noah, come thou and all thy house into the ark; for thee have I seen righteousness before me in this generation" (Gen. 7:1).** Here again is a *picture* of the righteous life of Christ warning a despicable world of sin. Because Christ was PERFECT in His generation—His Church, like Noah, will be delivered from the coming Great Tribulation!

After one has an awakened conscience to his sinful human nature—he must REPENT and come out of the world of sin. Then he should be BAPTIZED if possible, and receive God's HOLY SPIRIT (Acts 2:38). Noah's life is a *type* of the Christian experience.

Though he lived in a corrupt world, he was not defiled by their abominable sins. His FAITH in God and RIGHTEOUS life helped him escape the world of sin through the turbulent waters of the flood. Now he was in a new *regenerated* world.

Judgment had come upon a corrupt world, but Noah had been delivered by the "baptismal waters" of the flood! He was now in a new world of peace, characterized by the *rainbow*. This *peace* and *rest* in a regenerated world also characterizes the Millennium.

The Ark was Noah's families' haven of safety even as Jesus is the Christian's liberator. Yet in the Ark, the "clean" dwelt with the "unclean" beasts, just as the *righteous* must dwell with the *wicked* after regeneration in this life!

The day of the Ark's *resting* upon the new world is also highly significant. The "seventeenth day of the seventh month" is exactly the seventeenth day of the 1st month of the holy calendar! This being the day of *Christ's resurrection* is surely no coincidence! This will be explained in detail in volume 4 under "The Days Of Noah."

REGENERATION can only come upon acceptance of Jesus through *faith* in His blood followed by *repentance*. The Holy Spirit then coming to give *regeneration*. This being given Noah through the dove, a *symbol* of peace and gentleness of the Spirit.

Symbolically, the old world of sin has been judged and *washed* clean by the regenerating power of the flood waters.

Noah's blessings of regeneration are a *type* of the joys the Church experiences as being spiritually dead, then rising with Christ!

But what happens after freedom has come?

As the saying goes, is that all there is Alfie? Most assuredly not!

For now what does Noah do? **"Noah builded an altar to the Lord, and offered burnt offerings" (Gen. 8:20).** Like the "good seed" of Abel who offered up Burnt-offerings as testimony of obedience—so does Noah! Worship of the great God does not cease now that we are free from sin—it only begins!

Faithful Abraham

Abraham's life is a *pattern* of the FAITH a newly converted Christian must have after repentance and baptism. Adam's life represented *human nature* symbolically. His son Abel *figured* the spiritual man conquering human nature through *struggle* and *sacrifice*. Noah's life *parallels* one seeking *righteousness* after being called out of the world of sin! This is the newly converted Christian who understands the sinful tendency of human nature, and strives to subdue it. He understands the need for *water baptism,* symbolic of burying the old sinful way of life and the need for God's Holy Spirit in OVERCOMING sin.

Eventually, the spiritual child grows to perceive the need of FAITH to please his great God! This life of faith is perfectly *modeled* in Abraham.

Adam, the first man, lived in a world without God's Holy Spirit and was prone to sin. Righteous Abel overcame it! Obedient Noah was delivered from it! Faithful Abraham was called out of it, notice:

> **Now the Lord had said unto Abram, Get thee out of thy country, and from thy kindred, and from thy father's house unto a land that I will shew thee: And I will make of thee a great nation, and I will bless thee, and make thy name great; and thou shalt be a blessing (Gen. 12:1,2).**

Christians are also called out of this sinful world like Abraham!

But what was Abraham's reaction? Did he argue with his Creator? Did he ask a lot of philosophical questions? Let's read what the father of the faithful did: "**So Abram departed, as the Lord had spoken unto him..**" **(vs. 4).** This took a tremendous amount of *faith*! That is why Abraham is called the "father of the faithful"?

The apostle to the Gentiles elaborates on Abraham's example to all Christians:

Even as Abraham believed God, and it was accounted to him for righteousness. Know ye therefore that they which are of faith, the same are the children of Abraham (Gal. 3:6-7).

Paul sums up the promises made to faithful Christians in verse 29: **"And if ye be Christ's, then are ye Abraham's seed, and heirs according to the promise."**

Christians who have a deep abiding *faith*, even as Abraham, will inherit the same promises made to Abraham! These promises are far wider than we can imagine and contain physical as well as spiritual blessings.

It will take *faith* to leave the "old man" in us and start a "new life" in Christ. It will take *faith* to continue this life when trials and tribulation come. Abraham left a life in Babylon, *symbolizing* religious confusion. He left the "false religious idols," and practices behind and began worshiping God in TRUTH and SPIRIT! He is the *archetype* of a Christian's faith! Christians are admonished to do the same when the call comes from God if we want to be called Abraham's children!

But inherent *faith* cannot come unless *tried* and *tested* by the crucible of time. Abraham made many mistakes before he learned to trust God completely.

Instead of trusting in the omnipotent God when they were barren, Abraham and Sarah took matters into their own hands. Sarah encouraged Abraham to have a child by Hagar, his handmaid. This son was Ishmael, *symbolic* of deeds of the law through our own human strength.

Finally, Abraham and Sarah learned to *trust* God's will and eventually conceived Isaac when Abraham was nearly one hundred years old! Isaac is a *figure* of grace, being the "spirit of sonship"!

Only when the "bond-woman" and her son are "cast out" *spiritually* can fruit be born in Sarah. This is not by her own strength, but by *faith* in God's miraculous power! The promised seed of Isaac can only come after Abraham circumcises his flesh—or "cuts off" the old life of doubt spiritually.

Isaac—The Begotten Son

Isaac is the *archetype* of the Christian experience of SONSHIP! He is "the seed of promise" which is characteristic of all repetitive Christians!

Human nature, repentance, baptism, the Holy Spirit and faith, have been the sequence of spiritual maturity leading to SONSHIP!

During Isaac's youth, he was weaned upon *milk* even as neophyte Christians must be nourished by the Church before they can digest the *meat* of God's Word! As they grow to spiritual maturity, they begin to enjoy more of the experiences of *sonship*. Isaac's very name implies "laughter." But laughter and real joy can only come after SACRIFICE and pain!

The offering up of Isaac on Mount Moriah as a sacrifice to God—contained the *inward death* and *resurrection* that all potential "sons of God" must perform.

Moriah means "chosen of God" and it was here that Isaac's father offered him up as a sacrifice to the Eternal. Here is *portrayed* in vision—the *death* and *resurrection* of Christ. Abraham and Isaac are physical *carbon copies* of God the Father and Jesus Christ in offering up his only begotten son, even as Jesus, Isaac's life was given back to him.

Every Christian must also be willing to give up his life in service to God. We have been bought and paid for by the precious blood of Jesus Christ! That is the price of sonship into the God family! But we must now, even as Isaac *symbolically* [and Christ literally], offer up our lives as *living sacrifices* to our benevolent Father. We must *crucify* our old way of life—the human nature that would drag us down into the cesspools of this rotten world!

Can you see how the path of Christians is the same as God's own Son? How His very life must be relived in us? How sacrifice is a part of God's way of love—who on a higher platform gave His only begotten Son as a *sacrifice* for sin—out of love!

As we have shown, certain key women in the Bible represent *types* of Christian principles. Sara is *symbolic* of the New Testament of *grace*, while Hagar the Old Testament of *law*. But grace only came to Sarah after she understood higher principles. This took time and patience. Only then could Sarah begin to bear in her womb! Likewise, spiritual fruit can only be born through the crucible of time, knowledge coupled with faith!

Once these lessons are gleaned, much fruit can be garnered! After Sarah's death, Abraham takes Keturah (Heb. "sweet savour") to be his wife. Then, in Abraham's hundred and thirty seventh year, he begets *many* sons after a hundred years of virtual barrenness. This is a *type* of the "spiritual sterility" in us before sonship!

Here then is the underlying principle of true sonship—UNDERSTANDING! Isaac now succeeds his father's place after *faith* has come. For after faith, comes KNOWLEDGE as Peter exhorts: **"...add to your faith virtue; and to virtue knowledge..." (2 Pet. 1:5).** Peter further incites Christians to: **"...grow in grace, and in the *knowledge* of our Lord and Savior Jesus Christ..." (2 Pet. 3:18).**

The "spirit of sonship", as represented by Isaac, knows his father's will! He is no longer under a schoolmaster! As a genuine son, full of knowledge and understanding, he can do greater things to please his father. His sacrifices are well pleasing to the Father, even as the Captain of our salvation prepared the way, and received this heavenly exaltation: **"This is my son in whom I am well pleased" (Matt. 3:17).**

Isaac was forty years old when he married Rebekah and sixty when she had Esau and Jacob (Gen. 25:26). For twenty years, Rebekah was barren—but then Isaac cried out for God's help and: **"The Lord was entreated of him, and Rebekah conceived" (Gen. 25:21).**

But no sooner does Rebekah conceive than she is confounded as: **"The children struggle with her, and she said, if it be so, why am I thus" (Gen. 25:22).** Here again we find that inward battle within us continually rising in *the spirit of sonship*. Once again, as in Cain and Abel, we see the "inward strife" of *human nature* manifested by the birth of Jacob and Esau.

But this must be so prophetically! For even as "two manners of people" were in Rebekah's womb—this is an *abstract* of the "two natures" within each son of God. Isaac is the "spirit of sonship" and Esau the "work of the flesh" (Rom. 9:7-13). For, **"As it is written, Jacob have I loved, but Esau have I hated [loved less]" (vs. 13).** Here again, *symbolically* we have "the flesh lusting against the spirit, and the spirit against the flesh" in a classic wrestle mania of human nature! (Gal. 5:17).

Looking further into Isaac's "life of sonship", we can see his bride as a *prototype* of God's Church. After the nuptial of Isaac and Rebekah, we read where she is given, **"...jewels of silver, and jewels of gold, and raiment, and ...precious things" (Gen. 24:53).**

However, glory does not come immediately, for Rebekah is barren for twenty years. Her *counterpart* in the Church is also superficially barren. Ultimately, like Rebekah, she too will begin to multiply and be adorned in glorious jewels upon our Savior's return!

Jacob The Server

Jacob's life is a *replica* of the Christian life of SERVICE! The Old Testament Fathers of Abraham, Isaac and Jacob are all *types* of the *divine* nature in man, manifesting itself in the spirit. As Christians become more knowledgeable in the faith, they pass through these progressive stages of spiritual development.

Abraham was the life of *faith*, Isaac the spirit of *sonship*, now Jacob *symbolizes* the life of SERVICE. Faith and sonship were necessary prerequisites for service or bodily acts of performance. But service cannot manifest itself without a foundation of *knowledge*.

Jacob was not the firstborn of Rebecca, yet it was he who subdued his brother Esau and received the birthright promise (Rom. 9:10-13). Even in his mother's womb, he was distinguished as being higher than his brother. *Symbolically, h*e is the *"spiritual seed"* contending with the "flesh" once again.

As in the other stages of development leading to sonship, Jacob is not without chastening. Sarah had implanted seeds of haste in the mind of Abraham by conceiving through his handmaid. Now Rebekah stirs Jacob to practice deception in securing the birthright from his brother Esau. Both were futile

THE FOOLISHNESS GOD

efforts of SELF WILL, trying to usurp the sonship through impatience and lack of faith. We must learn from these examples and not take matters into our own hands! The lesson being, God will do His own work in His own time!

Jacob's very name [supplanter] was changed to Israel [prevailer] when he wrestled with God all night with a broken thigh. This is all characteristic of the divine life of a "broken spirit" and one willing to "take hold" and prevails! His is not so much a life of faith or sonship, but that of ACTIVE INVOLVEMENT of untiring *service*, reaching heights that were thought unattainable by the elect previously.

Esau represents a life of ignominy, who sells his very inheritance for a pot of lentils. This is a life of satisfying the flesh and not the spirit. For a moment of self gratification, he is willing to give up his *eternal birthright* without the blinking of an eye. This is the life of the flesh, beckoning to be satisfied for the moment without suffering for a season. This kind of mind rationalizes, "I can't eat my birthright, and I will die without food." Esau's life, and anyone who reasons thusly according to the flesh, is considered "a profane person" in God's eyes (Heb. 12:16).

Contrariwise, Jacob's life of service and overcoming hardship is manifested in his lengthy toil for the insidious Laban. Esau and Laban are both *superficial* of the flesh WARRING against the spirit.

Jacob agrees to toil in Laban's house for seven years for his daughter Rachel. But at length, when Jacob hopes to have her, Laban deceives him by substituting his older daughter Leah:

> **It came to pass in the evening, that Laban took Leah, and brought her to Jacob, and he went in unto her. And it came to pass that in the morning, behold, it was Leah. And he said to Laban, What is this that thou hast done unto me? Did I not serve thee for Rachel? Wherefore then hast thou *beguiled* me? And Laban said, it must not be so done in our country to give the younger before the firstborn (Gen. 29:23-26).**

What a dirty trick!

But Jacob served Laban seven more years, in drought by day and frost by night in order to have the love of his life (Gen. 29: 27;31:40).

This was truly a life of dedication and service!

As Hagar and Sarah are *archetypes* of the dispensation of *law* and *grace*, so are their successors in Leah and Rachel.

When Jacob's amazing life comes to an end, we can understand that the "spirit of service" has only come about as a result of his *weakness*. Only when Jacob is made weak by having his thigh out of joint does he become strong! Only when he becomes *humbled* in service for Leah, does he become stronger and more determined to have Rachel.

The apostle Paul reaffirmed this state of mind: **"...my strength is made perfect in weakness. Most godly therefore will I rather glory in my infirmities, that the power of Christ may rest upon me" (11 Cor. 12:9).**

This is the lesson of service—We must HUMBLE ourselves, and serve God in faith, not out of our human strength!

Joseph The Ruler

Joseph's life depicts the epitome of a Christian's reward! His was a life of suffering and trial—afterward richly rewarded by being given *power* to RULE!

After a life consisting of human nature, repentance, baptism, the Holy Spirit, faith, sonship and service—comes power to rule! These are the *seven* stages in the evolutionary process of attaining sonship!

Even as a youth, Joseph had dreams of *rulership*. Certainly everyone is familiar with the story of how Jacob [Israel] loved Joseph more than his other children and the coat of many colors he had made for him. Remember also, how Joseph had dreams of ruling over his brothers some day (Gen. 37:3-10).

Because of this, Joseph's brothers hated him and conspired to kill him. But Reuben intervened and the plot changed, as Judah had a brain storm to sell Joseph into bondage instead (verses 18-28).

While in Egypt, Joseph became highly favored by Pharaoh as a result of interpreting his dreams. Eventually Joseph became second only to Pharaoh in authority in the land. Afterwards he would help his starving family during a famine throughout the land.

Here is a life not of faith—for Joseph left his home not of his own accord, but by *faith* through conspiracy. Nor does he *serve* day and night to attain sonship as did Jacob. Although Joseph is none of these per se, his life definitely contains overtures of these virtues. His is a life of SUFFERING in the dungeons of Egypt before he is allowed to rule! This is the price all Christians must be willing to pay for rulership in the family of God!

One can readily see in Joseph the *parallels* to the life of Christ, and the path all Christians must walk! Recall how there have been two ways of life—[law and grace] *pictured* by successors of woman. Sarah and Hagar's seed produced Isaac and Ishmael. Rebekah's seed propagated Jacob and Esau. Jacob sired the twelve children of Israel through Rachel and Leah (Gen. 35:22-26). Leah's son Judah represents law as culminating in the Jews. Rachel's firstborn [Joseph] *symbolizes* the seed of promise and rulership!

Here is a *picture* prophecy of the life of Christ! Just as Joseph's twelve brothers [representing the nation of Israel] mocked and wanted to kill him—the Jews conspired to kill Christ. It was Christ's own people who rejected Him! Christ was stripped of His *robe* and sold for 30 pieces of silver, even as Joseph was rent of his *multi-colored coat* and sold in Egyptian slavery for twenty pieces of silver (Gen. 37:28). Both were cast into prison by trumped up charges—before appearing before the magistrates of the land. Joseph appeared before Pharaoh, while Christ was sentenced by Pilot.

But after a life of suffering and endurance—both were EXALTED above measure. Joseph and Christ became RULERS over the very people that conspired to kill them!

This also parallels the life of man Christians! Many Christians have been cast off by friends and family. Christians have been persecuted unjustly and been imprisoned both physically and spiritually by the world around us. But the day is fast approaching when we, like our heavenly Brother—shall be *exalted* to rulership over the nations with Joseph! (Rev. 20:6).

SEVEN STAGES OF SONSHIP

Summary

In a word, the lives of the patriarchs of old are but *cameos* of entering the divine family of God! God allows us to look at the physical to comprehend the spiritual. Given an analogy, because Mohammed cannot go to the mountain—the mountain of God's heavenly sanctuary has come to Mohammed in *replica*.

Through the lives of Adam, Abel, Noah, Abraham, Isaac, Jacob and Joseph—a finer detail of God's blueprint plan of salvation has been revealed to us.

Adam is the *human nature* in all of us that must be *repented* of as characterized by his son Abel. Abel realizes the need for repentance, as he struggles with it in the form of wicked Cain. He realizes that sacrifice is the way back to God through repentance!

Noah *symbolizes* the life of *regeneration* after repentance *through baptism* and receiving God's *Holy Spirit* to fight the battle of human nature. Abraham's life is one of *faith*, utilizing this fruit of God's Holy Spirit (Gal. 5:22). Once faith comes, *knowledge* must be added in order to avoid the pitfalls of human nature and to receive God's blessings—this spiritually represents Isaac.

Through Jacob's life we realize how to apply that knowledge toward *service*. Finally, in Joseph the reward of RULERSHIP is attained as a result of applying these *seven* stages of sonship in our lives!

The Good and The Bad Seed

Throughout the entirety of the Bible, like a fine thread interwoven into a web—are described two ways of life. The web of *life* is pictured in the "good seed" where the web of *death* is patterned after the "bad seed." From Genesis to Revelation, we shall witness this fabric of good and bad seed in the *prototypes* of men and women!

The "bad seed" began in the garden of Eden as the serpent [Satan] beguiled the woman. This was the *archetype* battle between Satan and Christ's Church [woman] to exist throughout the ages!

In the dispensations of God's plan to follow, we will recognize the two sons of Adam [Cain and Abel]; the two sons of Abraham

[Isaac and Ishmael]; the two sons of Isaac [Jacob and Esau] as these twain seeds of "good" and "evil."

One characterizes the natural carnal seed as culminating in the JEW—the other seed is the righteous spiritual seed resulting in the Christian Church! Oftentimes the trilogy of Adam, Satan and Eve will be played over in other lives which serve as models. Yet each with the same theme. Only the names of the characters change—but the same play continues!

There are times when the role of the serpent is cast in Pharaoh, Goliath, Herod and the False Prophet; etc. Christ's role is played by Adam, Abraham and David; etc. The Church's role is modeled by woman starting with Eve, Sarah and Rebekah; etc.

Satan continually worked through several woman in the Bible to entice the man to sin, as he appeals to their human nature. In fact, women are often used *superficially* of human nature as it tries to lure the man to sin.

From here on out their names will change and their character will be revealed through *symbol*, *emblem* or *type*. But the plan is still the same! Whether we speak of Adam, Enoch, Noah, Abraham, Joseph or David—they are all *types* of Christ! Whether we speak of Cain, Nimrod, Pharaoh, Saul, Goliath, Herod, or the False Prophet—they are all *types* of evil influenced by Satan!

How sweet is God's truth!

Here then in the first book of the Bible is God's master plan of salvation revealed!

Only the characters and their names will change in the remainder of the book. But the plan or outline is established here! Namely, the first Adam, his wife Eve, Satan the devil, and Jesus [the 2nd Adam] his redeemer.

The following are the *counterparts* of our original characters throughout Biblical history:

SEVEN STAGES OF SONSHIP

Christ/nature	Satan/nature	Church/nature
Adam	serpent	Eve
Abel	Cain	—
Enoch	—	Methusaleh
Noah	Ham	Shem
Abraham	Pharaoh	Sarah
Isaac	Ishmael	Hagar/Rebekah
Jacob	Esau	Rachel
Samson	Philistines	Delilah
Joseph	his brothers	Egyptian seducer
Moses	Pharaoh	Israel
David	Goliath/Saul	Bathsheba
Jesus	Herod	Mary

Chapter Fifteen

GOD'S PLAN REVEALED BY THE OLD COVENANT

The Old Covenant was written to create an anticipation of and pave the way for, the coming of Jesus Christ. It is the story of the Hebrew nation, dealing largely with events and urgencies of its own times. But all through the story there runs unceasing expectancy and prevision of the coming of ONE MAJESTIC PERSON, who would RULE and bless the whole world. This person, long before He arrived, came to be known as Wonderful, Counsellor, the Mighty God, the Prince of Peace (Isa. 9:6)—THE MESSIAH!

By the time we come to the end of the Old Covenant, the entire story of Christ has been pre-written and *pre-figured* in language and *symbol*, which, taken as a whole, cannot refer to any other person in history!

Let us take a closer look at the books of the Old Covenant [in summary] that prophesied the coming of the Messiah, His death and God's MASTER PLAN for mankind.

The Old Covenant was written for our example, so we could benefit from the mistakes that were made by the ancient Israelites. The physical examples given can help us to understand spiritual lessons as Paul exhorts: **"For whatsoever things were written aforetime were written for our learning, that we through patience and comfort of the scriptures might have hope" (Rom. 15:4).** In essence, the apostle Paul is emphasizing this important truth! The things that happened to ancient Israel were for our example and learning (1 Cor. 10:6).

The Father of Many Nations

Gen. 12:3   "In thee Abraham shall all the nations of the earth be blessed."

18:18   Here is a clear definite statement, repeated three times, to Abraham, that in him God was founding a nation for the express purpose of, through the nation—blessing all nations. Christ was to become the "seed" out of Abraham that the nations of the earth would receive salvation through! See also (Gen. 22:18).

The Promise Repeated

Gen. 26:4   Made three times to Abraham, it is here repeated to Isaac, and then to Jacob, that their seed would be a blessing to all nations. See also (Gen. 28:14).

To Rule All Nations

Gen. 49:10,11   "The Sceptre shall not depart from Judah ...till *Shiloh* come, and unto Him shall the gathering of the people be." He washed His garments in the blood of grapes. Here is the first clear, definite prediction that ONE PERSON would arise in Abraham's nation to *rule* all nations. Shiloh, He whose right it is. He would appear in the tribe of Judah. His garments washed in

GOD'S OLD COVENANT PLAN

the blood of grapes, may be a metaphorical fore-hint of His crucifixion.

The Star

Num. 24:17,19   There shall come a *star* out of Jacob. A Sceptre shall rise out of Israel. He shall have dominion.

A Prophet like unto Moses

Deut. 18:15-19   God would raise up a prophet like unto Moses, through whom God would speak to mankind. Evidently, another characterization of the Shiloh and the Star.

To Lead His People into The Promised Land

Joshua   This book seems to have no direct prediction of the Messiah, though Joshua himself is thought, in sense, to have been *typical* of Jesus. The names are the same, "Jesus" being the Greek form of the Hebrew "Joshua." As Joshua led Israel into the Promised Land, so Jesus will lead His people into the spiritual Promised Land!

A Type of David

1 Sam. 16   David was anointed King over Israel. From here on David is the central figure of Old Testament history. The most specific and most abundant of all Messianic prophecies cluster around his name. Abraham was the founder of the Messianic nation—David was founder of the Messianic family within the nation!

David Promised An Eternal Throne

11 Sam. 7-16   "Thy throne shall be established forever." Here begins a long line of promises that David's family should reign forever over God's people.

Immanuel—"God With Us"

Isa. 7:13,14   "O house of David...a virgin shall conceive, and shall bear a Son, and shall call his name Immanuel." This seems to say that some one, to be called Immanuel, will be born in David's family, of a virgin: evidently meaning the same personage as the Branch and the Wonderful Child (4:2; 11:1; 9:6). The name Immanuel implies the deity of the child, which means "God with Us." Plainly, Christ's virgin birth and god-head as Messiah are envisioned. This same title is quoted in (Matthew 1:23) in reference to our Savior.

The Wonderful Child

Isa. 9:1,2,6,7   "In Galilee...the people have seen a great light." "For unto us a Child is born, unto us a Son is given: and the government shall be upon His shoulder: and His name shall be called Wonderful, Counsellor, Mighty God, Everlasting Father, Prince of Peace. Of the increase of his government and peace there shall be no end, upon the throne of David." What a beautiful description of Jesus Christ!

The Branch of The Lord

Isa. 4:2-6   "In that day shall the Branch of the Lord be beautiful and glorious... A cloud by day...and a fire by night... A Tabernacle...and a place of refuge..." Here is a *fore-picture* of Jesus Christ springing up out of the family tree of David as a "Branch" growing up out of a stump— eventually becoming a towering Tree that would protect His people.

The Branch to Rule

Isa, 11:1-10   "There shall come forth a Rod out of the *stem* of Jesse, a Branch shall grow out of his roots." Jesse was David's father, and out of his loins would arise a shoot [Christ] that would RULE the world!

The Eternal King

Psalms   King David had been attributed to being the chief writer of the book of Psalms. This inspiring book contains many gems which predict the eternal reign of the Messiah to be born through David's family. It is evident from reading the Psalms, that they can be speaking of none other than the personage who 1,000 years later became Jesus Christ!

The Lord's Anointed

Ps. 2   "The Lord's anointed...I have set my King upon my holy hill of Zion...Thou art my Son...I shall give thee the nations for thine inheritance...Blessed are all they that put their trust in Him."

To Speak in Parables

Ps. 78:2   "I will open my mouth in parables." Jesus quoted this Old Testament verse in (Matthew 13:34,35) in fulfillment of this prophecy. This was to become His chief method of teaching His disciples.

To Suffer Gall and Vinegar

Ps. 69:21   "They gave me gall for my food, and in my thirst they gave me vinegar to drink." This prophecy was also fulfilled in the sufferings of Jesus Christ (Matt. 27:34,48).

To be Rejected by Israel

Ps. 111:22   "The Stone the builders rejected is become Head of the corner." Israel as well as world leaders rejected the Messiah. Jesus referred to Himself as the Stone the builders rejected (Matt. 21:42-44).

To be Betrayed by a Friend

Ps. 41:9   "My old familiar friend, in whom I trusted, who did eat my bread, lifted up his heel against me." The *prototype* of this event was that of David's trusted friend Ahithophel, while Judas was the *antitype*. Perhaps the original *prototype* of this event was that of the archangel Lucifer who once ate at God's table and later rebelled against God. Recall it was Satan who actually entered into Judas Iscariot!

To be Crucified

Ps. 22:1   Psalm 22 contains a *fore-picture* of the crucifixion 1,000 years before it

	happened. Notice carefully the wording. "My God, my God, why hast thou forsaken Me?" These were Jesus' last words to His Father (Matt. 27:46).
7-8	"All that see Me laugh Me to scorn, saying...He trusted in God, let God deliver Him." This is an exact quote of Christ's enemies as He hung on the cross (Matt. 27:43).
16	"They pierce My hands and feet." This was indicative of crucifixion as the manner of Christ's death (Jn. 20:20,25).
18	"They part my garments among them, and cast lots upon My vesture." Even this minute greedy detail was fulfilled to the letter by Christ's murderers (Matt. 27:35). Here we find a *picture forecast* of the death of Christ in intricate detail recorded one thousand years in advance!

The exact date of Crucifixion Foretold

Dan. 9:24-27	"From the going forth of the commandment to restore and rebuild Jerusalem unto the Messiah, the Prince, shall be seven weeks and three score and two weeks... and after the three score and two weeks...in the midst of the one week shall Messiah be cut off... to make reconciliation for iniquity and bring in everlasting righteousness."
	Through this prophecy, the prophet Daniel had given the exact date of the Messiah's death. After a 3 1/2 year public ministry, Jesus was "cut off" in the middle of a [prophetic] week—Jesus was crucified.

The Passover

Exodus 12

The deliverance of the nation of Israel out of Egyptian bondage was a *fore-picture* of the redemption through the death of Christ for every Christian. Christ became "the Lamb of God" who expired on the cross, at a Passover Feast, bringing eternal deliverance from sin: "For even Christ our Passover is sacrificed for us" (1 Cor. 5:7-8).

The Passover, Nisan 14, is a memorial of the death angel's *passing over* the homes of the Israelites in Egypt and sparing the firstborn. The sacrifice of the Lamb was a *shadow* of Christ, the true Passover Lamb and His sacrifice for our sins on that day. The Passover is now a memorial of both events (Lev. 23:5-6).

The Messiah's Sufferings

Isaiah 53:3

"He is despised and rejected of men; *a man of sorrows* and acquainted with grief...He hath borne our griefs and carried our sorrows...He was *wounded* for our transgressions, and *bruised* for our iniquities...with His *stripes* we are healed.

7

"The Lord hath laid on Him the iniquity of us all...He was *oppressed*, He was *afflicted,* yet He opened not His mouth. He is brought as a lamb to the slaughter...He poured out His soul unto *death*...and bore the sin of many...

10   "It pleased the Lord to bruise Him...to make His soul an offering for sin...and the pleasure of the Lord shall prosper in His hand...By knowledge of Him shall many be justified."

His Resurrection
The Feast of Unleavened Bread

Ps. 16:10   "Thou wilt not...suffer thy Holy One to see corruption." This is quoted in (Acts 2:27,31) as referring to the resurrection of Christ. The Feast, Nisan 15, commemorated the night in which God brought Israel out of Egypt. It was an annual Sabbath and the first of the seven days of Unleavened Bread.

These seven days began at sundown and continued through at sundown, the seventh day, Nisan 21, also being an annual Sabbath. These seven days depicted our complete deliverance [*seven* denoting *completeness*] from our natural tendency to commit sin.

The Wave Sheaf offering took place on the first day of the week [Sunday] after the weekly Sabbath during the days of Unleavened Bread. It *pictured* Christ, the "first of the firstfruits" from the dead, being accepted by the Father before the early harvest [the Christians of these last 2,000 years] could be reaped (Lev. 23:5-6).

The Light of the World

Isa. 60:2   "Darkness shall cover the earth."

1	"Arise, shine, for the light is come, and the glory of the Lord is risen upon thee."
20	"The Lord shall be thine everlasting light, and the days of thy mourning shall be ended."

The Gospel Era—Pentecost—Firstfruits

Joel 2:28,32	"I will pour out my Spirit upon all flesh...whosoever shall call on the name of the Lord shall be delivered." This is the time period before Christ's second coming in which the Gospel would be preached throughout the world. Pentecost, the 50th day from the day on which the Wave Sheaf was offered, is always on a Sunday during Sivan, the 3rd month; but the day of the month varies from year to year and must be counted.
	Pentecost *symbolized* the coming of the Holy Spirit and thus is a *memorial* of the *beginning* of the New Testament Church. In a larger sense it depicts the entire time of the New Testament Church from the arrival of the Holy Spirit till the soon to occur second coming of Christ—when the reaping of the first harvest of souls will occur (Lev. 23:15).

The Second Coming of Christ—Trumpets

Isa. 40:5	"The glory of the Lord shall be revealed, and all flesh shall see it together."
10	"The Lord God will come with a strong hand, and His arm shall rule for Him,"
11	"He shall feed His flock like a Shepherd: He shall gather the lambs with His arms,

and carry them in His bosom, and shall gently lead those that are with young." The Feast of Trumpets, the first day of the 7th month, points forward to that day when the last trumpet will sound and the dead in Christ shall rise to meet Him at His second coming. Christ will then put down the Devil's rule and set up His glorious Kingdom, the Kingdom of God, at Jerusalem, to spread progressively over all the peoples of the earth (Lev. 23:23-25).

The Day of Atonement

Lev. 16

Two goats were used in this ceremony. One was killed as a Sin-offering. The high priest laid his hands on the head of the other, called the scapegoat, confessing over him the people's sin. Then the scapegoat was led away, and let go in the wilderness.

Nine days after the Feast of Trumpets, on the 10th of Tishri is the Day of Atonement, *picturing* that day in the future when the responsibility for sin will be placed justly upon the head of the instigator of it— Satan the Devil! Mankind will then become "at one" with God or in complete accord. All sins having been forgiven and forgotten. The 10th of Tirshri was observed as a day of fasting, a day in which Israel "afflicted their souls" by abstinence from food and drink (Lev. 23:26-32).

The Millennium—The Feast of Tabernacles

Ezek. 47:1

"In visions of God...waters issued from under the Temple eastward.

12	A man who had a measuring line...measured a *thousand* cubits, and caused me to pass through the waters, waters that were up to the ankle... "Again he measured a *thousand*...and waters were up to the knees... Another *thousand*, and waters were up to the loins... "Afterward he measured a *thousand,* and it was a river that could not be passed through. And he said to me, Son of man, these waters shall go on and on to the sea. Whithersoever the waters come *everything shall live.*"

This pictures the Millennium [a *thousand year*] period of reeducation to truth and the main harvest of souls resurrected to eternal life! The Feast of Tabernacles began on Tishri 15 at sundown and continued seven days through Tishri 21, the first day being an annual Sabbath. These seven days *picture the Millennium* when the resurrected Christians, then immortal, will rule the earth under Christ (Duet. 16:13-17; Lev. 23:33-35).

Gentiles to be Included

Hosea 1:10	"In the place where it was said, Ye are not my people, it shall be said unto them, Ye are Sons of the living God," This shows the Messiah's Family [Elohim] will include all nations including Gentiles!

The Kingdom

Ezek. 34:22-24	"My servant David shall be shepherd of my flock....King over them...and be their prince forever."

37:24,25   This pictures the Millennium period of Christ's 1,000 year Kingdom, with David king over the House of Israel.

Resurrection of the Dead

Isa. 25:6-9   In this mountain of the Lord...will swallow up death in victory and wipe away tears from off all faces."

26:1,19   "In that day...thy dead shall live, my dead body shall rise...and the earth cast forth the dead." This *fore-pictures* the final event in the plan of Salvation, even after the Great White Throne harvest of souls, when death is swallowed up in victory, and the beginning of the New Heaven and New Earth.

The Last Great Day

Lev. 23:33-35   The day following the Feast of Tabernacles is called the Last Great Day and is a *symbol* of still a more joyous occasion in the future. The rest of the dead, those never having had their eyes opened to the truth in their former life, will be resurrected to mortality.

This will be a time when God's Holy Spirit will open the eyes of the spiritually blind. This day, like the Feast of Tabernacles pictures the Millennium, and those who overcome with the help of God's Holy Spirit will then be given immortality.

Eternal Life

Gen. 2:7-9   A tree of life *symbolic* of God's Holy Spirit was placed in the garden of Eden.

Gen. 3:22	Eternal life was *pictured* by the tree of life.
Rev. 2:7	"...to him that overcomes will I grant to eat of the *tree of life,* which is in the midst of the paradise of God."
Rev. 22:12-14	Christians will have a right to the *tree of life* because they keep His Commandments.
Deut. 28:15	God told ancient Israel, like Adam and Eve, two ways of life are set before them—blessings of [eternal life] or cursing that would lead to ETERNAL DEATH. The Choice was theirs—but, they must CHOOSE!
Gen. 3:7	Both Adam and Eve's eyes were opened [they understood] and they were naked (spiritually). It took God's sacrifice of an animal to clothe them.
Rev. 3:17	God uses clothing as an analogy to being naked spiritually or a lack of spiritual covering. God had to make a sacrifice [*symbolic* of Christ] to clothe the spiritual nakedness of Christians.

Calling

Gen. 2:18	Adam and Eve were the first human beings *called* to know about God's plan.
Gen. 7:1	God *called* Noah out of the corrupt world in which he lived.
Gen. 12	Abraham was *called* by the Eternal out of Babylon (confusion).

GOD'S OLD COVENANT PLAN

Gen. 19	Lot was *called* out of perverted Sodom (sin).
Ex. 1:7-22	Israel was *called* out of Egypt which is *symbolic* of sin and is called spiritually Sodom (Rev. 11:8).
Ex. 5:1	God was *calling* His people out of sin—"let my people go."

Repentance

Ex. 6:9	Israel failed to listen to Moses, and God called them a "stiffnecked" people.
Ex. 13:21	The Eternal led the way for Israel before they were baptized [in the Red Sea] just as He does Christians.
Ex. 14:17	God says of His vengeance: "...I will get me honour over Pharaoh [a *type* of Satan] and upon all his hosts (demons)."
Lev. 4	Israelites that sinned had to bring an animal to be offered as a sacrifice. They had to place their hands upon the head of the animal [*typifying* the transfer of their own sin] being transferred to the sacrifice [Christ] and receiving forgiveness.
Heb. 9:11-14	The sacrifice of Christ purges the conscience of Christians.
Ex. 12:13	The blood of the Lamb saved ancient Israel physically, even as Christ's blood saves Christians spiritually.
Lev. 13:1	People with leprosy were branded "unclean" in God's eyes until their *scab* went away. Christians who are sinning without repentance in God's Church are

	also "unclean" spiritually and are not to be fellowshipped with (1 Cor. 5:1-6). They are to be spiritually quarantined!
Lev. 13:47-55	If the leprosy didn't change, like unrepentant Christians—their garments were to be "burned" with FIRE! This is *symbolic* of the burning in the "lake of fire" for those who commit the unpardonable sin.
Lev. 20:9	Any Israelite who cursed his parents was to be put to death. This analogy holds true for those who curse their spiritual Father and Mother—God and His Church!

The Holy Spirit and the Unpardonable Sin

Gen. 25:30-34	Essau sold his birthright for a pot of lentils. This illustrates a New Testament principle for Christians. Our eternal birthright is the Kingdom of God—but we will receive it only upon repentance.
Heb. 12:15-17	Christians can lose their spiritual BIRTHRIGHT even as Essau, if they are foolish! Rueben lost his birthright through sin!
Num. 16	Korah's rebellion is *typical* of those who *rebel* against God's Church and its ministry. Korah rebelled against Moses and was swallowed up in an earthquake!
Num. 14:6-11	The closer the Israelites got to the *promised land*, the more they rebelled. This is analogous to Christians who will rebel against God's ways as we approach the conclusion of this age. Before Christians get ready to inherit God's *eternal* promised land—more trials and

GOD'S OLD COVENANT PLAN

	more rebellion will come upon the Church!
Deut.	The book of Deuteronomy is called "the 2nd law" because the 10 Commandments were *restated* just before the Israelites were to enter the physical promised land. This was 40 years after their parents were rejected to go into the promised land because of *rebellion*. Joshua, a *type* of Christ was their leader.
	This generation no longer ate manna, but meat. This is analogous to the "strong meat" (Heb. 5:14) that should be in a Christian's diet by studying God's Word. God's Word is where we learn how to "love our neighbor" as well as "obey" God. During the Feast of Tabernacles, depicting God's Kingdom on the earth—*strong drink* and *meat* were emphasized (Deut. 14:26).
Deut. 10:12-13	God's full requirement for Israel was "...to *fear* the Lord thy God, to walk in all His ways, and to love Him, and to serve the Lord thy God with all thy heart and with all thy soul."
Deut. 33:29	God told Israel, as He does zealous Christians: "Happy art thou, O Israel: who is like unto thee, O people, *saved* by the Lord, the shield of thy help, and who is the sword of thy excellency! And thine enemies will be found liars unto thee; and thou shalt tread upon their high places."
Isa. 59:16-17	"For he put on righteousness as a breastplate, and an helmet of salvation upon his head; and he put on the garments

THE FOOLISHNESS GOD

of vengeance for clothing, and was clad with *zeal* as a cloak."

Baptism

1 Cor. 10:1-2   The apostle Paul informs us that the crossing of the Red Sea by the Israelites was a *type* of Baptism. Notice: "And were all *baptized* unto Moses in the Cloud and in the [Red] sea.."

Ex. 14:19   Here we read where the angel who had gone before, showing the Israelites the way, now went behind them and their enemy, protecting them. And then God parted the waters of the Red Sea: "...and the waters were a WALL unto them on their right hand, and on their left" (verse 23). The LIVING WATERS of God are a WALL to Christians (Jn. 7:37-39).

The Holy Spirit

Ex. 28:30   The high priest of Israel had to wear the Urim and Thurim upon his heart [stones of *light* and *perfection*—Josephus] when he went into the holy place to ask for God's will. This "light" and "perfection" was *symbolic* of God's Holy Spirit which Israel did not receive as yet. They were a physical nation and decisions were made in a physical way. Today, God's ministers provide "light" and "truth" to His people.

Heb. 8:5; 9:23   The Tabernacle was patterned after God's throne in heaven. It was a *temporary dwelling place* where God dwelt and His Holy Spirit. See also (Rom. 1:19-20).

Christ's Return

Isa. 9:16 — Isaiah, Daniel, Job and Enoch all knew of God's plan in which Christ would return to the earth and set up God's government. See also (Dan. 7:13,14; Job 19:25-26; Jude 14).

The New Covenant

Isa. 55:3; 61:8
Jer. 31:33 — The New Covenant with Israel prophesied.

Isa. 56:5; 62:2 — Israel to receive a new everlasting name. See also (Rev. 3:12).

God to dwell with them Forever

Isa. 35:2; 60:19-20 — God will finally dwell with His children once again FOREVER! He will be the LIGHT instead of the moon and sun.

Summary

The Old Covenent is replete with line upon line, dot upon dot, stating the purpose of God's plan through the nation of Israel.

Israel was founded for the sole purpose of blessing all nations through Abraham's seed which eventually culminated in Jesus Christ!

The personage who ultimately became Jesus Christ was called *Shiloh*, and was to arise in the tribe of Judah. He was called *Star* and was to *rule* all nations—even as a star [the sun] rules the day. He was destined to be a *prophet* like unto Moses, through whom God would perform *mighty miracles* and speak to mankind.

Over and over He is called a King, to ascend in David's lineage, to be called the Branch, The Prince, The Anointed One, God's First-Born, Wonderful, Mighty God, and Prince of Peace!

Christ's virgin birth, coming, death and resurrection was also foretold thousands of years before it actually happened!

THE FOOLISHNESS GOD

The Messiah was to *speak in parables* and be rejected by His own people. He would be spit upon, mocked and *betrayed* by a friend for thirty pieces of silver. Then He would be led as a lamb to the slaughter.

It was prophesied in the Old Testament, that the Messiah would proclaim salvation unto the Jew and Gentile alike by starting a New Covenant. This New Covenant would guarantee the Holy Spirit which would enable one to accept Jesus as their personal Savior and to be mindful of God's way of love.

How could this fantastic *composite* of Christ's life and work be written centuries before it occurred by many different writers? How could anyone have known the intimate details of Christ's life and death ages in advance?

Simple!

The miracle of the ages can only be explained by the simple fact that ONE SUPREME MASTER HAND inspired the writing! The following table is from the *Companion Bible*, Ap. 3.

Genesis finds its Complement in Revelation

1. Genesis the book of the beginning.	1. Apocalypse, the book of the end.
2. The earth created (1:1).	2. The earth passed away (21:1).
3. Satan's first rebellion.	3. Satan's final rebellion
4. Sun, moon and stars for Earth's government (1:14-16).	4. Sun, moon, and stars, connected with Earth's judgment (6:13; 8:12; 16:8).
5. Sun to govern the day (1:16).	5. No need of the sun (21:20).
6. Darknss called night (1:5).	6. "No night there" (22:5).
7. Waters called seas (1:10).	7. "No more sea" (21:1).
8. A river for Earth's blessing 14).	8. A river for the Earth
9. Man in God's image (1:26).	9. Man headed by one in Satan's image (13).
10. Entrance of sin (3).	10. Development and end of sin (21,22).

GOD'S OLD COVENANT PLAN

11."No more curse" (22,3).	11. Curse pronounced (3:14,17).
12 "No more death" (21:4).	12. Death entered (3:19).
13. Cherubim, finally mentioned in connection with man (4:6).	13. Cherubim, first mentioned in connection with man (3:24).
14. Man restored (22).	14. Man driven out from Eden (3:24).
15."Right to the Tree of Life" (22:14).	15. Tree of life guarded (3:24).
16. No more sorrow (21:4).	16. Sorrow and suffering enter (3:17).
17. Man's religion, luxury, art, and science in their full glory, judged and destroyed by God (18).	17. Man's religion, art and science, resorted to for enjoyment apart from God (4)
(18). The Beast, the great rebel, a king and manifested anti-God the river of Babyon (13-18).	18. Nimrod, a great rebel and king, and hidden anti-God, the founder of Babylon (10:8,9).

19. A flood from God to destroy an evil generation (6-9).	19. A flood from Satan to destroy an elect generation (12).
20. The Bow a token of God's covenant with the Earth (9.13).	20. The Bow, betokening God's remembrance of His covenant with the Earth (4:3; 10:1).
21. Sodom and Egypt, the place of corruption and temptation (13,19).	21. Sodom and Egypt again [spiritually representing Jerusalem) (11:8).
22. A confederacy against Abraham's people overthrown (10	22. A confederate against Abraham's seed overthrown (12).
23. Marriage of first Adam (2:18-21).	23. Marriage of last Adam (19).
24. A bride sought for Abraham's son [Isaac] and found (24).	24. A Bride made ready and brought to Abraham's Son (19:9). See (Matt. 1:1).
25. Two angels acting for God on behalf of His people (19).	25. Two witnesses acting for God on behalf of His people (11).
26. A promised seed to possess the gate of his enemies (22:17).	26. The promised seed coming into possession (11:18).
27. Man's dominion ceased and Satan's begun (3:24).	27. Satan's dominion ended, and man's restored (22).
28. The old serpent causing sin, suffering, and death (3:1).	28. The old serpent bound for 1,000 years (20:1-3).
29. The doom of the old serpent pronounced (3:15).	29. The doom on the old serpent executed (20:10).
30. Sun, moon, and stars, associate with Israel (37:9).	30. Sun, moon, and stars associated again with Israel (12).

Chapter Sixteen

GOD'S PLAN REVEALED BY THE FIRST FIVE BOOKS

There is a very interesting *similarity* between the experiences of the ancient Israelites and New Testament Christians—that weaves a fine thread throughout the Bible. The first five books of the Bible show the *parallel* between the experiences of the ancient Israelites and New Testament Christians.

It took 50 years for the Israelites to cross the river Jordan after coming out of Egypt. Israel could not truly enjoy life until they crossed the river Jordan into the promised land.

Crossing the river Jordan had a deep *spiritual* meaning as to *why* Jesus was baptized in the Jordan river by John the Baptist! John represented the difference between the Old and New Testament—REPENTANCE!

Recall how WATER is *symbolic* of REPENTANCE! The very first miracle Jesus performed was to change WATER into WINE! At the Passover, Jesus explained that wine represented His blood *symbolically*.

After REPENTANCE, a person wanting to become a Christian, should if possible be BAPTIZED in WATER, as foretold by the apostle Peter on the day of Pentecost (Acts 2:38). One only begins this process after accepting the BLOOD of Jesus Christ as their personal Savior!

The Feast of Tabernacles *pictures* the rejoicing of the sons of God crossing the Jordan into the promised land spiritually!

Genesis: The book of *Genesis* records the CALLING of Abraham to receive a special BIRTHRIGHT. This calling and promise culminated in "the children of Israel." Christians are called to inherit a special BIRTHRIGHT promise also—that of inheriting the Kingdom of God. Abraham is the father of the Christian spiritually.

Exodus: The book of *Exodus* records how Moses helped the children of Israel out of Egyptian slavery. After eating the Passover *(symbolic* of accepting Christ as their deliverer from sin) Moses led the Israelites out of Egypt. Egypt *symbolizes* the world of sin and Israel is *symbolic* of a Christian coming out of the world of SIN and bondage. A Christian's taskmaster is the world pulling him down, human nature and Satan the devil! The Israelites were actually BAPTIZED in the Red sea (1 Cor. 10-12).

Christians, like Israel were to be a special peculiar people to God on earth. A kingdom of priests and kings (Ex. 19:6; 1 Pet.2:9; Rev. 1:6, 5:10). That is why Christians are being judged by the Royal Law (Jas. 2:8)—Royalty is for KINGS!

Perhaps the greatest lesson Christians can learn from Israel's experience as recorded in Exodus is FAITH! Three days after Israel crossed the Red Sea and went into the wilderness of Shur, they found no water (15:22).

When they finally found water at Marah, it was *bitter* and unfit for drinking (vs. 23). Israel began to complain to Moses, saying, "What shall we drink"? (vs. 24). God heard their cry and gave then water (vs.25).

Approximately six weeks later, Israel again was without water and began to complain once again (17:1).

Three months after leaving Egypt, Israel came to Mount Sinai (19:1). If one follows a Bible map of the route Israel took leaving Egypt—it is quite apparent that this route was a much longer one than logically necessary. God knew what He was doing however, for by going this longer route, Israel was spared having to go through enemy territory.

The lesson to be learned here for Christians, is that we must be patient and FAITHFUL to God's chosen servants who are guiding His work today. Like Israel, Christians must ENDURE hardships, and most importantly follow God's leaders into the spiritual promised land!

Leviticus: The book of *Leviticus* shows the relationship of God to His people and to each other.

Israel was told to get SIN out of the camp and to "love their neighbor as their self " (19:18).

The dietary laws of chapter eleven told Israel what to eat and what not to eat. This *symbolized* the fact that Christians need to survive on spiritual [clean] food, and can get sick and die from wrong doctrines that can defile their mind (unclean food). People were classified as either "clean" or "unclean" depending upon their spiritual condition (5-6). Those who had sinned were "unclean" until they repented and offered a sacrifice.

Individuals with leprosy were unclean till their scab went away (13:1) This was *typical* of those who leave the Church and go back to their old sinful ways. In God's eyes they are "spiritually unclean" until repentant. In a type of quarantine, the apostle Paul told faithful Christians to avoid them (1 Cor. 5:1-6). Furthermore, if the leper's scab didn't change [like people] who are unclean—their garments [flesh] will be burned! (13:47-55).

Numbers: The book of *Numbers* deals with the problems [TRIALS] the Israelites experienced in the wilderness. They were given just enough food and water to get through their trial. Israel had to *depend* on God to lead and guide them by following the "pillar of fire" in the cloud (9:15-18).

Their *survival* depended upon their OBEDIENCE to God. The Israelites kept hearing a lot of promises, "You're going to go into the promised land" but saw no immediate delivery— they had to have FAITH!

Likewise, Christians must go through many trials, and, in FAITH, be obedient to God before entering into eternal life!

Deuteronomy: The book of *Deuteronomy* known as "the 2nd Law" was given to the children of the first generation of rebellious Israelites. The promise given to Abraham, Isaac and Jacob was about to be fulfilled. Now, the Israelites had learned to keep God's laws and were to teach them to their children (6:5-10).

Israel had now learned that **"...man does not live by bread only, but by every word that proceedeth out of the mouth of the LORD..." (8:3).** God said:

> **And now, Israel, what doth the Lord thy God require of thee, but to fear the Lord thy God, to walk in all his ways, and to love Him, and to serve the Lord thy God with all thy heart and with all thy soul. To keep the commandments of the Lord, and his statutes, which I command thee this day for thy good (10:12-13). Circumcise therefore the foreskin of your heart, and be no more stiffnecked (10:16).**

Before Israel could cross over the Jordan river, they had to learn obedience to ALL of God's laws, notice:

> **And he said unto them, set your hearts unto *all* the words which I testify among you this day, which ye shall command your children to observe to do, *all* the words of this law. For it is not a vain thing for you; because it is your life: and through this thing ye shall prolong your days in the land, whither ye go over the Jordan to possess it (32:46-47).**

Whether a Christian crosses over *spiritual Jordan* to the other side [eternal life] is also dependent upon being faithful to God!

Christians will cross over the Jordan spiritually once Christ returns to secure the land for them. Once they cross spiritual Jordan, they, like Israel, will have to clear out the land of their enemies. The spirits in high places [demons] will be removed by Christ so all of physical and spiritual Israel can dwell safely forevermore!

Freedom—A Process

Today, the world is crying out for freedom. This only proves the strongest motivation in man is not a job, sex or food—it is the desire to be FREE!

Sin is the opposite of freedom for it enslaves one into bondage. The Bible tells us that the experiences ancient Israel encountered were for us to learn vital spiritual lessons (1 Cor. 10:6).

Through the experiences of ancient Israel, Christians can learn the process of obtaining *spiritual freedom* even as they obtained *physical freedom*. God tested Israel's obedience from the very start after leaving Egypt. They actually took the long route to the promised land so God could test their attitude of faithfulness!

The Eternal told the children of Israel through Moses, to follow the fiery cloud. Sometimes the cloud went in opposite directions of the holy land. Yet God did this to PROVE whether or not Israel would be true to Him (Ex. 16:4).

God kept Israel in the wilderness for 38 years before they could enter the promised land, and removed all of them that were disobedient to Him (Deut. 2:14). Israel had to learn to be *faithful* to God, as well as Moses, God's chosen servant!

There are two basic lessons Israel had to experience before God allowed them to receive physical salvation or FREEDOM in the promised land. All Christians will have to ultimately go through the following similar experiences to attain *spiritual salvation*:

1) **Slavery**—The children of Israel were slaves in Egypt or in bondage to sin. Christians were also in *bondage* to spiritual sin before being *redeemed* like Israel by God Almighty. A Christian's taskmaster is the world around him pulling him down.

2) **Servitude**—Israel had to be good *faithful* servants to God and Moses before being allowed to inherit the promised land. The *unfaithful* and *disloyal* were not permitted to enter the physical promised land. Likewise, Christians today must be *faithful* and loyal to God's chosen leaders. God gave Israel just enough food and water to survive upon—it is the same with us.

Freedom only came to Israel when they crossed the Jordan river—the only thing that prevented them from obtaining FREEDOM! Remember, Jesus was baptized in the Jordan by John who preached *repentance*—and is an example for all Christians following His footsteps to salvation!

The only thing preventing Christians from obtaining spiritual FREEDOM is being *unfaithful* to God in keeping His Royal law of love.

It is by the "law of liberty" (Jas. 1:25), that a Christian will be judged (Jas. 2:12). This will determine if we will be set FREE to enter the spiritual promised land or not. The only thing that can hinder our crossing over *spiritual* Jordan—is the baptismal bridge of repentance!

The 7 Days of Creation and God's Seven Thousand Year Plan

There is a theory, although highly speculative, that God's entire plan is a Sabbatical plan. There were the seven days of creation...six by work and the seventh of rest. Recall, the number 7 signifies "spiritual perfection" or finality in the Bible. There are Seven Churches, 7 Seals, 7 Trumpets of the 7th Seal, and 7 annual sabbaths or Holy Days that the Lord gave to the nation of Israel. There was a Sabbatical year every 7th year. Following this pattern of seven, some early church Fathers believed that God's plan for mankind runs 7 thousand years!

According to this belief, God has allotted approximately 6000 years for humanity to go its own way. These six millenniums of human civilization are nearly over. Christians believe that God is going to intervene in world affairs by sending His Son, Jesus Christ back to the earth at some point— to start God's Kingdom that will have l000 years of peace.

The pattern for this little-understood plan is given in the first two chapters of Genesis. It is the WEEK of seven days. As God originally set time in motion, man is given six work days followed by a day of rest. In (Hebrews 4:4, and 11) the seventh day is mentioned as a *type* of the peaceful rest...l000...year rest...that will follow the present age of human labor and futile struggle to master the earth. The Millennium, then, is compared with a "day" of the week.

Observe that after Christ's intervention, the time of that peaceful rest under His rule is specifically termed **"A thousand years" (Rev. 20:4).** If the last "day" of God's 7000-year plan is 1000 years according to this theory, then the preceding six days which He has allotted for mankind to work out his own ideas would amount to 6000 years.

Now notice your Bible. Many Bibles are complete enough to contain chronological charts showing that human life was created slightly more than 4000 years before Christ. And almost another 2000 years have elapsed since...making nearly 6000 years of human civilization to date. In addition, the trend of world events is now proving we are very near the time the Scriptures have always said Christ will return...when the probability of world destruction would become a reality (Matt. 24:22). Six thousand years of human history have almost been completed.

Peter also wrote that a day in God's Plan is as "a thousand years," and "a thousand years" of human civilization as ONE day of His planned week of SEVEN 1000-year days (11 Pet. 3:8). The Greek word for "as" here is translated "about" in (Mark 5:8;9).

It was believed by some early Church Fathers that Peter knew that Christ would intervene shortly before the close of 6000 years of human struggle and slavery—and that God would send Jesus Christ to set up His government to rule during the seventh thousand-year period—a millennium of peace, a sabbatical rest!

As for the seventh year land rest, the seventh day weekly rest was **"...a sabbath of *entire rest*...for all time" (Lev. 16:31).** Because the weekly sabbath *envisions* the seventh 1,000 year rest period of man's history on earth—each day equaling 1,000 years—the seventh year land rest *pictures* this same 1,000 years of the land's rest!

As we continue our study of the *types* throughout this series in the other volumes, we shall see how the prophecies revolve around the sabbatical cycles as well!

What a beautiful *model* of the Millennium!

Many Jews were aware of God's 7,000 year plan from the scriptures, as the 1903 *Jewish Encyclopedia* states under the article "Eschatology" V, p.211:

> **The Perso-Babylonian world-year of twelve millenniums, however, was transformed in Jewish eschatology into a WORLD-WEEK OF SEVEN MILLENNIUMS corresponding with the week of Creation, the verse 'A thousand years in thy sight are but as yesterday' (Ps.90:4) having suggested the idea that the present world of toil is to be followed by a SABBATICAL MILLENNIUM, 'the world to come.' Of these six millenniums were again divided, as in Parsism, into three periods: the first 2000 years devoid of the Law; the next 2000 years under the rule of the Law; and the last 2000 years preparing amid struggles and through catastrophes for the RULE OF THE MESSIAH.**

Here is what the *Encyclopedia Britannica*, eleventh edition, article "Millennium" p. 459, relates concerning first century Jews:

> **The view most frequently expressed there...is that the Messianic kingdom will last for one thousand (some said two thousand) years. 'In six days God created the world, on the seventh He rested. But a day of God is equal to a thousand years (Ps. 90:4). Hence the world will last for six thousand years of toil and labor; then will come one thousand years of Sabbath rest for the people of God in the kingdom of the Messiah.' This idea must have already been very common in the first century before Christ.**

What Early Church Fathers Wrote

Barnabas, one of the early Church Fathers, and a companion of the apostle Paul, wrote an epistle which is not included in the

THE FIRST FIVE BOOKS

canon of scripture—but describes this 6000 year plan of God. He wrote:

> **Attend, my children, to the meaning of this expression: He finished in six thousand years, for a day is with Him a thousand years, and He himself testifieth, saying, 'Behold this day shall be a thousand years.' Therefore, children, in six days, that is, in six thousand years, shall all things be accomplished. And what is that he saith, And he rested the seventh day; he meaneth this: that when His Son shall come, and abolish the season of the Wicked One, and judge the ungodly, and shall change the sun and the moon and the stars; then he shall gloriously rest in that seventh day (Chapt. 13:3-6, *Epistle of Barnabas*).**

An apocryphon book of the Old Testament, entitled *The Book of the Secrets of Enoch*, written between A.D. 1-50, alludes to the seven-day millennial design, and proves that the millenarian design of the creation-week did not originate with Barnabas. It says thusly:

> **And I blessed the seventh day which is the Sabbath...God shows Enoch the age of this world, its existence of seven thousand years.**

The apocalyptic work, *The Books of Adam and Eve*, written around the first century A.D. describes Michael the archangel counseling Seth:

> **Man of God, mourn not for the dead more than six days, for on the seventh day is a sign of the resurrection and rest of the age to come; on the seventh day the Lord rested from all His works.**

Another Jewish apocalyptic work from the latter half of the first century A.D. known as *2 Baruch*, also describes the Messiah's return in sabbatical language:

> **And it shall come to pass, when He has brought low everything that is in the world, and has sat down in peace for the age on the throne of His kingdom, that joy shall be revealed, and *rest* shall appear.**

Toward the end of the second century, Irenaeus, the bishop of Lyons, wrote on the subject. In his youth, he had heard Polycarp preach. His work, *Against all Heresies*, refers to the Millennium in a number of passages. He drops this bombshell on us: **"For in as many days as this world was made, in so many thousand years shall it be concluded" (5:28.3).** After citing various prophecies about the Kingdom on earth (5.34.1-4), he notes that these prophecies are to be taken literally (5.35.1).

Hippolytus of Rome, in the early third century, wrote a commentary on the book of Daniel. Like so many others, he believed God would intervene after 6000 years of human history:

> **And 6,000 years must need be accomplished in order that the Sabbath may come...For the Sabbath is the type and emblem of the future kingdom of the saints, when they shall reign with Christ, when He comes from heaven, as John says in his Apocalypse: (4.23).**

The *New Shaff-Herzog Encyclopedia of Religious Knowledge*, vol. VII, p. 376, says of the early church fathers: **"The early fathers most commonly looked for the second advent at the end of 6000 years of the world's history."**

In the late third century, Victorinus of Pannoia wrote a commentary on Revelation in which he shows his acceptance of the Millennium. Elsewhere he similarly writes, **"Wherefore, as I have narrated, that true Sabbath will be in the seventh millenary of years, when Christ with his elect shall reign" (Defab. mun.).**

The Decline and Fall of the Roman Empire by Gibbon, vol 11, p. 546, 1899 edition also reveals this wonderful 7,000 year plan of God.

During the first three centuries, the belief that our Lord would return to the earth after six thousand millennia was so strong, no less than 23 early church fathers including Justin Martyr, Tertullian, Victoranios and Methodius taught it.

How interesting that in our day, at the very time that 6000 years have elapsed, the world is threatened with extinction of life. Man, capable as never before, to destroy himself completely, by the nuclear bomb, germ warfare, or chemical warfare.

How interesting that the population is running over, and we cannot meet our food supply now! Our air and water is polluted, and we have used up much of our tillable, or arable land. It is just a matter of time before we would destroy ourselves!

But thank God, this will not happen! Jesus said Himself, that when we see these things taking place, He would come again (Matt. 24).

Throughout history it is apparent that the Great God of heaven has foretold the length of sojourn that His people would be held in shackles to the world around them. Abraham was told the exact number of years that his children would remain in bondage in Egypt, before being delivered through the Exodus. It seems only fitting that the Eternal would also inform His chosen how long they would be held captive to this present evil world and being delivered through a future Exodus upon our Savior's return.

It is no mere coincidence that the 4th Commandment makes mention of the creation week because it is very significant to God's 7000 year plan.

How marvelous is our Great Creator God!

God's Plan Revealed In The Creation Week

There is quite a remarkable revelation of God's plan revealed in the creation week. But this revelation can only be understood in conjunction with the Holy days God gave the nation of Israel. Each of *the 7 days of creation* parallel the meaning of *the 7 annual Holy days*. We will study each of the Holy Days in detail in Volume .3.

Day No. 1 and Passover

God said in Genesis 1:3, **"Let there be light".** This is a different Hebrew word than used in verse 14 for "lights." The apostle Paul quotes (Genesis 1:3 in 11 Corinthians 4:6), and equates this "light" with Jesus Christ. Notice:

> **For God, who commanded the light to shine out of darkness, hath shined in our hearts, to give the light of the knowledge of the glory of God in the face of Jesus Christ.**

Jesus said Himself He was "the light of the world" in John 8:12: **"I am the light of the world. If you follow me you will not walk in darkness."** This analogy carries further in the understanding of why God created the "darkness" after the "light" and why God called it "darkness." The Hebrew word for "darkness" in (Genesis 1:5) means "to deviate, or turn from the right or straight line." The word "day" in the Hebrew means "movement, or disturbance."

That is why Christians are called "the children of light" in (Ephesians 5:8) and are told to "come out of the world of darkness" (11 Cor. 6:14; 1 Pet. 2:9).

This truth is found in (John 12:35; 1 John 1:7,2:9), as well as countless New Testament scriptures. Notice John 12:35-36:

> **Yet a little while is the light with you. Walk while ye have light, lest darkness come upon you for he that walketh in darkness knoweth not whither he goeth. While ye have light, believe in the light, that ye may be the children of light.**

With this understanding, we can now understand when Christ died on the cross as the LIGHT of the world, that *darkness* came over all the earth (Lk. 23:44). Truly, Christians are the "light of the world, and should let their light shine before men" (Matt. 5:14-16).

When the New Heaven and New Earth is created there will no longer be any need for the sun, nor the moon for the lamb [Jesus Christ] will light up the city (Rev. 21:23,22:5).

Clearly, then, the Light of (Genesis 1:3) represents Jesus Christ, the Lamb of God represented by the first annual holy day PASSOVER.

Day No. 2 and Unleavened Bread

On day number 2 God made a firmament [air] that divided the water which was under the firmament [oceans, rivers, lakes] from the *water* that was above the firmament [clouds]. The firmament here is AIR! God called this firmament [air] heaven (Gen. 1:8). There are 3 heavens that the Bible speaks of, but this *heaven* is the earthly atmosphere. The Hebrew word means "to set" or "place" "to arrange".

How does this second day correspond to the next annual holy day in God's plan—the 2nd Day of Unleavened Bread picturing "BAPTISM"? Simply this—The AIR contains oxygen which we all need in order to sustain life.

Baptism is the start of God's sustaining life to the new Christian. We read in (John 20:22) that Jesus breathed on them just after His resurrection and said, **"...receive ye the Holy spirit"**.

This event took place before the day of Pentecost when they were to receive the POWER of the Holy Spirit. This was only a little "down Payment" so they could start understanding God's spiritual truths. It was the start of God's seed in them which "sets" "places" and "arranges" a Christian in Christ's Church.

Day No. 3 and Pentecost

What happened on the third day of creation is outlined in (Genesis 1:9-12). There we read where God let dry land appear to produce *vegetation.* The next feast in God's plan is PENTECOST—the firstfruits. Genesis 1:10 shows that the waves brought forth the land or raised it up so *vegetation* [fruit] could take place. This analogy is used in describing a Christians growth as being "tossed to and fro"—finally producing fruit! This corresponds to the *trials* one must endure to develop *character,* before one can enter God's eternal Kingdom!

Genesis 1:11 shows an interesting order of "grass," "herbs" and "fruit" as *analogous* to a Christians growth. In (1 Peter

1:24) God describes human flesh as grass. Herbs are used for healing properties (Rev. 22:2). In the spiritual *analogy,* a Christian is "fleshly" before converted, then his mind is "healed" by a miracle from God's Holy spirit, then he can start producing "fruit".

Christians cannot produce fruit unless they are firmly grounded in good soil. The Parable of the Sower in (Matthew 13) shows this very clearly. The only individual that produced fruit was on good ground.

In (Psalm 104:5-9, and Jeremiah 5:22) God says that the *seas* will not be able to overcome the land and destroy it. This also is significant as it relates to a Christian never being *tempted* more than he is able to bear (1 Cor. 10:13).

Thus, we see that the 3rd day of the creation week is *symbolic* of the TRIALS a Christian will have to go through, but not more than he can bear to produce FRUIT! God called the dry land earth (Heb. *powder)* or something that can be molded. In (Revelation 21:1) we read that there will no longer be any more need of any sea after the new earth is made. The sea is constantly changing the earth (*symbolic* of trials changing a Christian to produce fruit). Then, we will no longer need to be changed—because we will be made PERFECT through the resurrection!

Day No. 4 and Trumpets

On the 4th day God made TWO GREAT LIGHTS—the greater light [sun] to rule the day, and the lesser light [moon] to rule the night (Gen. 1:16). These lights were for signs, seasons, days, and years (vs. 14).

As already noted, Jesus is described as the LIGHT in Genesis 1:3, and in (Malachi 4:2) we read concerning Jesus' return **"...the Sun of righteousness arise with healing in his wings..."** Here, the physical sun is used to describe Jesus Christ. However, the dream that Joseph was given, as interpreted by his father Jacob, in which he saw a woman clothed with the Sun, having the moon under her feet and a crown of 12 stars upon her head had a different meaning. Jacob interpreted the the Sun as representative of himself [the Father], and the moon his wife (Gen. 37:9).

One can easily *parallel* the physical to the spiritual, as God the Father would represent the Sun and Jesus Christ the Moon [or the Church]. This analogy is used in (Psalm 19) in describing Jesus, the Bridegroom as the sun. Clearly, Jesus can be represented as either the sun or the moon for as He said, **"...if you have seen the Son, you have seen the Father"**!

The sun *radiates* light as a transmitter, but the moon does not radiate light by itself, rather it *reflects* light! Just as the physical sun emanates light via the moon's reflection on the other side of the planet, Jesus was a reflection of God the Father, even as the Church is a reflection of Jesus. While Jesus walked the earth, God the Father was not visible, but was rather *reflected* by His Son's example. After His death, Jesus' example was emulated by His spiritual Body—the Church!

If the Father represents the sun in (Genesis 1:16) as the greater "light", then it follows that Jesus and His Church must be represented by the moon. The moon "reflects" the light from the sun, even as Christians must "reflect" the light of Jesus Christ before all men, by letting their light shine. Then shall the righteous [Christians] shine forth as the sun (Matt. 13:43). Then shall the "light of the moon" be as the light of the sun (Isa. 30:26).

Just as the sun RULES the moon (Gen. 1:16,18) so does God the Father rule Christ (1Cor. 11:3; Eph. 4:6-15), and Christ RULES His Church. His Church is a sign—a witness to the earth! They are the ones who are sounding the TRUMPET of alarm as did Christ to this Satanic age. Soon, Christ will return to the earth for His Church—fulfilling the Day of TRUMPETS as is *symbolic* of the 4th day of creation.

Even as the physical sun brought the light of day from the darkness of night on the *fourth* day of the "creation week"—Jesus brought the light of TRUTH out of the darkness of evil after 4,000 years. Surely this is not merely coincidental!

Day No. 5 and Atonement

The next holy day in God's wonderful plan is the day of ATONEMENT which *pictures* the putting away of Satan and the marriage of the Church to Christ. The fulfillment of this event will speculatively take place at the Millennium's conclusion when Satan is destroyed forever!

It was on the 5th day of creation that all the animals "clean" and "unclean" were created. Many of these animals were used to describe or depict spiritual characteristics of certain individuals, as viewed through God's eyes. Swine for example are used to describe unrepentant sinners. Satan is described as a "roaring Lion", while the dove was a *symbol* of peace in God's Holy Spirit.

All these were to grow together and multiply. But some day Jesus will separate the sheep from the goats, the "clean" from the "unclean", and Satan will be destroyed.

Christians will then be able to be married to Christ! They will then be AT-ONE—with God forever!

Day No. 6 and The Feast of Tabernacles

It was on the sixth day of creation that man was created in God's "image" and "likeness." This is highly significant as this relates to the FEAST OF TABERNACLES when man will finally *rule* the earth in the "image" and "likeness" of God for one thousand years.

The Feast of Tabernacles *portrays* a time of tremendous harvesting of those who have developed through trial and testing into the very IMAGE and LIKENESS of the family of God.

Day No. 7 and The Last Great Day

You will recall it was on the 7th day that the Godhead rested. Sabbath means "to rest." Jesus Said in Matthew 11:28, **"Come to me... and I will give you rest."**

On the LAST GREAT DAY, Jesus said:

> **If any man thirst, let him come unto me and drink. He that believeth on me, as the scripture hath said, out of his belly shall flow rivers of living water (Jn.7:37).**

It is very significant that only after the Sabbath was created were the rivers named! These rivers have already been explained to represent the flowing of God's HOLY SPIRIT to the earth!

THE FIRST FIVE BOOKS

The 7th day correlates to the Last Great Day in that ALL the family of God will finally rest *after* ALL His work is completed! God's work will be completed on earth after the Millennium when everyone has had the opportunity to drink of the river of life!

New Book available on Amazon

www.ingramcontent.com/pod-product-compliance
Lightning Source LLC
Chambersburg PA
CBHW070533010526
44118CB00012B/1126